Forming Ministers
or Training Leaders?

Forming Ministers or Training Leaders?

An Exploration of Practice in Theological Colleges

ANTHONY CLARKE

RESOURCE *Publications* • Eugene, Oregon

FORMING MINISTERS OR TRAINING LEADERS?
An Exploration of Practice in Theological Colleges

Copyright © 2021 Anthony Clarke. All rights reserved. Except for brief quotations in critical publications or reviews, no part of this book may be reproduced in any manner without prior written permission from the publisher. Write: Permissions, Wipf and Stock Publishers, 199 W. 8th Ave., Suite 3, Eugene, OR 97401.

Resource Publications
An Imprint of Wipf and Stock Publishers
199 W. 8th Ave., Suite 3
Eugene, OR 97401

www.wipfandstock.com

PAPERBACK ISBN: 978-1-7252-6351-2
HARDCOVER ISBN: 978-1-7252-6349-9
EBOOK ISBN: 978-1-7252-6350-5

06/10/21

"Those engaged in the important work of ministerial formation and training, and others interested in it as a possibility, will find much to embrace in this study. Based upon the emerging practices and theological reflection of a particular context and tradition, the book nonetheless draws upon a broad range of parallel experiences to propose a distinctive approach that many will wish to endorse."

—**NIGEL G. WRIGHT**
Principal Emeritus, Spurgeon's College London

"Anthony Clarke has written an accessible, exquisite, and nuanced account that traces the formational dynamics in ministerial training. His writing ranges well beyond the frontiers of his own denomination, and with care, wisdom, and rich insight, he excavates the landscape for teaching pastoral practice and expanding pastoral imagination. In an ecclesial climate where many pastors and clergy can feel they are held captive by the increasingly functional demands of administration, coupled to financial burdens and all the attendant anxieties related to church growth, mission, and evangelism, it is a breath of fresh air to encounter a truly wise scholar who can see a way forward for renewal and reinvigoration. I commend this work for careful and considered reflection—for all who want to understand and enrich our sense of formation for ministry."

—**MARTYN PERCY**
Dean, Christ Church, Oxford

"Ministers reading this book will be prompted to reflect on how their assumptions about what they do are still formed by their initial ministerial education. Theological educators will be prompted to reflect on whether they are forming ministers for a church that no longer exists. A book that will provoke fresh and lively conversations about ministry."

—**HELEN CAMERON**
Research fellow, Centre for Baptist Studies,
Regent's Park College, Oxford

"Among many books about the practice of Christian ministry, this one is exceptional. The author asks how this practice is shaped by another—the practice of preparation for ministry—and he relates the two practices, drawing on his own rich experience and a penetrating theological analysis. The whole is interwoven by an original account of the replacement of the idea of 'training' for ministry by the 'formation' of the minister, making this an indispensable study of ministry for today."

—**PAUL S. FIDDES**
Professor of Systematic Theology, University of Oxford,
and Principal Emeritus and Senior Research Fellow,
Regent's Park College, University of Oxford

"Many years ago, I 'trained for ministry' as a Baptist, and had that process occurred a generation earlier I would have been 'theologically educated.' Now, the language used is quite rightly 'ministerial formation,' and Anthony Clarke's fascinating book fleshes out what that might mean for Baptists . . . I have followed Anthony Clarke's research at a distance, and this book's roots in empirical research provides evidence for what he proposes, and which I enthusiastically endorse . . . This book is an important contribution to the work of discovering what such formation might look like in the twenty-first century, and deserves to be read not just by those whose task is to provide that formation, but all who seek to offer ministry in Christlike ways—whether they be Baptists or not—as part of a community of practice."

—**PAUL GOODLIFF**
General Secretary, Churches Together in England

To colleagues
in churches and in college,
staff and students
from whom I have learnt
and with whom I have reflected,
collaborated and shared hospitality

Contents

Preface | ix
Acknowledgements | xiii

1. Introduction | 1
   Practice and the Pastoral Imagination
2. The Practice of Ministry | 23
3. The Practice of Preparation | 42
4. Exploring Practice and the Pastoral Imagination | 71
   An Example of Empirical Research
5. Discerning a Pastoral Imagination | 84
   Some Findings Among Baptist Colleges
6. Discerning a Pastoral Imagination | 109
   Some Findings Among non-Baptist Institutions
7. Towards a Theology of Formation for Baptists | 133
8. Towards a Pastoral Imagination | 156
9. Towards a Renewed Practice of Ministry | 175

Appendix 1: Core Questions in Empirical Interviews | 185
Bibliography | 187
Index | 199

Preface

THIS BOOK BEGAN LIFE as a thesis for the DMin degree through the University of Chester, which I took as part of my own continual professional development. It was a piece of practitioner research located in the context of my own practice as Tutor in Pastoral Studies at Regent's Park College, a role I have had occupied since 2006. It was written from the context of change, both from denominational reviews, university restructuring and government funding and from wider changes in theological education; it was also written out of the experience of being responsible for those preparing for ministry at Regent's Park College, a role I have immensely enjoyed and which has always been stimulating and rewarding. In many ways it is a book about how I might develop my own role and work further.

One of the great benefits of teaching in a theological and ministerial context is that it offers another opportunity to reflect on your own experience and practice of ministry; the necessity of teaching others pushes your own thinking further and deeper. And so I feel I have a much fuller grasp of issues around ministry now than when I first returned to Regent's as a tutor. If only I had known all this when I left college as a student! Within the work at college, one of the subjects that always produced lively debates in class was about leadership, and not just with ministerial students. Over the years we have hosted a number of days for members of churches where our students serve as "Ministers-in-Training" to visit college and to gain a better insight into what happens in this part of the lives of "their MiTs". As part of these days I would "teach' a class using material that I had used with the students and often I choose to use material around leadership; the discussions were illuminating and sometimes quite concerning. It is out of these experiences that I developed the ideas that are named in the book as the "leadership paradigm" and the "ministry paradigm". The book then explores ideas of ministry and leadership, arguing that, in the face of the

Preface

challenge posed by leadership language and thought, it is better to reclaim a historic and contemporary Baptist understanding of ministry best understood through what I describe as a "dialectical" model of ministry.

Part of my role involves producing documents, such as brochures for those exploring a call to ministry, handbooks for those current students and submissions as part of an inspection process. Rarely did I start with a blank piece of paper, but adapted and updated existing documentation. What soon became clear was that a wide variety of terminology was used both by different people but also within the same document; was I engaging in teaching, education, training, formation? This prompted me to explore both historically and more systematically the language that was being used, partly as a way of deciding for myself on the most appropriate terminology. So in the book I chart the history of preparation for ministry among Baptists and explore the contemporary developments in language, suggesting that while no one word has gained universal support, the description of "formation" rather than "training" is the most appropriate to use.

Then as I read further into questions of both the practice of ministry and the preparation for ministry I developed an increasing sense of dissatisfaction that recent debates have tended to separate out a discussion about the preparation for ministry from an understanding of ministry itself; literature tended to concentrate on one or the other. My desire was to find more ways to connect the practice of preparation and the practice of ministry together. While the thesis, and so the book, is set up as a question, I readily acknowledge that I always approached the discussion with significant ideas already being formed in my mind; there is a sense that the title was never meant to be an open question for me. My own thinking was moving over time to stress formation as the preparation for ministry. But training for leadership was, and still is, a significant alternative way to think of the process of preparing for ministry. While my own thinking was already moving in this clear direction, the reflection on practice in the thesis allowed me time and space to articulate my own developing views. While there are a number of alternative ways of articulating my role I would now talk very clearly that I am involved in forming minsters.

The original DMin research focused on an in-depth empirical study of the Baptist colleges in England and Wales alongside a sample of other non-Baptist colleges and courses, and while some of the detail of this empirical research has been removed from the book for ease of reading, particularly detailed footnotes drawing on transcripts of interviews, the central findings

Preface

are still important to the argument of the book. The other nine theological institutions involved in the empirical research kindly supplied to me numerous documents many of which were not in the public domain. While I make reference to these in the footnotes I have not included all this material in the bibliography as it is not publicly accessibly.

So drawing on the literature around ministry, leadership and the work of theological colleges, and the initial empirical research, while also engaging with current expressions on trinitarian theology, my hope in this book is that I can offer not a Baptist theology of formation, as if totally distinct from any other denomination, but a theology of formation for Baptists, exploring the way that a college might seek to shape those preparing for ministry which in turn will shape their on-going practice of ministry.

Acknowledgements

RARELY IS A BOOK written that is not shaped by a wide variety of interactions with other people, and this book is no different. And I am grateful to a number of people who have played an important role as the ideas expressed here have developed. As mentioned earlier, this book began as a DMin thesis in the University of Chester, with Revd Dr Nigel Wright as my supervisor. I am grateful to Nigel for his friendship, wisdom and support during the years of writing a doctoral thesis part-time while working in a demanding role alongside this. This work was as tutor at Regent's Park College and I am grateful for all the friendship and support of colleagues at college during that time and since.

In particular I value immensely the conversations around ministry and formation with those colleagues with whom I have shared most directly in the work of preparation for ministry: Rob Ellis, the college Principal, Myra Blyth, Nick Wood and Carol Murray as fellow tutors. The very first discussion of a DMin on this theme came in my first professional development review. This has been a truly collegial experience making Regent's such a formative place to work, and as we have planned the curriculum, discussed documents and prepared for a variety of self-assessment and review processes so we have engaged in collective theological reflection about our shared work, and those reflections have fed into this book in a variety of ways.

The book draws theological ideas from a number of places, but in particular it engages with the trinitarian theology of Paul Fiddes, himself a former tutor and Principal at Regent's Park. While expressed in the book in the academic tradition of referencing his published works, the influence has been much deeper and more personal than that, and I am deeply grateful for Paul's friendship and encouragement alongside the many conversations about the theological themes within the book.

Acknowledgements

Two shorter papers connected to the theme of the book have already been published. In 2014 I edited a book of essays in honour of Paul Fiddes, *For the Sake of the Church: Essays in Honour of Paul S. Fiddes,* and also contributed a chapter entitled "A Trinitarian Theology of Ministerial Formation." This gave an initial opportunity to engage with the way that the work of Fiddes might be put in dialogue with ministerial formation. Then in 2015 I rehearsed some of the historical material in the article "How Did We End Up Here? Theological Education as Ministerial Formation in the British Baptist Colleges," *Baptist Quarterly*, 46:2 (2015) 69–97. There is some overlap between the material in this book and both these articles and I am grateful for the opportunity to use some of the material again here, but the articles retain their integrity as pieces of work in their own right.

The original DMin and so the book could not have happened without the willingness of various colleagues to engage in the empirical research. I am deeply grateful for those colleagues from the other Baptist colleges who were both willing to give time to me but also open up their colleges to this process of reflection. Being part of a wider community of practice among fellow Baptists engaged in preparing for ministry has been encouraging and insightful and alongside the more formal empirical research there have been numerous other conversations which have contributed to my own thinking. I have always found the annual gathering of British Baptist tutors a stimulating occasion. I am equally grateful to those from the non-Baptist theological institutions who were also willing to engage with the empirical research, in some cases based on an existing relationship but in other cases responding to a researcher they did not know. Some degree of vulnerability was required in these different contexts, without which the project could not have happened.

Alongside those more clearly named, there are a whole range of people who in some way have shaped who I am as a minister and tutor. Since I was ordained in 1991 I have been minister of two churches, Oxlow Lane Baptist Church in Dagenham and South Oxford Baptist Church; and I have been a member at two others, John Bunyan Baptist Church, Oxford and Cornerstone Baptist Church, Thame. These have all been contexts for the exercise of ministry and reflection on that ministry, which never happens in a vacuum—and I am grateful for the supportive and stimulating places all these churches have been. It is also now over twenty years since I first put my toe in the water of academic teaching, taking the occasional class. Since

Acknowledgements

then I have had the privilege of engaging with numerous students who, as they rightly do, have pushed and challenged and argued for different ideas. All this has been grist to the mill of my own ongoing thinking, and so it is to all those colleagues and students, named and unnamed to whom the book is dedicated with grateful thanks.

As has been the case for all my published work, my father, Revd Jim Clarke, read the final draft as a willing proof reader and I am thankful again for his meticulous help which helped improve the final manuscript. Finally, my gratitude as always to my wife, Amanda, and my three children for their love and support.

1

Introduction
Practice and the Pastoral Imagination

It was Monday morning. We had moved into a freshly decorated house and had begun to get to know neighbors. On Saturday the church had been more than full for an inspiring ordination and induction, and yesterday I had preached my first sermon as an ordained minister. And as I sat at my new desk, mug of coffee in hand, I thought to myself: what do I do now?

THIS HAS BEEN THE core of a conversation I have had at various times over the years I have been involved in ministry both with others and with myself! It may rarely be expressed in quite such explicit terms, but this has been a fundamental question of those who have settled in a church after finishing a process of preparation for ordained ministry. What should be done—now, today, first? The existential nature of the question may strike deeper among Baptist ministers, the majority of whom are inducted into sole pastorates without a "senior" colleague to direct them and more recently the timing of such questioning may have been brought earlier, as the majority of Baptist ordinands already exercise ministry while preparing for ordination, some in a sole pastorate context. It is a question at many levels, and while seemingly a very practical question it is one of significant theological depth.

Forming Ministers or Training Leaders?

It is a clearly question about the practice of ministry. I recall the Monday morning after my own ordination and induction service in 1991; I was now the minister of a small church in Dagenham on the borders of East London and Essex. My wife and I had been quite recently married and she had left for the daily commute into London. I had a very empty diary and the clear assumption was that I would fill it and knew how to fill it. What was I going to do with my day? But it is, of course, much more than a question about activity. Within the specificity of daily tasks are woven deep questions about a self-understanding and theology of ministry, out of which practice emerges and which practice then continues to shape a developing theological understanding. Neither practice nor theology remain static. It is, therefore, a question that remains constant through a lifetime of ministry, emerging perhaps more clearly at particular points, such as beginning a new ministry, but nevertheless always present: who am I as a minister, and what should I be doing now in response to my calling?

In this particular scenario it is also a question about the practice of preparation for ministry which has enabled, encouraged and shaped the practice of ministry both leading up to an ordination and induction and beyond. So while these fundamental and existential questions remain throughout a life of ministry, there is a sense that they are most acute and pressing the first time they need to be asked. Before settling in Dagenham, I trained for ministry in a more traditional college-based setting, having some, but more limited, placement experience. Having left college aged 24 to accept a call to a sole pastorate, I had limited experience of church life and, especially, in those early months I was doing many things for the first time. But I did have three years of theological education and preparation for ministry on which to draw to help answer my own questions about what to do, now.

Finally it is also question about the way that these two practices are connected, and this is the central conversation I hope to develop in this book, a conversation that seems to me needs to be pursued more rigorously than it has been in the past. As someone who has now spent half his ministry working in a theological college preparing men and women for ministry, my experience is that that these two questions are not frequently asked together, so the answers can inform each other. There are books that explore ministry and how this might be practiced, but these tend not to discuss the process of preparation, and there are books that explore the

Introduction

practice of preparation for ministry but these often make assumptions about the nature of the ministry to be practiced.

Andrew Mayes, for example, in some important research into the preparation for ministry within the Church of England can use terminology such as priest, minister and leader interchangeably, as if there were no theological distinction.[1] The material from the ecumenical Quality in Formation Panel is intentional in not offering any particular theological understanding of the practice of ministry, seeking rather to ensure that each institution offers preparation appropriate to the breadth of traditions within the sponsoring church.[2] Paul Goodliff, in his earlier exploration of the influence of a sacramental theology of ministry, does begin to make some links between the teaching of tutors and the theology of ministers, but does not explore what might be a distinctly Baptist approach.[3] In his later book *Shaped for Service*,[4] more recently published, Goodliff makes much more of a connection between formation and ministry, drawing on similar ideas of practice to those pursued here, developing this connection at greater depth. But there is still work to be done on how these two practices shape each other, and while there will be some clear resonances with Goodliff's work, who is a friend and colleague, this book will offer a much more detailed discussion of the actual practice of preparation for ministry.

My aim in this book, then, is to bring and hold together these two distinct areas and practices, the practice of ministry, particularly but not exclusively as exercised in a local church, and the practice of preparation for this ministry, exploring how our understanding of one shapes and contributes to our understanding of the other. As in all writing, this book emerges from a particular context which shapes the whole way it has been written. Various aspects of this context will appear through the book but it would be helpful to mention two at the beginning.

The first important aspect of context is recognizing who I am. I come to explore these questions as a Baptist minister who has served two congregations and is still engaged, to a more limited degree, in the practice of ministry in a local church. I also come now as a tutor at Regent's Park

1. Mayes, *Spirituality in Ministerial Formation*. From a Baptist perspective Tidball explicitly admits to using "the terms 'ministry', 'leadership' or 'pastoral leadership' as interchangeable" (*Ministry by the* Book, 14).

2. Quality in Formation Panel, *Quality Assurance and Enhancement in Ministerial Education* and *Quality Assurance and Enhancement in Ministerial Formation*.

3. Goodliff, *Ministry, Sacrament and Representation*.

4. Goodliff, *Shaped for Service*.

College part of the University of Oxford and a member of the Baptist Union of Great Britain, having significant responsibility for preparing ordinands. I approach the subject from a particular denomination and with a particular role within it. This book also began as a DMin thesis for the University of Chester, which I undertook as a long-term part-time project to give me an opportunity to stand back from the specific details and day to day activities involved in being a college tutor and ask more fundamental questions, which arise from and are shaped by practice. Since the DMin was submitted in 2016 I have continued the reflection process in response to a changing context.

I come, therefore, in academic terms as both a practitioner-researcher[5], engaged in the practices of both ministry and the preparation for ministry, and also as a researcher-practitioner, an academic in the University of Oxford, involved in teaching on and researching in the practice of ministry. I seek to be both a "scholar-practitioner" and so to "integrate scholarship into . . . practice and generate actionable knowledge"[6] and also integrate practice into scholarship as a practical theologian. This book is thus offered as the fruit of my own reflection on our practice at Regent's Park College.

The second aspect of context is to recognize the significant and developing degree of change during the course of the original research and the writing of the book, indicating something of the fluid nature of the context. When I returned to Regent's Park College as a tutor I was struck by the changed pattern of preparation for ministry from my own experience as a student there fifteen years earlier, which had been a traditional three-year college-based course focused on the final honors school of the Oxford BA, with a very heavy weighting towards biblical studies and systematic theology. And then over the last fifteen years working as a tutor at the College the broader context has changed significantly again. Four of these changes are important to highlight here.

First there has been the broader change in culture with well documented accounts of the decline of the church. While there have been discussions about the appropriateness of particular language, such as post-Christian, the wider cultural context in the UK in which ministry is exercised reflects a growing separation between the lives of many and the life of the church. Even though there is some evidence of a broader engagement with churches during the Covid 19 pandemic the trend over recent

---

5. See Fox, Martin and Green, *Doing Practitioner Research*, 1–2.
6. Coghlan and Brannick, *Doing Action Research in Your Own Organisation*, 8.

Introduction

decades has been clear. One result of this has been the increasing call for a less traditional and more pioneering approach to church and ministry, to enable churches to engage with very different social demographics to those of current members. A concomitant response from theological colleges in the way they prepare ministers was advocated at the turn of the millennium by Robert Banks[7] and the case for a stronger more missional approach continues to be made.[8]

Second, and partly in response to the first change, there have been particular moments within my own denomination, the Baptist Union of Great Britain, when there have been initiatives to review the nature of ministry. There was an initial attempt to set up an overall review body together with working groups in the Autumn of 2013, which then developed in to *The Ignite Project* in 2015, and discussions about, and the implementation of the recommendations of *The Ignite Report* are still ongoing. These mirror similar reviews of ministry in other UK denominations.[9] During this period the British Baptist Colleges withdrew from the United Kingdom Ecumenical Inspection process for theological colleges under the auspices of what is known as the Quality in Formation Panel (QiFP), and established its own peer review process, which prompted further reflection by the British Baptist Colleges on their own practice.

Thirdly, there have been major changes to the broader higher education context in the UK, related to the teaching and financing of theological study. The launch in 2014 of the Common Awards by the Church of England and its ecumenical partners in collaboration with Durham University was significantly driven by the financial crisis in theological education created by changes in the UK Government's policy towards the funding of Higher Education. Financial pressures have led to the closure of significant theological institutions, especially Heythrop College in 2018 and St John's College Nottingham in 2019 as well as presenting significant challenges to others.[10] The general introduction of tuition fees has also impacted the

---

7. Banks, *Reenvisioning Theological Education*.

8. See, for example, Cronshaw "Reenvisioning Theological Education and Mission Spirituality."

9. The Ministries Committee of the Methodist Church in the UK produced *The Fruitful Field*, as a consultation document in 2011 which led to significant streamlining of their preparation for ordination. The Church of England established a process called *Resourcing Ministerial Education* which first reported in 2015.

10. See the discussion in "Bible College: Yesterday, Today, Forever" in *Christianity* February 2015.

study of theology more generally. In 1998 £1000 a year top up tuition fees for undergraduate study were introduced in the UK—previously all first degrees in higher education had been free for students. This was increased to £3000 a year in 2006 and then to £9,000 in 2012—being then the full fees and highest amount that a University could charge for undergraduate courses—financed mainly through student loans. Research from the British Academy shows that there has been a sharp decline in numbers of undergraduates studying Theology and Religious Studies in English public Universities since the introduction of full fees in 2012 but with some increase in students at private institutions, which are often either denominational or from a particular theological tradition.[11]

The report also notes that some changing patterns are part of a much wider development in British Universities that have seen degrees reworked within a religious studies perspective, and theology departments renamed or incorporated into wider departments or schools around broader historical or sociological studies. As part of these broader developments the name of the Faculty of Theology in the University of Oxford, of which I am a member, was changed to the Faculty of Theology and Religion, together with a new final honors school degree in Theology and Religion which began in the 2016/17 academic year. The unifying nature of theology implicit in such a move is thus the methodology of religious studies, which raises important questions about the wider theological task being developed in a college such as my own.

And fourthly it has been a time of continuing change in teaching practices. The increasing move away from a college providing a residential community in which students and staff live, work and worship together to a more dispersed model of students engaging together regularly for learning has led to developing patterns of teaching. By far the largest of the independent theological colleges in the UK, St Miletus, works entirely on a non-residential basis. Patterns of teaching around block weeks, online methods and a "flipped classroom"[12] have developed. The Covid 19 pandemic brought sudden pressure for teaching to move to an online platform and one of the lasting impacts of this experience may be a new balance of teaching and learning, and new and creative ways of engaging with virtual classrooms.

---

11. See The British Academy, *Theology and Religious Studies Provision In UK Higher Education.*

12. See Bergmann and Sams, *Flip Your Classroom.*

Introduction

Writing while still in the midst of the pandemic, it will require a return to some kind of "normality" to create the space to assess these developments.

The work of ministry and preparing for ministry have been affected by these ongoing changes. What seems clear is that having been through a period of considerable change, such change will be continuing into the future too, and thus the need for ongoing reflection on how we prepare for future ministry. This book aims to be one contribution to how we may best continue our thinking about preparing people for ministry in God's church in these changing contexts.

EXPLORING PRACTICE

One term that I have been using frequently so far and will be important in the book is that of "practice," and over recent years the term "practice" has become an increasingly significant concept in both sociology and theology. The influential work of Alasdair MacIntyre[13] describes practice as much more than a procession of unconnected individual events, or a series of technical abilities driven by instrumental needs, but as a "coherent and complex form of socially established co-operative human activity through which goods internal to that form of activity are realized"[14] and as such is something which is both shared with others and persists over time. He offers the example of playing chess, a complex co-operative activity, and suggests that the internal goods realized by this practice are excellence in chess.

Building on MacIntyre's work a number of writers have developed a more explicitly theological understanding of practice.[15] Dorothy Bass and Craig Dykstra, for example, suggest that, while MacIntyrean in basis, the distinct theological turn in their own understanding of practice is to replace MacIntyre's stress on "internal goods" with goods orientated towards God and God's intention for creation. So, they suggest, a practice must "pursue a good beyond itself, responding to and embodying the self-giving dynamics of God's own creating, redeeming and sustaining grace"[16] and be "a sustained, co-operative pattern of human activity that is big enough,

---

13. MacIntyre, *After Virtue*.
14. MacIntyre, *After Virtue*, 187.
15. See, for example, Bass and Dykstra, *For Life Abundant*; Dykstra and Bass, "A Theological Understanding of Christian Practices"; Tanner, "Theological Reflection and Christian Practices"; Forrester, *Truthful Action*.
16. Bass and Dykstra, *For Life Abundant*, 30.

rich enough and complex enough to address some fundamental feature of human existence."[17]

An alternative approach is found in the work of the leading French Social Theorist Pierre Bourdieu who explores, among other things, the relationship between individuals as those who on the one hand are shaped by their history and the givenness of the structures around them and on the other are those capable of more spontaneous individual agency. Bourdieu argues for a complex dialectic in which practices are neither unchanging responses to "rules" given within cultural structures, nor entirely the product of individual or communal agency[18] and he describes this dialectic as a *habitus*. For Bourdieu this is understood fundamentally at the level of the individual, although he recognizes the "homogeneity" that exists within a group,[19] and like MacIntyre there is significant stress on that which persists and continues. A *habitus*, for Bourdieu, in what is a somewhat opaque phrase, derives from "structured structures predisposed to function as structuring structures"[20] and is "a present past that tends to perpetuate itself into the future by reactivation in similar structured practices."[21] In other words, while there is some space in Bourdieu's thinking for individual change and novelty, the prevailing sense is on continuity in our actions which are structured and shaped by our past into the present. Furthermore, Bourdieu recognizes that what might appear to be spontaneous responses are always, to some degree, shaped by our habitus. He draws on a sporting image that top sportsmen and women know instinctively what to do in different situations, they have a "feel for it," without having to think rationally through their response. They play out of their *habitus*. Bourdieu suggests that this is true in life as we respond to new situations out of the *habitus* we have developed and that has developed us.

The practical theologian Elaine Graham draws on Bourdieu to offer the same kind of mediation between determinism and voluntarism while offering a reading of Bourdieu which places greater stress on the agency of the individual.[22] Graham explores further the possibility for novelty

---

17. Dykstra and Bass, "A Theological Understanding of Christian Practices," 27.
18. Bourdieu, *The Logic of Practice*, 53.
19. Bourdieu, *The Logic of Practice*, 58.
20. Bourdieu, *The Logic of Practice*, 53.
21. Bourdieu, *The Logic of Practice*, 54.
22. There are readings of Bourdieu which see in his work a greater emphasis on the more closed structuring nature of the *habitus*, and are thus in some contrast to Graham.

Introduction

and development within the structured and structuring structures; for her *habitus* is "thus conceived as the residuum of past actions, a deposit of past knowledge and practice" but specifically one that "is always available as the raw material for creative agency or "regulated improvisations."[23] Following Graham's reading of Bourdieu, practice may be described in performative terms which involves both the given and the creative.[24] Playing jazz music has been used as an example of this, where the deep structures of music form the deposit of accumulated past knowledge which is essential for the possibility of successful improvisation.[25]

The importance of these discussions is that those in ministry are engaged in a practice. What a minister does over time is not a random set of actions, but if studied and analyzed will have distinct patterns to it. It is these patterns that make it a practice. Drawing together the various perspectives above I offer an understanding of practice that will be used throughout this book that can be described as structured, co-operative and creative: there is certainly an important element of individual and spontaneous agency to my practice (creative) but my understanding of ministry has been worked out and shared with others (co-operative), and the person I am has been shaped in certain ways by my own history and by others who have interacted with me, which significantly affects my spontaneous actions (structured).

We can begin to see the importance of this by returning to our initial scenario about what to do on the first day of ministry. One response is to suggest that the way it is framed already places too much stress on individual agency. Ministry is a practice shared with others contemporaneously and historically, persisting over time and concerned for the external goods of the mission and kingdom of God and so one answer to the question posed here is: "do what ministers have always done." Yet ministry is also performative, in creative and sometimes unexpected ways, which, in response to the call of God, break from the established patterns. A second, and contrasting answer, to the scenario then would be: "do what the context demands now."

See, for example, Fiddes, "The Body as Site of Continuity and Change," 263–65.

23. Graham, *Transforming Practice*, 102–3, with reference back to Bourdieu, *The Logic of Practice*, 57.

24. Graham, *Transformative Practice*, 97–104.

25. See, for example, Buschart and Eliers, *Theology as Retrieval*, 268–69.

Forming Ministers or Training Leaders?

We see here the tensions both between structure and creative agency but also between the corporate and the individual. The concept of ministry I want to explore in this book will be firmly rooted in the mission of God and the ministry of Christ in which the church and individuals are called to participate. There is, therefore, a necessary givenness which is both structured and structuring and which persists over time. Yet it will be rooted in the mission of God who "is about to do a new thing"[26] and calls God's people in radical and unexpected ways. This is one important way of negotiating the tensions between more "inherited" forms of church and ministry and more "pioneering" ones, since all are rooted in the same mission of God and ministry of Christ.

Equally, while Bourdieu is surely right that all of us carry our own *habitus*—as embodied, internalized and forgotten history—MacIntyre's stress on the co-operative nature of practice helpfully rebalances this approach so that our *habitus* is also corporately shaped and open to change. The practice of ministry in any tradition will, therefore, be a constant negotiation between the givenness of ministry as it is both historically and corporately mediated, that is both structured *and* co-operative, and the creative performance from the agency of the individual.

So a fundamental argument and assumption through the book is that ministry can best be understood and described not as a random set of unconnected individual actions but as a co-operative practice, which persists over time and provides something of a corporate and structured *habitus* within which the individual minister may creatively improvise.

If there is this "givenness" in the practice of ministry that is both structured and co-operative then a process of preparation for ministry can be expected to be one way through which the structured and co-operative practice of ministry is mediated. To "do what ministers have always done" requires being inducted into the practice of ministry. In other words, *habitus* is not simply that unique collection of experiences that have shaped the person I am, although these must always be recognized, but something more corporate and intentional. Historically and ecumenically quite different practices of ministry can be discerned, not simply because of individual creative agency, but because there have developed quite distinct shared understanding and approaches. To draw on MacIntyre's example of playing chess, over time different versions of the game have developed and as individuals we are gradually inducted into one of these versions of the game,

26. Isaiah 43:19.

Introduction

which we then learn to play with our own creative flare. We might expect that Baptist ministry is one such version and one such approach to ministry that has been shaped and developed historically over the past 400 years.

The overall understanding of practice I have explored above can then be applied not only to ministry itself but also to the whole process of preparation for ministry. The work of preparing others for the exercising of ministry is a practice which itself will be both structured and co-operative, within which there is room for creativity and individual agency. Such an understanding of practice can apply to both the overall work of an institution and also the more specific work of a tutor, shared with a variety of classes over time.[27] The individual agency of a tutor happens in the context of co-operative action with colleagues and the structured practice of the institution, and the wider practice of the institution will be shaped in contemporary and historical perspective, through its particular theological and ecclesiological commitments. But, again, within these co-operative, structuring structures there is space for creative improvisation both as colleges develop particular patterns and individual tutors establish distinct pedagogical practices.

THE PASTORAL IMAGINATION

A second important term I utilize through this book is that of the "pastoral imagination." This was first developed by Craig Dykstra and then further refined in a book, *Educating Clergy*, by Charles Foster and others. Dykstra first introduces this notion of the pastoral imagination to describe the overall approach of a minister to pastoral practice as it develops over time. It is, he suggests, "a way of seeing into and interpreting the world which shapes everything a pastor thinks and does," which is both a gift but also deeply shaped by professional practice.[28] The pastoral imagination, therefore, is the particular and distinct way that *ministers* see and approach their pastoral practice *as ministers* and this can be compared with the "legal mind," a way of seeing and thinking that is particular to that profession or the "artistic imagination," common and unique to artists.[29]

While recognizing the individuality involved in pastoral practice—and Dykstra bases his comments on his personal observations of "good"

27. Foster, Dahill, Goleman, and Tolentino, *Educating Clergy*, 28, 372.
28. Dykstra, "The Pastoral Imagination," 2.
29. Dykstra, "The Pastoral Imagination," 1.

pastors—Dykstra strongly stresses the co-operative and structured similarity, shared among "good" ministers but distinct from other professions. He suggests that "pastoral ministry may require a complexity and integrity of intelligence that is as sophisticated as is needed for any kind of work," this being a "kind of internal gyroscope and a distinctive kind of intelligence."[30] So, for Dykstra, and following MacIntyre, a pastoral imagination could be described as one that is shared with others, persists over time, and is co-operative and part of the structuring structure that shapes ministry in a more universal way.

Dykstra's interest here is less the connection between the pastoral imagination and preparation for ministry but more with the practice of ministry itself, giving practice significant epistemological significance, for

> it is always forged . . . in the midst of ministry itself, as pastors are shaped by time spent on the anvil of deep and sustained engagement in pastoral work. It is the actual practice of pastoral ministry . . . that gives rise to this particular and powerful imagination.[31]

Foster, *et al.*, intentionally build on Dykstra's concept and language,[32] but do so in a way that offers a greater emphasis on diversity and individual agency rather than structure, but also begins to link the practice of preparation with the practice of ministry. Recognizing the diversity of seminary education they broaden the terminology, referring throughout to a "pastoral, priestly or rabbinic imagination."[33] While stressing that there is something shared about the practice of "clergy," as professionals with leadership responsibilities in their communities who act as agents of God, integral to their research project is the exploration of diversity of approaches and so a diversity of pastoral imaginations.

The research question behind their work explores the connection between the practice of preparation and specific pastoral imaginations, asking how seminary educators foster among their students a particular pastoral, priestly or rabbinic imagination.[34] They conclude that

---

30. Dykstra, "The Pastoral Imagination," 1. See Dykstra, "Pastoral and Ecclesial Imagination," 51.

31. Dykstra, "Pastoral and Ecclesial Imagination," 41–42.

32. Foster *et al.*, *Educating* Clergy, 12–13. There is also an institutional partnership between the Carnegie Foundation which sponsored the research in this book and the Lily Endowment of which Dykstra was the vice-president.

33. Foster et al., *Educating Clergy*, 13.

34. Foster et al., *Educating Clergy*, 13.

Introduction

seminaries do seek to form the disposition or *habitus* of a given religious or intellectual tradition within their students, suggesting Dykstra does not place enough responsibility for a pastoral imagination on seminaries, and offering a gentle and respectful correction;[35] ordinands enter "the community of the seminary educator's practice as apprentices,"[36] rather like apprentices of a master craftsman.

Yet Foster, *et al.*, although exploring a variety of Christian and Jewish traditions, still tend to work with a generic understanding of ministry applied across denominations. The fact that the book is titled *Educating Clergy*, with no apologetic for, or discussion of, the theology already conveyed in such language, indicates that their work does not pay enough attention to the way that the deep-seated concept of ministry, at the heart of any pastoral imagination, varies too.

Drawing on the foundational work of Dykstra and the developments of Foster *et al.* I propose a particular, refined, understanding of the pastoral imagination, which I will use as the central concept for joining together the practices of ministry and preparation for ministry. I propose, then, an understanding of the pastoral imagination as:

- the fundamental way of seeing into and interpreting the world which shapes everything a pastor thinks and does;
- co-operative and structured, sharing in aspects of ministry that will be universal across the church, but also shaped within a particular and distinct church tradition;
- creative and contextual, allowing space for the interplay between the co-operative and structured, the individual agency and personality of the minister and the particular context in which ministry is practiced;
- shaped both by the practice of ministry itself and the practice of preparation within the particular *habitus* of an institution;
- forged in the interplay between the practice and theology of ministry, for there is no neutral understanding of "ministry," leading to a constant dialectic between the practice of ministry and an underpinning theology of ministry itself.

---

35. Foster *et al.*, *Educating Clergy*, 23.
36. Foster *et al.*, *Educating* Clergy, 372.

A METHODOLOGY

The original DMin thesis was conducted as a piece of practitioner-research, understanding practice as the bearer of theology and concerned with the interplay and mutual shaping of theology and practice. I assumed an overall philosophical stance that might best be described as critical realism,[37] which combined what Maxwell describes as "ontological realism and epistemological constructivism."[38] I took the position that the different expressions of the practice of ministry are in fact different ways of participating in the one mission and ministry of God in Christ, a more realist approach, thus grounding practice in the prior reality of God rather than the subjective approaches of individuals and institutions, while recognizing that all knowledge both of the participants and the researcher is provisional and partial, a more critical aspect.

While seeking to develop a more fluid and flexible use of research methods appropriate to this unique context,[39] integrating insights from a range of empirical approaches, the original research drew particularly on three aspects of research methodology: Ethnography and the practice of participant observation, Organizational Studies and Theological Action Research.

Ethnography and Participant Observation

The work here sits within the broader scope of ethnography, particularly through the practice of participant observation. Mary Clark Moschella describes ethnography as immersing oneself in the communal and ritual life of a group in order to gain an understanding of this group in which participant observation is the hallmark.[40] The principal aim of ethnography is to lead to greater knowledge and more nuanced understanding,[41] particularly of the shared patterns of values, behavior, beliefs, and language of an entire social group,[42] although it may also lead to challenge and change. Key features

---

37. Cameron and Duce, *Researching Practice in Ministry and Mission*, 29–30.
38. Maxwell, *A Critical Approach for Qualitative Research*, 6.
39. Swinton and Mowat, *Practical Theology and Qualitative Research*, 50.
40. Moschella, "Ethnography," 225.
41. Moschella, "Ethnography," 226.
42. Creswell, *Qualitative Inquiry and Research Design*, 68.

of ethnographic research include observation, conversation, making field notes, qualitative interviews and the collecting of relevant documents.[43]

Participant observation is an established anthropologically-based approach to exploring the wider life of a particular community. It recognizes that observation of human communities requires some element of participation and that participation always allows opportunities for observation. Participant observation increasingly recognizes the importance of interviews or focus groups,[44] since "observation rarely grasps the intentions behind people's behavior."[45] Important aspects of ethnography within my research will be my own position as a participant observer, already immersed, as a "complete member," in the life of Regent's Park College and the collaborative partnerships within the Baptist Union and observing as an "outsider" other Baptist colleges and a number of other non-Baptist institutions. I seek to engage with the lived world of others within the empirical research, and gain a greater understanding of the entire social world of British Baptist preparation for ministry. I am also concerned with the establishment of new knowledge, which, as Cooperrider and Srivasta, suggest, has a "generative capacity"[46] therefore shaping my own practice, the practice of the college, and potentially the wider denomination. Yet, as a piece of practitioner-research that begins with the desire to reflect and develop my own practice, and with the limited immersion possible in the other Baptist colleges there are other aspects which cannot be understood in straightforward ethnographic terms.

Organizational Studies

The connections with organizational studies are particularly around the practice of researching one's own organization. Coghlan and Brannick describe this as research conducted by a "complete member" of an organization, "contextually embedded" and immersed in what Donald Schon has famously described as the messy and confusing "swampy lowlands" of practice.[47] What is particularly helpful about this approach is the recogni-

43. Bryman, *Social Research Methods*, 432.
44. See Moschella, "Ethnography," 225.
45. Cameron and Duce, *Researching Practice*, 60.
46. Cooperrider and Srivasta, "Appreciative Inquiry in Organisational Life," 130. The authors are seeking to rehabilitate the place of theory in social transformation.
47. Coghlan and Brannick, *Doing Action Research*, 4, 121.

Forming Ministers or Training Leaders?

tion of the unique role that the practitioner-researcher plays, the shadow side of any organization that an "insider" may have access to beyond the public view, and the constant need for reflexivity within the researcher who naturally and rightly brings his or her own understandings and commitment to the project.

Yet the evaluative nature of my own research which is understood to be a key aspect of researching one's own organization,[48] was more limited. For example, I explored the *intentions* of different colleges and courses in encouraging a particular pastoral imagination rather than evaluated their *successes,* and the research was not related directly to a process of organizational change[49] and there was no official reporting procedure in place.[50] Yet the whole of this book is about what I do on a week by week basis and so begins as fundamentally a piece of reflection on my own practice, recognizing that my developing practice has already shaped some of the theological conclusions to which the book leads. It is a book that is derived from practice in order to better develop that practice.

Theological Action Research

Reason and Bradbury define the overall wider methodology of action-research as:

> a participatory, democratic process, concerned with developing practical knowing in the pursuit of worthwhile human purposes ... [which] seeks to bring together action and reflection, theory and practice, in participation with others, in the pursuit of practical solutions to issues of pressing concern.[51]

Key features of action-research methodology are a collaborative / participative approach throughout, a particular cyclic methodology, a problem-solving approach to the contemporary situation and a prior commitment to action.[52] What is particularly helpful about action-research

---

48. Fox et al., *Doing Practitioner Research,* 66.

49. Coghlan and Brannick, for example, stress strongly the place of transformational change as a goal of the research, *Doing Action Research,* 121–30.

50. Fox et al., *Doing Practitioner Research,* 74.

51. Reason and Bradbury, *Handbook of Action Research,* 1.

52. See also Coghlan and Brannick, *Doing Action Research*; Brydon-Miller et al., "Why Action Research?" 9–28; Norman, "Theological Foundations of Action Research for Learning and Teaching," 114–40.

Introduction

methodology is this commitment to action as the outcome of research, its insistence on participation and an inherent concern for human flourishing. Fox *et al.* also develop their understanding of practitioner-research as an aspect of action-research[53] which connects with the aspect of action-research Coghlan and Brannick describe as self-study of the researcher.[54]

While sharing something of the praxis-oriented approach within a socially constructed epistemology, and sharing the desire for the extrapolation of useful knowledge,[55] fundamental aspects of this action-research methodology were not developed here. My concern was not to solve a problem but to reflect on practice in a more open way;[56] it was not to make a particular action more effective or to seek large-scale transformational change of the organization; it was not to build on behavioral science and the cyclic model which tests action and reflects on it as part of the process.

Building on this broader action-research methodology Theological Action Research is an approach developed by Helen Cameron *et al.*[57] that seeks to develop theology in "four voices." The "four voices" methodology was originally developed as "a single methodological and theological vision"[58] to keep theory and practice connected together. Cameron *et al.* describe theological action research as "a partnership between an insider and outsider team to undertake research and conversations answering theological questions about faithful practice in order to renew both theology and practice in the service of God's mission."[59]

It is a praxis-orientated methodology that explicitly combines the wider understandings of both action-research and practical theology, particularly drawing on systematic empirical research conducted collaboratively and patterns of theological reflection. Cameron *et al.* suggest five key characteristics to their methodology,[60] all of which will be helpful in different ways. First it is "theological all the way," rather than adding theological

---

53. Fox *et al., Doing Practitioner Research*, 48.
54. Coghlan and Brannick, *Doing Action Research*, 126.
55. Coghlan and Brannick, *Doing Action Research*, 16.
56. In this it shares the concerns of Cooperrider and Srivasta, "Appreciative Inquiry", that action-research's prior commitment to fixing what is broken could be better expanded to include what the authors describe, more positively, as "appreciative enquiry".
57. Cameron, Bhatti, Duce, Sweeney, and Watkins, *Talking About God in Practice*.
58. Cameron *et al., Talking About God*, 32.
59. Cameron *et al., Talking About God*, 63.
60. Cameron *et al., Talking About God*, 51–60.

reflection to empirical data that is otherwise seen as devoid of theology; any empirical data already contains embedded theology. Secondly, theology is disclosed through the conversational method. Thirdly theological action research looks for the formative transformation of practice and fourthly it allows practice to contribute to the transformation of theology, which sets up the vital dialectic between theory and practice that will be at the heart of this book.

The final and most innovative aspect of this methodology is the development of "four voices" which in particular enables research to be "theological all the way" and to combine theory and practice. The four theological voices that Cameron *et al.* identify are: the formal (the voice of the academy), the normative (the voice of the particular denomination as it speaks authoritatively), the espoused (the expressed self-understanding of a particular group) and the operant (the theology embedded in the group's practice).[61]

Cameron *et al.* suggest that theological action research could be conducted apart from the methodology of the "four voices" and that the "four voices" description of theology has value beyond theological action research.[62] More recently Cameron and Duce offer the "four voices" approach as a particular methodological response to the connection of theory and practice without it being linked specifically to theological action research.[63] This book follows this development and utilizes the "four voices" as its overarching methodology, in distinction from the fully developed pattern of theological action research as a collaborative process, in an approach that engages with organizational studies, action-research and ethnography, but remains distinct from all of them. Key to the research and this book, then, was the generation of these "four voices" to enable a subsequent conversation between them.

My assumption, based on my own experience, was that no theological college will be neutral in respect to the future ministry of its ordinands but through a theological vision, shared history and the particular practices of its tutors any theological college will be seeking to encourage a particular pastoral imagination in its students. An important task was to test this assumption by seeking to identify the operant and espoused practice of the preparation for ministry of a number of different theological institutions, both Baptist and others. The precise details of how this was done

61. Cameron *et al.*, *Talking About God*, 53–55.
62. Cameron *et al.*, *Talking About God*, 51.
63. Cameron and Duce, *Researching Practice*, xxx.

Introduction

are set out in chapter four, but involved investigating both the expressed understanding of these theological colleges (the *espoused* voice) and the theology embedded in their practice (the *operant* voice). This was partly formalized into the first of two empirical research questions: what is the pastoral imagination which the Baptist colleges individually are seeking to inculcate in their students?

Historically and anecdotally it has been the distinctive approaches within the five Baptist colleges in England and Wales that have been stressed, and perhaps exaggerated, rather than any similarities, although a more recent perspective suggests that these differences have largely disappeared in reality if not in perception.[64] Exploring, then, what has been a contentious issue and building on pastoral imaginations discerned in the individual colleges, a further research area was to identify elements within the practice of the five Baptist colleges that may be considered co-operative and aspects of a wider structuring structure. Therefore, I compared the *operant* and *espoused* voices identified in the five Baptist colleges with the *operant* and *espoused* voices from a sample of non-Baptist institutions leading to a second empirical research question: is there a particular combination of practices and elements of a pastoral imagination that could be considered distinctly Baptist?

Although Cameron *et al.* refer to a normative voice, in reality the nature of Baptist ecclesiology, with its strongly congregational basis, means that any attempt to offer such a normative voice on ecclesiological issues is immediately challenged and undermined by this very ecclesiology. This, therefore, requires some refinement of these "four voices." The one document that can be claimed to have *normative* status among Baptists is the relatively brief Declaration of Principle reworked into something like its present form in 1904 and with the content settled in 1938.[65] This is the document that all churches, ministers, colleges and associations agree to and affirm in joining the Baptist Union. In addition to the Declaration of Principle, there are other documents of significance which might be better described as a *representative* voice rather than a *normative* one, in that they have emerged from a wider process of reflection and deliberation within the Baptist Union and so have some sense of shared ownership, but *represent* a wider, collective view rather than being one which can be imposed on others in any normative

---

64. So suggests Goodliff, *Ministry, Sacrament and Representation*, 45.
65. A very minor change in 2009 altered Holy Ghost to Holy Spirit.

sense. A further important part of the book seeks to identify what might be considered a *representative* voice among British Baptists.

Particularly significant among these documents, for our purposes, are papers and reports that have been agreed by the Baptist Union Council. Such reports might be categorized into two historical groups: those between 1948 and 1969, which Goodliff describes as "the foundational documents"[66] and then a later grouping from 1994 onwards, which were mostly received by the Baptist Union Council rather than accepted. In addition to these more formal documents the views of a variety of Baptist theologians, including Goodliff himself, as leader of the Ministries Team of the Baptist Union of Great Britain until 2014, offer personal representative voices into the debate as those who have engaged in wide discussion and shaped on-going practice within the wider Union. These sources are brought together in a description of a Baptist *representative* voice.

Set in Higher Education contexts the Baptist colleges themselves are deeply engaged with the *formal* voice of the academy, and there are many theologians who have contributed to the way Baptists have understood theology and preparation for ministry. But among a variety of contributions to the formal voice drawn into the theological discussion, I have chosen to engage with and make particular use of the contribution of Paul Fiddes, one of the most significant contemporary Baptist theologians who has written extensively on Baptist ecclesiology and the doctrine of God both on the more specific discussions about ministry and also on a wider and deeper theology of the practice of preparation. The work of Fiddes will be used to develop a theological underpinning for the practice of preparation.

The key conversation, then, between the "four voices" will be between the theology embedded in the *operant* practices of the Baptist colleges and a sample of other institutions, the theology these colleges and institutions *espouse,* the *representative* developments within the Baptist Union and the *formal* voice in the theology of Paul Fiddes.

My aim, then, was to engage in a piece of practitioner-research that reflects on my own practice, is reflexive throughout, draws on the wider understanding of participant observation and especially on my existing participation in Regent's Park College and the wider Baptist Union, and utilizes, with some refinement, the "four voices" developed by Cameron *et*

---

66. Goodliff in fact describes the reports from 1957 to 1969 as "foundation documents" and considers the 1948 report as part of an ecumenical imperative, but his narrative both connects these strongly together and recognizes the more settled gap between 1969 and 1994. See, *Ministry, Sacrament and Representation*, 30 and 34.

Introduction

al., with the aim that both theology and practice are transformed. Within this research I was seeking to establish new knowledge with the expectation that the "generative capacity" contained in such knowledge will impact my own work, the work of the college and also the life of the wider denomination. As such, it sits between the more action-orientated approaches of action-research and the more knowledge-based approaches of ethnography.

A SYNOPSIS OF THE BOOK

My aim in this book is to explore the practice of ministry, the practice of the preparation for ministry and the connection between them through the concept of the pastoral imagination. I turn first, in chapter 2, to the understanding of the practice of ministry held generally, but not exclusively, by British Baptists through a literature review of key contemporary Baptist writers and important Baptist reports and papers. This will also offer something of a representative voice in the debate on the practice of ministry. I focus particularly on the current debate about understanding ministry through the paradigm of leadership, suggesting that "ministry" and "leadership" each convey a distinct *habitus* and offering my own preference for the *habitus* of ministry.

I then turn, in chapter 3, to the understanding of the practice of preparation for ministry exploring the historical development of practice and language in Baptist settings and also in the wider ecumenical context through a further literature review which also draws on both significant unpublished papers and the documents of QiFP, once again establishing something of a representative voice. I conclude by contrasting "training" and "formation" offering my own preference for the *habitus* of formation.

In chapter 4 I build on the overall methodology outlined above and set out the particular methods employed in the empirical research that explored the operant and espoused practice of the five Baptist colleges in England and Wales together with five non-Baptist institutions. Chapters 5 and 6 offer the findings from this research and discuss the practice of preparation for ministry embedded in the different institutions, and in particular I suggest the pastoral imagination that emerges from both espoused and operant theologies.

In chapter 7 I bring together theology and practice through a conversation between the espoused and operant voices of chapters 5 and 6 with the representative voice from chapters 2 and 3, in dialogue with the formal voice found particularly in the work of Paul Fiddes. Out of this conversation, and particularly drawing on Fiddes' work, I offer a new contribution to theory in the form of a distinct, trinitarian theology of formation for Baptists that combines the current representative position with the empirical research and is firmly rooted in a doctrine of God.

In chapter 8 I also combine practice and theology by reflecting on my own practice, exploring the nature of the practice of preparation and a proposed pastoral imagination preparation to guide the practice at Regent's Park College, and considering some of the implications for my own practice. Finally in chapter 9 I conclude by returning to the practice of ministry itself in the light of all that I have said about the preparation for ministry and the theoretical understanding of practice and the pastoral imagination set out in this opening chapter, seeking to ground the discussion by offering some initial answers to the question raised at the start of this chapter about beginning in ministry.

2

The Practice of Ministry

WHAT SHOULD BE DONE—now, today, first? This is the question with which we began. The way any minister responds to this challenge will be shaped contextually but also by the particular minister's underlying understanding of the role of ministry, which may be partly implicit and partly explicit, partly structured and partly creative, and this complex but fundamental underlying sense of ministry I have described as the "pastoral imagination."

This question about what should be done is set here within the framework of ordained ministry. Baptists over the centuries have, like most denominations, always recognized the particular calling and role of some—the few—within the wider church—the many.[1] The theology, language and practice connected to this exercising of ministry has changed, but the Baptist tradition has clearly affirmed both the ministry of all in the local gathered congregation and the particular ministry of some, whom it has often described, amongst other terms, as "ministers." In recent decades, as part of the continual debate about ministry, two contrasting issues have been particularly dominant, both in the literature and also in my experience of working with ministerial students: the practice of ministry as leadership and the understanding of ministry as sacramental. Both would have significant impact on the way a minister responds to the challenge of beginning and sustaining a ministry.

In this chapter I will explore how this changing and contested practice of ministry among British Baptists has been understood by exploring

---

1. See Goodliff, *Ministry, Sacrament and Representation*, 24–25.

the *representative* voice as set out in Baptist documents and expressed in a range of contemporary Baptist authors and then will begin to set out arguments that the most helpful pastoral imagination is built on the concept of ministry rather than that of leadership.

A DIALECTICAL MODEL

Over the last 70 years reports within the Baptist Union of Great Britain have continually stressed that ordained ministry is always appointed by Christ, from above, yet is called by the local church, from below.[2] In 1994 the Baptist Union Council received a report from the Doctrine and Worship Committee, entitled *Forms of Ministry Among Baptists: Towards an Understanding of Spiritual Leadership*, which summarized and reiterated an understanding of ministry endorsed through various Council debates earlier in the twentieth century. The thrust of this understanding is that the ministry of "the few" who are set-aside in a particular way is rooted both in the ministry of God in Christ and emerges from the ministry of the whole church.

> Ministry is exercised by the whole Church as the Body of Christ, which thus 'preaches the Word, celebrates the sacraments, feeds the flock and ministers to the world'; but some individuals are called to spiritual leadership, exercising forms of ministry in a representative way on behalf of the whole.[3]

I suggest that this might best be described as a dialectical model of ministry in which the ministry exercised by all and by the few stands in creative tension. Further it may justly be termed the *representative* position of the Baptist Union in the twentieth century, finding support both historically and in contemporary writers as well as, significantly, in documents agreed by the Baptist Union Council, and, as such, stands against both the wider catholic tradition, rooted in the historic episcopate and the patterns of newer churches, dependent on the role of apostles.

A leading voice in articulating, expounding and developing such a view of ministry is that of Paul Fiddes. One of Fiddes' first published works was devoted to this issue,[4] and he has returned to it often since; Fiddes was

---

2. Goodliff, *Ministry, Sacrament and Representation*, 47.
3. Baptist Union of Great Britain, *Forms of Ministry Among Baptists*, 17, quoting The Baptist Union of Great Britain, *The Baptist Doctrine of the Church*, 8, 89.
4. Fiddes, *A Leading Question*.

also a long-serving member of the Doctrine and Worship Committee of the Baptist Union Council, its Moderator in the early 1990s during a time of particularly contested thinking and a significant contributor to various of the key reports. Fiddes argues for this careful balance between the whole gathered church and those it sets aside for ordained ministry, and contrasts this with, on the one hand a hierarchical model, found in both secular and some church contexts, and on the other hand an employment model, in which the minister is simply at the behest of the congregation.[5] Rather he argues for "the offering of trust" in which "oversight flows to and fro between the personal and the communal, since the responsibility for 'watching over' the church belongs both to *all* the members gathered in church meeting and to the pastor."[6] Fiddes considers this dual oversight to be rooted theologically in the overall rule of Christ, and finds support for such a position in the seventeenth century confessions.[7]

David Bebbington also describes how early Baptists saw themselves as the whole gathered church sharing in the kingly ministry of Christ, as well as his priestly ministry, so that it is the believers together who "have all power both of the kingdom and priesthood immediately from Christ,"[8] while also practicing "a form of high churchmanship" which gave an important role to elected leaders to feed, govern and serve.[9] Bebbington explains how early Baptists like Smyth and Helwys disagreed with the radical puritans who entrusted authority, and the keys of the kingdom, to the church officers alone, instead holding in tension both the high place of the whole gathered church as the spouse of Christ who rules with her husband and the significant responsibility of the few called to serve and govern.[10] He then suggests that in the nineteenth century the more positive influence of the Brethren and the more negative response to the Oxford Movement led to a lower estimate of the place of the few in this dialectical understanding.[11]

---

5. Fiddes, *Tracks and Traces*, 84–87.
6. Fiddes, *Tracks and Traces*, 87.
7. Fiddes, *Tracks and Traces*, 87–91.
8. Bebbington, "An Historical Overview of Leadership in a Scottish Baptist Context," 15, quoting Smyth, *Differences of the Churches of the Separation*, 315.
9. Bebbington, "An Historical Overview," 16.
10. Bebbington, "An Historical Overview," 15–16.
11. Bebbington, "An Historical Overview," 16–17.

Forming Ministers or Training Leaders?

Nigel Wright seeks a similar kind of balance in his suggestion of ministry as "inclusive representation" in a "deliberately irenic"[12] paper first written when he became the then moderator of the Doctrine and Worship Committee towards the end of the 1990s.[13] Wright wanted to uphold a view of ministry which did not exclude the ministry of the many, which some saw as under threat, but still sought a particular role for ordained ministers.[14] In Goodliff's survey of the current understanding of Baptist ministers 95.9% would use representative language to describe their role, by far the greatest consensus,[15] and Haymes, Gouldbourne and Cross reaffirm that "there can be no ministerial function apart from the church, for there is no ministry apart from the church, and the ministry does not exist over against the church."[16]

This particular position has been further refined in two ways. First, while the importance of having particular individuals set aside in some ministry role has been stressed, such individuals have generally been seen to be for the *bene esse* of the local church but not essential. On the one hand Bebbington suggests that for the first Particular Baptists a local church would not be complete without both "officers" and members; the influential, and deeply ecumenical, Ernest Payne in the middle of the twentieth century argued for the necessity of ministers;[17] and Nigel Wright offers one of the strongest contemporary arguments, suggesting that "they are almost necessary but not quite absolutely."[18] Yet on the other hand the more general position among British Baptists has affirmed the importance of elected lay-leaders and the significant contribution of ministers, but does not make these theologically necessary. A Baptist church with just members is still a church. This shapes the dialectical model in a particular way.

Second, Fiddes argues that one of the distinctives of those individuals who exercise *episkope* is that they represent the wider universal church

---

12. Goodliff, *Ministry, Sacrament and Representation*, 55.

13. Wright, "Ministry: Towards a Consensus," reworked as "Inclusive Representation; Towards a Doctrine of Christian Ministry."

14. Rob Ellis suggests that Fiddes and Wright reach a similar position from different starting points, Wright drawing more explicitly on New Testament texts and Fiddes building on a doctrine of the Trinity, in "'The Leadership of Some . . .'" 77.

15. Goodliff, *Ministry, Sacrament and Representation*, 182.

16. Haymes, Gouldbourne and Cross, *On Being the Church*, 156.

17. See Payne, *Fellowship of Believers*, 39.

18. Wright, *Free Church, Free State*, 173.

bringing more of the length and breadth of the universal church to the local congregation.

> We should resist the view that the minister's authority is simply delegated from the local church meeting. The minister has been commissioned by Christ, and he or she comes into the local situation from the life of the church world-wide.[19]

Whatever language is used to describe other officers in the local church, and the traditional term deacon has in many places been supplemented or replaced by elders or leaders, Fiddes argues for a clear distinction, although not in rank or status, between those "lay" leaders of a congregation and those ordained to the office of minister, which again could be described in representative terms, this time representing the universal church.

This concept of a Baptist minister being a minister of the universal church while practicing ministry in a local congregation becomes established, after a number of historical disputes, in these foundational documents in the middle part of the twentieth century. In the eighteenth century debate developed between Daniel Turner and John Gill, with the former arguing that a minister was a minister of the church in general and so able, occasionally, to preach and preside in other churches, while Gill strictly limited the practice of ministry to the one local church.[20] In the twentieth century Arthur Dakin, then Principal at Bristol Baptist College, published an account of ministry which argued strongly for restricting those called Baptist ministers to those serving in the pastorate of a local church, who should be re-ordained on moving pastorate, and thus for excluding others from such a title, including College Principals! Ernest Payne, who had recently moved from Regent's Park College to become the Baptist Union's General Secretary, responded with a more universal vision of ministry.[21] By 1969 and the report on *Ministry Tomorrow*, while there was still a strong privileging of pastoral ministry in a local congregation, there was clear support for an understanding of the practice of ministry which was broader and among other things involved representing the universal church. This also shapes the dialectical model, but in a different and contrasting way.

While there is clear evidence that this dialectical model establishes itself as the *representative* voice, it is Fiddes who expresses this tension most

---

19. Fiddes, *Tracks and Traces*, 95.
20. See Goodliff, *Ministry, Sacrament and Representation*, 25.
21. See Payne, *Fellowship of Believers*.

clearly and creatively, stressing how this is a distinctively Baptist approach. Clearly there are significant ecumenical connections, both in the way that the ministry of "the few" is described through the Reformed understanding of the ministry of Word and Sacrament, which is prevalent among leading Baptist thinkers during these decades,[22] and in the way that the language of the priesthood of all believers has been developed more widely among other Protestant churches, in which the "laity" have found a much more significant place.[23] Yet ultimately this dialectical model, in which the few and the many share in the task and practice of oversight, remains a distinctly Baptist contribution to ecclesiology and ministry.

> The liberty of local churches . . . is not based on a human view of autonomy or independence, or in selfish individualism, but in the sense of being under the direct rule of Christ who relativizes other rules. This liberating rule of Christ is the foundation of what makes for the distinctive "feel" of Baptist congregational life, which allows for spiritual oversight (episkope) both by the *whole* congregation gathered together in church meeting, and by the minister(s) called to lead the congregation. This oscillating movement between corporate and individual oversight is difficult to pin down, and can lead to disasters when it begins to swing widely from one side to another, but is based in taking the rule of Christ seriously.[24]

A LEADERSHIP CHALLENGE

Although there have always been differing understandings of ministry among Baptists, this dialectical approach has been particularly challenged in recent years by an increasing stress on the practice of leadership. The foundational documents and the wider tradition does not at all resist the language of leadership to describe this oversight, for ministers "are appointed to the tasks of leadership and this leadership is to be recognized by the church,"[25] but they understand it in this particular dialectical way.

22. Goodliff, *Ministry Sacrament and Representation*, 30–33, 46–47.

23. So, World Council of Churches, *Baptism, Eucharist and Ministry* stresses the role of the whole people of God. See also the report from the Church of England Faith and Order Advisory Group, *The Mission and Ministry of the Whole Church*.

24. Fiddes, *Doing Theology in a Baptist Way*, 22; see also Ellis, "The leadership of some."

25. *Doctrine of the Ministry*, 13. In Goodliff's research 80% agreed with the statement that ministry is "the role of pastoral leadership."

In his recent book on ministerial formation Paul Goodliff begins, interestingly, by stating that the "nature of leadership in the church has always been contentious," but never been more starkly put as in the present. "For a few," he writes, "an improvement in the quality of its leadership is the answer to most of the church's woes, while for others 'leadership' is a taboo subject, promising little but a wholesale capitulation to the spirit of the age: secular, commercial and shallow."[26] While certainly agreeing with his sense that the question of ministry as leadership is one of the pressing questions for the contemporary church, and thus this chapter, my own sense and experience is that these two pulls on the dialectical model have not been equally strong.

It seems to me that there has been quite a small minority voice which has argued that Baptist ministers should not be described as leaders at all, for leadership resides only in the gathered congregation, rather than in this dialectical model.[27] Yet in recent decades the most significant challenge has come from the positive adoption of leadership language,[28] at times as a deliberate attempt to rebut this rejection of ordained ministers as leaders.[29] A survey of the more recent popular literature that pertains to ministry, suggests that the language and concept of "leadership" has become increasingly dominant, especially within the evangelical wing of the church.[30] Among Baptists this leadership challenge arises from a complex blending of theology and cultural influence, but three key factors are significant.

Internal Baptist Reflections

One challenge comes from internal Baptist reflections on the nature of ministry and church life. A key proponent of this among British Baptists has been Paul Beasley-Murray, whose most extended contributions came

---

26. Goodliff, *Shaped for Service*, xv.

27. For example, Hale, "Down with Leaders."

28. Ellis is amongst those who suggest that we are now in a "leadership paradigm" ("The Leadership of Some," 71).

29. See the correspondence between Hale and Beasley-Murray, *Baptist Times* between February 18th and March 18th 2011.

30. For wider discussions of the developing of leadership thinking see, for example, Banks and Ledbetter, *Reviewing Leadership*; Grundy, *What's New in Church Leadership?* Quicke, *360-degree Leadership*.

in the 1990s, but who still exercises influence today.[31] Beasley-Murray's starting point is that he believes he is writing in the context of a crisis in church and so a crisis in ministry.[32] This crisis is experienced both as an encroaching clericalism and also as the wider adoption of an employment model resulting in a significant number of ministers being regarded simply as paid workers at the behest of the church's every whim,[33] although it seems that Beasley-Murray is drawing on anecdotal evidence for his description of the underlying issues. His response is to think differently about ministry. The language of ministry should be reserved for the whole church, to protect the Baptist understanding of the priesthood of all believers,[34] while the language of leadership should be used for those who are set apart, thus avoiding a particular clerical approach to the role of the few.[35] All are called to ministry but only some are called to leadership.[36]

Beginning with the three New Testament lists of gifts, Beasley-Murray claims they all included leadership (although he recognizes that the language is not explicit), and so concludes that it is "fair to argue that this concept of leadership is the distinguishing concept between the ordained ministry of the church and the general ministry of the church" and among a plurality of local church leaders the distinctive role of those who are ordained is to be the "leader of the leaders."[37] Ordained ministers serve God, but lead the church and "no ministry in the church is more important than pastoral leadership."[38]

This increasing stress on leadership language exemplified by Beasley-Murray is seen in a number of places. Similar language is adopted by Nigel

---

31. Beasley-Murray, *Dynamic Leadership* and "The Meaning and Practice of Ordination" in Beasley-Murray (ed.), *Anyone for Ordination?* Beasley-Murray has also been Chair of Ministry Today and the newly formed College of Baptist Ministers. He has recently published the e-book *Living Out The Call* in which many of these themes are re-emphasized.

32. Beasley-Murray, *A Call to Excellence*, 1–5; Beasley-Murray recognizes that he draws mainly from examples in the USA to support his point.

33. Beasley-Murray, *Dynamic Leadership*, 11.

34. Beasley-Murray, *Anyone for Ordination*, 164–65.

35. It is perhaps a little ironic then that Beasley-Murray referred to himself as Senior Minister, and is chair of two organizations for ministers!

36. A colleague at Spurgeon's College, Mike Nicholls, writes in a similar vein, that the term minister should be abandoned, and Union structures be renamed, for example, to the Leadership Recognition Committee in "Ministry—Mean What You Say," 14.

37. Beasley-Murray, *Anyone for Ordination*, 162–63.

38. Beasley-Murray, *Anyone for Ordination*, 172.

Wright who has the subheading "the leadership of some and the ministry of all" in the chapter "Ministers and Members" in *Free Church, Free State*,[39] although the content of the chapter overall holds on more strongly to the dialectical model. Michael Quicke, another former Principal at Spurgeon's has drawn significantly on leadership ideas in *360-degree Leadership*,[40] and the work of Bill Allen and Viv Thomas,[41] who have both taught at Spurgeon's, and Derek Tidball[42] former Principal at London School of Theology, has also been influential. Clive Burnard in a recent doctoral thesis, which examined the ministry of a former BUGB General Secretary, suggests that Baptist views on congregational governance can exist in a healthy tension with a biblical view of leadership,[43] but his overall stress is significantly on the role of the few as leaders.

Most passionately Brian Winslade argues for a different kind of relationship between ministers and members within a Baptist ecclesiological polity.[44] Winslade, a New Zealand Baptist minister who has also worked in Australia and USA but whose thinking has begun to influence British Baptists,[45] insists that he is not "advocating an alternative to Baptist congregationalism" but seeks "new ways of expressing congregationalism in the emerging twenty-first century that will better position Baptist churches for the primary task of mission."[46] It is this missionary focus rather than a particular process of decision-making and discernment which, for Winslade, is at the heart of Baptist ecclesiology.[47] Offering a particular, and somewhat polemic, view of the development of early Baptist practices as deeply shaped by the rise of parliamentary democracy—despite the fact that in the early seventeenth century such a small percentage of the male

---

39. Wright, *Free Church, Free State*, 160.

40. Quicke, *360-degree Leadership*.

41. Allen, "Pathways to Leadership" and also, "Pathways to Leadership" in Adair and Nelson (eds.), *Creative Church Leadership*; Viv Thomas, *Future Leader*.

42. Tidball, *Builders and Fools: Leadership the Bible Way* and *Ministry by the Book*.

43. Burnard, "Transformational Servant Leadership as Exemplified in the Ministry of the Reverend Doctor David R Coffey," 66.

44. Winslade, *A New Kind of Baptist Church* and reworked from his doctoral thesis "Prioritizing Mission Within a Baptist Polity."

45. See the review of his book by Beasley-Murray, *Baptist Times*, February 18th 2011, in his "Let's not be Afraid to Learn Lessons from New Zealand," and in his *Living Out The Call*, as well as the doctoral work of Burnard.

46. Winslade, *A New Kind of Baptist Church*, 6.

47. Winslade, *A New Kind of Baptist Church*, 4–5.

population had a vote suggesting that Baptist practice was rather more counter-cultural[48]—and a rather stereotypical portrayal of current Baptist church life as trapped in the intricacies of parliamentary democracy according to "Robert's Rules," Baptist ecclesiological practices are seen as both culturally bound and no longer fit for purpose in the face of the challenges of contemporary culture.

But most significant is Winslade's insistence that while congregational governance protects the local congregation from outside authority,

> the doctrine of the priesthood of all believers can be a subtle belief in the leadership of none or, worse still, the leadership of all. Congregational government does not imply congregational leadership and congregational management.[49]

Governance is the responsibility of the few, the elders, and Winslade advocates a contemporary secular model that explicitly equates the elders of a church to the company board and the senior minister as the CEO.[50]

While these various authors can be carefully nuanced about the way the few exercise leadership, in terms of being persuasive but not demanding, servant-hearted not over-bearing,[51] there has been a tendency that reaches its climax in Winslade to radically recast the relationship between the few and the many. Here there is no mutual sharing of oversight but the clear, if compassionate, leadership of the few. This leadership challenge brings with it two further consequences.

First, it provides impetus towards a more functional view of ministry. While earlier foundational documents tended to eschew a very ontological view of ministry, a strongly functional view is also a distinct and significant development. This more functional view of ministry can also be seen as integrated in a classic evangelical position, which "does not particularly require a separated ministry so much as an enthusiastic laity."[52] Understanding ministry as leadership emphasizes tasks that are much more compatible with the practice of leadership in "secular" contexts.

---

48. Holmes, *Baptist Theology*, 102, notes that the 1832 Reform Act increased suffrage to 10% of the male population!

49. Winslade, *A New Kind of Baptist Church*, 4–5.

50. Winslade, *A New Kind of Baptist Church*, ch 10.

51. Tidball is typical in stressing that leadership that "is hierarchical, authoritarian, abusive, singular or exalts personality . . . would not be legitimate" (*Ministry by the Book*, 238).

52. Goodliff, *Ministry, Sacrament and Representation*, 55.

Second, while rejecting a clerical paradigm that reserves certain aspects of ministry to those who are ordained, it substitutes this for a leadership paradigm with a strongly hierarchical basis that divides a congregation into leaders and followers,[53] so that the majority of the church are then followers of the few or even single leader. This language offers a very different lens through which to view the relationship between the few and the many, in which a sense of shared discipleship and ministry is replaced by this dominant leadership structure. In order to avoid the employment or clerical model writers such as Beasley-Murray and Winslade have moved towards a more strongly hierarchical one that tends to set service and leadership apart.[54]

External Ecclesial Pressures

Influence on Baptist understandings also comes from other denominations and churches, whether that be from the evangelical wing of the Church of England, the Restorationist stream in the United Kingdom, or the teaching and literature of American churches. Within this there is the clear tendency, that reflects cultural leadership studies, to treat the question of leadership as a discrete and independent subject, with its own theological rationale, further shaping the communal ways that leadership is being understood across denominations. The result of this has been the sharp separation of the study of leadership from ecclesiology. The recent book by British Baptist Michael Quicke, *360-degree Leadership*, is typical in considering leadership as expressed in a variety of recent American publications from a generic standpoint, rather than a clear ecclesiological one.[55]

One of the significant influences on many local Baptist churches is the material from Willow Creek, an independent evangelical church near Chicago, and its Senior Pastor Bill Hybels. Hybels' book, *Courageous Leadership*, typical of the genre, offers biblical and theological rationales but with no ecclesiological grounding. Hybels' central thesis is the importance of the few in the life of the church and the failure of this to be sufficiently recognized. So he insists that "all over the world, people have never been led . . .

---

53. See, for example, Quicke, *360-degree Leadership*, 4, 70, quoting approvingly from John MacGregor Burns and Warren Wilhelm.

54. Beasley-Murray, *Dynamic Leadership*, especially 32–36.

55. Quicke, *360-degree Leadership*: There is a hint, 58–59, of ecclesiology in advocating corporate discernment.

I believe that the great tragedy of the church in our time has been its failure to recognize the importance of the spiritual gift of leadership."[56] One area, for example, where this influence is expressed is that of choosing other officers or leaders. Whereas in the dialectical model and in more traditional Baptist patterns the responsibility lies firmly with the congregation who both nominate and elect, there seems a growing desire among ministers to be able to pick their team to complement their own gifts or for "the few" to take full responsibility for discerning who else should join this group.[57]

It may be that the dislocation of leadership from ecclesiology is part of a wider post-denominational movement that seeks to locate faith, church and ministry in biblical patterns that seek to be culturally relevant but end up being acontextual. The reality is of course that there is an operant ecclesiology at work in all churches, embedded in structures and practices even when that is neither acknowledged nor explicitly developed. Willow Creek, for example, does have an explicit ecclesiology as an independent church with a governing Board of Elders, which the church understands to be the Biblical model,[58] rather than based on congregational government. The development of its practices of leadership and ministry has happened in this very specific ecclesial setting, and so to adopt certain practices involves bringing with them implicit ecclesial understandings.

It is significant that Winslade openly admits, in a way that reflects the practice of others, that larger Baptist churches develop what is in effect a nuanced "presbyterian" form of governance, although he seeks to argue that in doing so the church still upholds a congregational polity.[59] Such a construction of membership and ministry, influenced by presbyterian, episcopal or apostolic polities, challenges and moves away from the dialectical model which is rooted in an explicit and foundational congregational ecclesiology, the heart of a representative Baptist understanding of the church.

---

56. Bill Hybels, *Courageous Leadership*, 67.
57. See Hybels, *Courageous Leadership*, 80–86, for advocacy of such a policy.
58. See, http://www.willowcreek.org/governance, accessed 12th May 2014.
59. Winslade, *A New Kind of Baptist Church*, chapter 12. It is only presbyterian in that the local church is governed by elders rather than being part of a wider denominational presbyterian structure.

Wider Cultural Developments

The third, though interconnected, area of influence comes from wider cultural developments, both in more general patterns of modernity and post-modernity, and in the more specific development of leadership studies. It is, of course, too simplistic to categorize this as a divide between the secular and the Christian, as both are often woven together. Robert Greenleaf's influential development of "servant leadership," for example, emerged from his role within a "secular" company, AT&T, but he writes both as a CEO and shaped by his Christian faith. While it is often recognized that it is important that wider cultural practices are not simply and uncritically baptised into church structures, it is questionable whether such caution has always been adopted. In particular, as suggested earlier, leadership theory has tended to see itself as a discrete subject which can be developed either from first principles or as reflection on practice and experience, creating a significant disconnect with an ecclesiologically rooted understanding of ministerial oversight.[60]

Among contemporary Baptist thinkers, Paul Goodliff in particular has drawn on the MacIntyrean analysis, which has categorized modernity in terms of therapist and manager, to explore the way that developments within late modernity and post-modernity have significantly shaped the understanding and practice of ministry.[61] Seeing the way that these trends identified by MacIntyre have shaped the church, Goodliff concludes that an older tradition of attentiveness to God has been "replaced by the activist, the managerial, the administrative tasks of running an organisation called the church."[62] Goodliff suggests that the combination of evangelical activism and the "false god of visible success" has significantly contributed to contemporary understandings, which has led to judging ministerial practice by an instrumental effectiveness, expressed as "the ability to lead and manage a local church in pursuit of growth in numbers, and it must be acknowledged, financial support."[63] This effectiveness, he suggests, may

---

60. See Banks and Ledbetter, *Reviewing Leadership*, chapter 4; for an early and incisive caution against reading modern leadership patterns into the ministry of Jesus see Cadbury, *The Peril of Modernising Jesus*.

61. MacIntyre, *After Virtue*, 29–30, suggests that modern western culture is shaped by three "characters", which stand as metaphors for cultural developments and emphases: the therapist, manager and rich aesthete.

62. Goodliff, *Ministry, Sacrament and Representation*, 132.

63. Goodliff, *Ministry, Sacrament and Representation*, 139.

be coined in terms of church growth or ministry as leadership,[64] and his conclusion is that it has resulted in a particular kind of malaise.[65]

The leadership challenge is thus both widespread and significant. Whereas few Baptist ministers and churches have adopted this approach to the extent that Winslade encourages, my own experience points to the widespread influence of these ideas in the shaping of much contemporary practice.

A SACRAMENTAL TURN

Yet there is also evidence of more recent changes in a different direction and in a significant move away from a more functional understanding of ministry, which Goodliff describes as a "sacramental turn."[66] Goodliff's work offers both a narrative and systematic account of the twists and turns which led to an increasing suspicion of the more traditional language of "Word and Sacrament" in the mid-twentieth century with a pull towards a more functional direction, and then, under the influence of a small number of significant college tutors and principals, a move towards embracing some kind of sacramental understanding of ministry.

His empirical research suggests that 56.8% of Baptist ministers consider ministry to be a sacramental office and 76.3% consider their ordination to the Christian ministry to be shared with other traditions, thus somehow representing the universal church.[67] Looking more closely at the data Goodliff concludes that there is strong evidence of a change from the 1950s to 2000s with a clear trend towards an increasingly sacramental understanding of ministry, although the group which showed the most functional characteristics and least sacramental ones were those who were at college in the 1980s, which further reinforces the sense of the functional turn before the sacramental one.[68] Goodliff's own current assessment is that among Baptist ministers there would be "a centre of gravity around about the notion of a representative individual and some kind of light sacramentalism."[69]

---

64. Goodliff, *Ministry, Sacrament and Representation*, 140.

65. For further theological critique of the stress on management see Pattison, *The Faith of the Managers* and "Management and Pastoral Theology".

66. Goodliff, *Ministry, Sacrament and Representation*, 60–61.

67. Goodliff, *Ministry, Sacrament and Representation*, 182.

68. Goodliff, *Ministry, Sacrament and Representation*, 86.

69. Personal interview, 17th July 2013.

Goodliff offers a number of reasons that have influenced this change, including the development of a more open evangelicalism, the influence of charismatic and ecumenical partners and a more general adoption of post-liberal theology mediated again by college tutors.[70] In particular Goodliff identifies the work of Eugene Peterson as having a significant impact in calling ministers away from "modernist and functionalist concerns for managing the church"[71] to an older and deeper view of ministry, and he concludes that "the resurgence of sacramentalism might be seen as a reaction to an overly managed church and a too functional view of ministry."[72]

As always there is a spectrum of views with John Colwell, a tutor at Spurgeon's from 1994 to 2009, arguing for the strongest sacramental position of an indelible ordination,[73] with milder versions adopted by Paul Fiddes,[74] Nigel Wright[75] and Stephen Holmes.[76] As the majority position moves along the spectrum from more functional to more sacramental this may have consequences for the way the dialectical model or leadership paradigm are worked out, although further research would be required. It is certainly true that Baptist writers who would embrace and encourage a more sacramental understanding have, to varying degrees,[77] argued for a more dialectical model of ministry. Goodliff in addition suggests that a functional approach has proved inadequate in the task of forming ministerial virtues as part of the preparation for ministry.[78] It would seem that the leadership model, while being adopted and espoused by some, is increasingly perceived as inadequate by others and is being challenged by a more sacramental view of ministry.

---

70. Goodliff, *Ministry, Sacrament and Representation*, 7.
71. Goodliff, *Ministry, Sacrament and Representation*, 130.
72. Goodliff, *Ministry, Sacrament and Representation*, 149.
73. Colwell, *Promise and Presence*, 222.
74. Fides, *Tracks and Traces*, 101–2.
75. Wright, *Free Church, Free State*, 169–71.
76. Holmes, "Towards a Baptist Theology of Ordained Ministry," 258–62.
77. So Colwell, Fiddes, Holmes, Goodliff and Ellis. Wright is perhaps the most willing to embrace aspects of the leadership paradigm.
78. Goodliff, *Ministry, Sacrament and Representation*, 142, and this is a central thesis in *Shaped for Service*.

Forming Ministers or Training Leaders?

MINISTERS OR LEADERS?

There is not in the literature any simple contrast between ministry and leadership and the vast majority of Baptist writers adopt some understanding of the way ordained ministers exercise leadership. Whether ordained ministers should have a role in pastoral leadership is not the significant question. What is at stake is the way that the "few" and the "many" are related in contemporary Baptist church life, and whether the representative position within the Baptist Union in the twentieth century, which I have described as the dialectical model, will be modified or replaced.

Recognizing that there is a spectrum of thinking and not just two distinct views, we may still suggest that "ministry" and "leadership" each offer quite distinct pastoral imaginations. They are both ways of understanding practice that are structured, co-operative and creative, seeking to be rooted in God's coming in Christ, sharing with others in an approach to ministry that persists over time, as well as being contextual and giving space for individual creative improvisation. They are both shaped by the interplay between the practice, theology and language used. As such then ministry and leadership each develop their own *habitus*, which continues to structure and shape those who indwell them.

In etymological derivation, "minister" derives from the word for servant, based on the Latin translation of the Greek word *diakonos*. Theology embedded in the language of ministers and deacons suggests all are servants. "Leader", at least its most common secular terminology, is not used in the New Testament for those set apart in the Christian Church.[79] On the other hand, in contemporary use, while some hear the word "minister" in an overly clerical sense, others may hear the word "leader" in an overly authoritarian way, and we noted earlier the tendency to rename those traditionally called "deacons" as elders or leaders. Language is not neutral and will contribute to the overall *habitus* that is developed.

Regarding the detail of the practice of ministry, the Baptist Union reports during the twentieth century focus their understanding on preaching the Word, presiding at the sacraments, pastoral oversight and pastoral care. Such an understanding has developed co-operatively over time but has roots deep in Baptist history, with early Baptists focusing on feeding the flock, preaching and praying, and with administering the sacraments and

---

79. *Archon* is used 36 times in the New Testament but never to describe those in the church.

pastoral oversight being added in time.[80] Most recently, with the interesting addition of the outward focused emphasis on evangelism, it has been expressed as:

> The essence of such ministry will always be that of 'bearing the Word', that is to say, proclaiming, teaching and interpreting for today the Word of God spoken in Jesus Christ and witnessed to in the Holy Scriptures. This Word is to be applied to all people through pastoral care, evangelism or teaching by those who are instructed in the beliefs and practices of the Christian faith and able to be reliable guides.[81]

This contrasts with the much greater stress on strategy and management which has accompanied a more functional stress on leadership. This is not to deny the place of the practices listed above but Beasley-Murray's categorization, for example, of ordained ministers as "leaders of leaders" positions ministry more within this management category even though preaching and pastoral care may remain central tasks. In a recent Oxford MTh thesis by one of my former students, Gareth Garland undertook some empirical research in which he correlated the practice of ministry of a sample of Baptist ministers in one geographical area with their more functional or more sacramental espoused understandings of ministry. His findings suggest a greater emphasis on management and delegating among the more functional group and a greater emphasis on pastoral care and incarnational mission amongst the more sacramental group.[82] All this then adds further to our reflection on what a minister might do in a new pastorate.

The pastoral imagination, then, within the ministry *habitus* would seem to understand ministerial practice more strongly around "bearing the Word" in worship, preaching, evangelism, and pastoral care. This paradigm intentionally uses the same language of the few and the many to stress that these practices are fundamentally shared and prefers the historical language rooted in *diakonos*, recognizing that as meanings work in complex ways, there may be no obvious title that clearly conveys the radical servant nature at the root of the words. Using language with this dual focus may run certain risks, of being misinterpreted so that the "obvious" Baptist theology of

---

80. Goodliff, *Ministry, Sacrament and Representation*, 26.

81. Baptist Union of Great Britain, "An Agreed Statement on Ministry".

82. Garland, "Anyone Can? An Exploration of Ordained Baptist Ministry as one of Word and Sacrament."

the priesthood and ministry of all becomes lost,[83] but holds onto the clear dialectical model.

The pastoral imagination that emerges from the leadership *habitus*, on the other hand, contrasts the calling of the few and the many, categorizing some as leaders and the rest as followers, and while wanting to hold on to the epithet of servant, it is the noun "leader" qualified by the adjective "servant" that remains dominant. Oversight is not shared between the few and the many but resides firmly in the few, together with a much greater emphasis on the tasks of management.

As a structuring structure a pastoral imagination provides a fundamental framework within which creative ministry develops. We can expect our opening question—what do I do?—to be answered quite differently within a pastoral imagination shaped by either "leadership" or "ministry".

Later chapters in the book will add theological depth to an argument about the nature of ministry and ministerial formation, but I have begun here to lay the foundations for this understanding on a more historic basis. I have argued that from their early origins Baptists have held an understanding of ministry and the relationship between the few and the many that is best described as a "dialectical model". This was an intentional model, distinct from other groups, even other radical Protestants, that was based on a careful and creative tension between the kingly rule of the whole congregation and the gift of the few who exercise oversight. In distinction to Winslade's caricature of early Baptist history this was a counter cultural development somewhat ahead of its time. While the precise way that this dialectic has operated has changed and developed, the fundamental nature of that dialectic has remained, and is expressed in a variety of representative documents and writers.

In terms of ministry as a practice that is co-operative and shared with others over time into which we are inducted and which then acts as a structuring structure or *habitus*, there is, I suggest, a distinctly Baptist approach. There are ways that this is being challenged by some writers explicitly and implicitly from within the leadership paradigm, but I argue that, rather than being out of date in a contemporary context, it remains as relevant and in some ways as counter-cultural as in the past. This distinctly Baptist approach is best expressed with the language and paradigm of ministry that holds intentionally to a creative tension between the ministry of the many together

---

83. This is Beasley-Murray's claim, "The Ministry of All," 158, although one hopes that what is obvious is remembered!

The Practice of Ministry

with the representative ministry of the few. This, as I have suggested, does not mean that there is no leadership; in this understanding ministers, deacons / elders and a whole congregation exercise leadership. But as an overall description of the role of the few called by God, ministry is the most appropriate language. At the heart then of a distinctly Baptist approach to a pastoral imagination is this dialectical understanding of ministry.

Reflecting on my own ministry over thirty years, this is the *habitus* into which I was inducted. First by being a member of a local Baptist church and being shaped by its practices; then by a process of preparation in College for ordained ministry; and more recently, as is often the way, the calling to teach others allowed me to reflect on my own practice and understanding and make explicit what was hitherto much more implicit.

"What do I do?" This was our opening and overarching question. Eugene Peterson offers one of the clearest and most compelling answers, an answer I have often drawn on in teaching and ordination sermons, when he calls for those set aside in ministry to be attentive to God and help others be attentive to God too.[84] If those new in ministry might be shaped by a *habitus* which is shared with others and persists over time, to do somehow what ministers do, then we might answer this by suggesting that what ministers do is to be attentive to God in, with and through the congregation.

---

84. Peterson, *Working the Angles*, 2.

3

The Practice of Preparation

"What should I do?" I have suggested in the previous chapter that the pastoral imagination revealed in the answer to this question would be quite different if shaped more around the *habitus* of ministry or the *habitus* of leadership, and began to argue for a *habitus* of ministry. A number of factors will be involved in shaping the way an individual minister responds to this question, but Goodliff's research has clearly shown that preparation for ministry in Baptist colleges has shaped students' understanding of ministry, and so we can expect that the pastoral imagination or *habitus* of a new minister will have been partly shaped by their experience of the process of preparation. If we understand ministry as a practice in the way outlined in chapter 1, then we can expect the process of preparation as a key time in which ministers engage with the broader practice of ministry, that is as something shared and co-operative that persists over time.

There has been this preparation for ministry for a considerable period of church history,[1] and for the majority of Baptist history too.[2] The majority of new ministers settling in Baptist churches and entering into the Register of Nationally Accredited Ministers of the Baptist Union have been prepared in one of the five colleges in membership with the Baptist Union, although, within the freedom of a local Baptist church to call its own minister, at the

---

1. See Mayes, *Spirituality in Ministerial Formation*, chapters 1 and 2 for a survey of such preparation through Christian history.

2. Bristol Baptist College, the oldest Baptist ministerial college in the world, was founded in 1679, actually beginning in 1720.

time of writing three other routes existed.[3] Some exercise ministry having studied in a variety of other contexts, principally non-denominational Bible Colleges. Such people could apply to the Residential Selection Conference to be considered for acceptance onto the Register. Secondly, in 2006, the London Baptist Association launched a Portfolio Route, designed for those already exercising ministry, who needed further preparation for ministry if they were to be accredited, but for whom patterns and programs of formation in the context of one of the Baptist colleges were not deemed appropriate. At the time of writing this is limited to London, and it is focused on those ministering in a variety of ethnic churches although other Associations have expressed interest in the scheme. Thirdly, it was possible to apply to transfer into the Register from a different Baptist Union or a different denomination recognized by the Baptist Union of Great Britain. Such a range of pathways into Baptist ministry is likely to lead to varying pastoral imaginations, although exploring this particular issue is beyond the scope of this book. Instead, I will focus here on the work of the five Baptist colleges as they seek to prepare new ministers.

There have been significant changes to the practice of the Baptist colleges over the last thirty years, in line with developments more widely in the preparation for ordinands. In this chapter I will explore how the practice of preparation for ministry among Baptists has developed historically, including more contemporary initiatives, through engaging with the limited published literature, important unpublished papers from those involved in the Baptist colleges, and the influence of patterns of ecumenical inspection. I will then begin to set out arguments for an understanding of the practice of the preparation for ministry as formation.

DIVERSE TERMINOLOGY

Up until this point I have consistently used the language of "preparation" to describe this practice, looking for a more neutral and descriptive word in the midst of linguistic and pedagogical diversity. In reality varied language has been and is used to describe the process of preparation, language which again has been both contested and which carries embedded theology.

---

3. Figures in the Baptist Union of Great Britain *Ignite* report suggest that 72.6% of current active ministers were prepared for ministry in a BUGB Baptist College.

Forming Ministers or Training Leaders?

Alongside wider terms such as growth, learning or development, the three key descriptors have been education, training and formation.[4]

"Theological education" has been particularly connected with the cognitive dimension of learning expressed in terms of knowledge and understanding. The connection of theology with academic education goes back to the very origins of universities, and while it has been a broader term, there was a tendency, certainly within the twentieth century, to equate theological education with preparing ordained ministers. Building on this strongly cognitive understanding, one unnamed Baptist College Principal from the 1960s is reported to have said "train a man's (sic) mind and the rest will take care of itself."[5] While educational philosophy itself has developed and there is a broader and more foundational epistemology in many contemporary accounts, which argue that education engages the whole person in all their dimensions and relationships,[6] understanding the term to derive from the Latin *educere*,[7] to lead or draw out, the language of education still tends to retain its cognitive stress.

"Ministerial training" became the most common description of this process of preparation in the latter half of the twentieth century. The 1960s and 1970s in particular saw a reaction to the perceived heavily academic bias of the colleges and this led to the development of intentional courses in pastoral studies, which explored more practical aspects of ministry. Corresponding to a greater stress on the development of skills in other aspects of education, this became a significant feature of the way the practice of preparation was rethought during these decades. It is language which is still widely used, and for Baptists it is embedded in the denomination description of those in the process of preparation as "Ministers-in-Training".

The language of "formation" has its roots in the Catholic tradition in the mid-eighteenth century, particularly in French religious orders, where formation is occasionally applied specifically to the development of ordinands in spirituality and holiness,[8] and was first used in an ecumenical con-

---

4. For another summary account of these developments with different emphases see Goodliff, *Shaped for Service*, 28–37.

5. Quoted by Taylor, "The Free Churches Selection and Training." Taylor also comments in 1982 that it was not that long ago in the 1950s that remarkably little practical training was given, just degrees in theology, 2nd lecture on "The Theology of Spiritual Formation" at 14th Atlantic Seminar in Theological Education.

6. See, for example, Astley, *The Philosophy of Christian Religious Education*, 38–39.

7. As opposed to the Latin *educare* meaning to bring up or train.

8. Mayes, *Spirituality in Ministerial Formation*, 35–38, who suggests that no research

text in the 1965 World Council of Churches *Gazzada Statement* on "laity formation".[9] It then begins to make its mark in the Protestant churches in the late 1970s, and is the language which has become increasingly significant, indeed dominant in some circles.[10] The language of formation allows for a stress on both the place of spirituality and character in the practice of preparation and also on the way that various diverse aspects are integrated together. Reflecting on all three linguistic descriptions a Baptist Union document states:

> Ministers are not simply 'trained' in skills required, or 'educated' in the academic discipline of theology and its many sub-disciplines. While both are certainly major components of ministerial courses, there is a third area, one concerned with character and spirituality, ethics and human relationships, that is essential to ministry. When these aspects are added to the development of skills and the acquisition of knowledge and understanding, there is a complex mix that is generally referred to as 'formation.'[11]

But the above quote raises a number of important questions about the use of language. First, it proposes three aspects to the overall preparation, two of which are labelled as training and education, and linked to practical skills and cognitive knowledge, but the third is left untitled. Sometimes, as we will see, this third area is described as "formation", so that the whole process is one of training, education and formation. But confusion arises because all three terms are also used to describe the whole process as well as particular aspects of it. Second, it suggests that this complex mix is "generally" referred to as formation, but it remains unclear who is thought generally to use the language in this way, although Baptists would seem to be included. Third, a further unspoken implication is that while this may be contemporary practice it has not always been so, but the document offers no account of how Baptists in particular have reached this point. I offer such an account below.

---

into the origins and development of "formation" has been published.

9. Raiser, "Fifty Years of Ecumenical Formation," 440.

10. In addition to Mayes' work see Worthen, *Responding to God's Call* and Shier-Jones (ed.), *The Making of Ministry*.

11. Baptist Union of Great Britain, *Patterns of Ministry Among Baptists: A Review of 'The Register of Covenanted Persons Accredited for Ministry,'* 11.

AN AGREED LANGUAGE? THE EMERGENCE OF THE FORMATION PARADIGM

The origins of a formation paradigm in the eighteenth century Catholic Church are developed in and after Vatican II, with some of the texts referring explicitly to different aspects of formation, and also more generally referring to the development of spirituality as distinct from academic study.[12] Reflections on the spiritual formation of Catholic ministers in the USA explicitly develops this language,[13] which comes to fruition in the 1992 Papal Encyclical *Pastores Dabo Vobis* from John Paul II. This uses formation language as the dominant paradigm and refers to human, spiritual, intellectual and pastoral formation. These have since become the dominant four categories in Catholic thinking.[14]

Additional evidence of its roots in Catholicism comes from John Henry Newman in the middle of the nineteenth century, in his lectures in support of a new exclusively Catholic university in Dublin. He brings together the intellectual and spiritual in a university setting in a way that has significant modern resonances. He speaks of the way "a habit of mind is formed which lasts a life-time"[15] and that a university education quite explicitly concerns the formation of character. Mike Higton summarizes Newman's understanding of university education, based on his experience at Oxford and hopes for Dublin, as "a school of intellectual virtue, forming its students as human beings, citizens and professionals"[16] and as "formation in counter-cultural intellectual virtue: in patient questioning and the pursuit of coherence or integrity."[17]

Other significant developments come in a number of interconnected and mutually dependent ways. In 1977 the World Council of Churches produced their new journal, *Ministerial Formation*.[18] It attempts no definitive definition, yet an early edition suggested this was a holistic process

---

12. Mayes, *Spirituality in Ministerial Formation*, 42.

13. See Hughes, *Preparing for Church Ministry* and the report of the Task Force of the National Federation of Seminary Spiritual Directors, *Spiritual Formation: Current Issues* referenced in Edwards Jr, "Spiritual Formation in Theological Schools."

14. Mayes, often works with these categories; *Spirituality in Ministerial Formation*, 172–74.

15. Newman, Discourse 5 "Knowledge its Own End" in *The Idea of a University*, 129.

16. Higton, *A Theology of Higher Education*, 80.

17. Higton, *A Theology of Higher Education*, 90.

18. The first edition appeared in January 1978 and it continues to be published.

involving: intellectual resourcefulness, awareness of God and sensitivity to real human problems, the assimilation of appropriate skills, enrichment in exemplary spirituality and a commitment to congregations and people.[19]

Around the same time in the USA the Association of Theological Schools responded to the increasing sense of the paucity of spirituality in theological colleges both in the formal curriculum and in the wider life of students and staff with a two-year research project that culminated in the 1980 report, "Spiritual Formation in Theological Schools: Ferment and Change."[20] It offered its own definition of "spiritual formation":

> Anything can contribute to our spiritual formation, including the critical tradition of belief we normally call academic theological education and the personal identity/role development involved in pastoral formation. But intentional spiritual formation is distinguished from these by its up-front focus on conscious means of cultivating attentiveness to grace, especially to the called out Christ-nature, in our individual and corporate life.[21]

Such concerns were then taken up in the so-called "Theological Education Debate" from the early 1980s onwards and, in reaction to contemporary experience that was seen as fragmented and overly cognitive, ways of speaking of the wider process of theological education that drew on formative language were developed. So, for example, responding to the critique and challenge set by Edward Farley, Richard Neuhaus edited papers from a symposium under the title *Theological Education and Moral Formation*.[22] A similar contemporary parallel is the work of James Smith, who argues more generally that Christian colleges and universities in the United States have been too concerned about information rather than formation, and that education needs to be more deeply formative.[23]

In 1987, the Church of England produced a significant report on the future of Ministry, *Education for the Church's Ministry*, often known as *ACCM 22*,[24] which begins their tentative use of formation language. This is consolidated in subsequent years by the reports, *Theology in Practice*

---

19. Sapsezian, "Exploring the Nature of Ministerial Formation," 20–21.
20. Edwards Jr, "Spiritual Formation in Theological Schools."
21. Edwards Jr, "Spiritual Formation in Theological Schools," 10.
22. Neuhaus, *Theological Education and Moral Formation*.
23. Smith, *Desiring the Kingdom*, 221.
24. Church of England, Advisory Council for the Church's Ministry, *Education for the Church's Ministry*.

and *Integration and Assessment*.[25] Likewise, the Methodists discussed the preparation for ordained ministry in some depth through their report, *The Making of Ministry*,[26] which leads to formation language becoming the dominant language adopted at the Methodist Conference in 1999. A major further development was the consultation and reflection process that produced *Formation for Ministry within a Learning Church* in the Church of England, often known as the Hind Report after its chair Bishop John Hind, which sees formation as the "overarching concept that integrates the person, understanding and competence" and not just one aspect of the whole.[27] The developing nature of the process can be seen in the way the second and final version of the report uses formation language to a much greater degree than the first published drafts.[28] Frances Ward connects this development within Anglican documents with the rejection of a particular, "banking" model of education and the adoption of new perspectives from adult education and life-long learning.[29]

Yet formation language has not been universally adopted within the Church of England. Initial documents from the most recent review entitled *Resourcing Theological Education* suggest this will consider initial ministerial education and different training pathways. The language of theological education has a long history and, by avoiding ministerial language, may appear more inclusive. Formation language is present in the new review but appears to be more downplayed and is not developed further. So one publication from this review, *Resourcing Ministerial Education: A Guide to New Financial Arrangements* (published in 2017), uses predominantly training language, although formation and education both appear in a much more limited way, with no discussion of the interplay between terminology.[30]

Baptists appear to be early adopters of this language, although Baptist ecclesiology means it is harder to follow the development through a

---

25. Church of England, *Theology in Practice* and *Integration and Assessment: The Report of an ABM Working Party on Educational Practice*.

26. Church of England, Ministerial Training Policy Working Group, *The Making of Ministry*.

27. Church of England, Archbishops' Council, *Formation for Ministry within a Learning Church*, 29.

28. For a fuller account of these developments see Mayes, *Spirituality in Ministerial Formation*, chapters 3 and 4.

29. Frances Ward, *Lifelong Learning: Theological Education and Supervision*, 73.

30. Church of England, Ministry Division, *Resourcing Ministerial Education*.

normative voice of denominational documents.[31] In fact there is a very intriguing reference to the work of Hugh Evans, Principal at Bristol in the later part of the eighteenth century as "forming them able, evangelical, lively, zealous ministers of the Gospel."[32] More recently, the most significant figure was Michael Taylor, an initial member of the WCC PTE Commission, a regular contributor to *Ministerial Formation* and whose previous study at Union Theological Seminary, New York connects him to the American context. Taylor, it seems, becomes the conduit from international and ecumenical developments to the wider Baptist denomination in the UK.

He writes in 1979 that one of the perplexities that remained was "how to form persons and not just train minds or develop skills."[33] In 1982, in a series of lectures, Taylor explores the different uses of the word "formation" and the scope of its meaning, asserting his preference for the term personal formation (spiritual formation seeming to separate out the spiritual from the rest of life), by which he means the entirety of the process of preparing for ministry as an aspect of the on-going formation of the people of God. Yet he concedes that "we do, in my world, pay lip-service to formation in the more all-embracing sense to which I have referred."[34] In 1983 Taylor gave a paper to the Baptist Colleges' Staffs' Conference on "Ministerial Formation" and the following year's conference followed the theme of "Formation of Persons for Ministry" and "Education as the Formation of Persons."[35]

The adoption of formation language was not and is not total. Articles in the magazine of the Baptist Ministers' Fellowship, *The Journal*, in the 1990s reflect on developments in ministerial training with no mention at all of formation,[36] and in my own experience the preparation in college is much more commonly described as ministerial training. But there have been significant changes in the practice of preparation that have moved away from the more dominant cognitive model to one which embraces this

---

31. It is perhaps for this reason that Mayes' quite extensive review of formation language makes no mention at all of Baptists!

32. Quoted in Ellis, "Being a Minister: Spirituality and the Pastor", 57.

33. Taylor, "The Free Churches Selection and Training."

34. Taylor, 1st lecture, 14th Atlantic Seminar in Theological Education, 6. A letter from Brian (presumably Haymes, a tutor at Northern) to Taylor as Principal in 1982 reveals the debate among staff there about the language, with the language of training still dominating but with a growing belief in the language and idea of formation.

35. Minutes of The Baptist Colleges Staffs Conference.

36. See, Nicholls, "An Evaluation of Church-based Training," and Weaver, "Developing Patterns of Ministerial Training."

"complex mix". This has often been represented by the language of "head, heart and hands" and "knowing, being, doing" or the now common image of three interlocking circles (figure 1 below), that seem to have emerged in Baptist thinking through the work of Bill Allen when he was tutor at Spurgeon's College.[37] This interconnection between knowledge, character and skills corresponds to the cognitive, normative and practical "apprenticeships" identified in clerical and other professional education by Foster et al.,[38] and, to some degree, to the cognitive, affective and volitional aspects of education.[39]

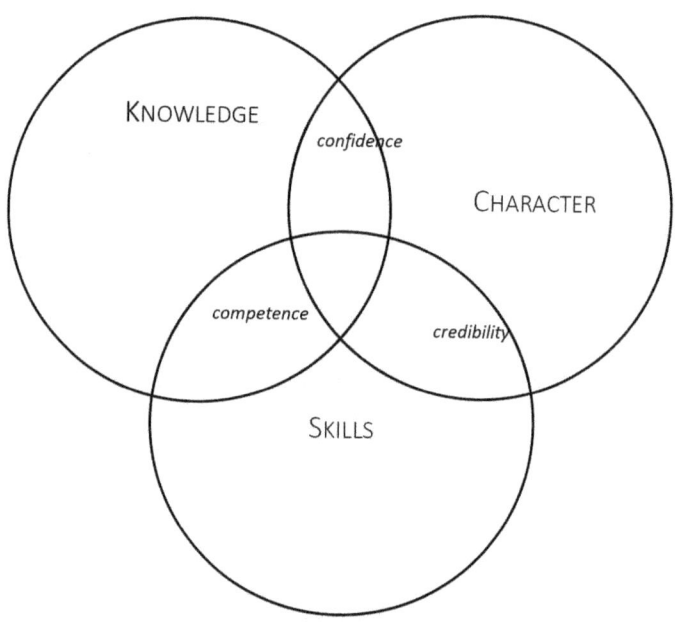

Figure 1: Venn diagram of integrating preparation for ministry

Although the last twenty-five years have seen a move into the formation paradigm there is not yet a clearly and universally accepted use of language. Three important aspects stand out.

37. The origins of this model are in Allen's PhD, "Pathways to leadership."
38. Foster et al., *Educating Clergy*, 406.
39. See Astley, *Learning in the Way*, 35–37.

The Practice of Preparation

First, the word "formation" itself, as we have seen, is used in two contrasting ways: it may indicate a distinct third area of preparation which particularly centers around issues of spirituality and character, but it may also indicate the whole process of preparation of which education and training and the development of character are aspects. So the paper "Ministry and Mission: Direction of Travel" as part of the Common Awards process is typical of much documentation in that it uses formation in both these ways.[40]

Secondly, the words education, training and formation are, at times, all used interchangeably to describe the whole process of preparation. A document on restructuring the Union's Accredited list in 1998 can refer simply to ministerial formation without any further explanation,[41] assuming that such language would be understood. Yet other Union documents and articles by college staff from the same period will refer simply to ministerial training,[42] and a report on the colleges and the Union can use education, training and formation, seemingly interchangeably, and although it explicitly proposes a holistic practice of preparation, training language significantly dominates.[43] *The Ignite* Report, from 2015, uses the language of formation and training, but it is the language of formation that is more prevalent. The Baptist Union website in 2020 uses almost predominantly the language of training.

Within this diversity it is also possible to trace a common way that language has developed in all of the colleges. For example, earlier versions of student handbooks predominantly use training language, which has been gradually changed to place more emphasis on formation.[44] In a survey of the websites of the British Baptist colleges in the summer of 2012, there was very little mention of ministerial formation and the majority of colleges simply referred here to ministerial training, despite other significant internal documents stressing formation. By 2020 there is an increased use of ministerial formation on the same websites, although both nomenclatures are used and there begins to be some distinction as some Colleges

---

40. Church of England Ministry Division, "Ministry and Mission: Direction of Travel," 3–4.

41. Baptist Union of Great Britain, "Towards a New List."

42. See, for example, Wright's work in Baptist Union of Great Britain, "Ministry: Towards a Consensus" in 2000.

43. Baptist Union of Great Britain, *Partners Together: The Colleges and the Rest of the Baptist Union of Great Britain—Report of the Union/Colleges Partnership Task Group*.

44. Mayes concludes that there has been the same gradual change in language in Anglican colleges.

use predominantly formation language and others that of training. It may be that there is some sense that "training" communicates more easily with those outside of the colleges and its use is intentional, or it maybe that the language used simply reflects the particular experience of the individual writing that particular text and is somewhat unintentional.

Thirdly, as well as confusion and variety there has also been some resistance or reluctance to use the language of formation. The URC nationally has been much more cautious of formation language, considering it to suggest an elitist and ontological understanding of ministry.[45] This alerts us to the theological presuppositions about the nature of ministry behind developments in patterns of formation and the important link between the practice of preparation and the pastoral imaginations that it shapes. Certainly the language of formation with its person-centered and holistic stress fits easily with an understanding of ministry as "being" as well as "doing". For some, the fact that the language has emerged from the Catholic tradition has not been helpful.[46] Others, while embracing the holistic concept, are concerned that formation may too easily be seen as "conformation" to a predetermined pattern, suggesting too great a centralization by ecclesiastical authorities, or that a college can do more in three years than is possible.[47] Foster *et al.*, prefer to use "clergy education" as the overarching description, aware of the limits of "formation" language, but formation still plays a key role, as they suggest it does in any professional identity.[48]

This confusion of language is also exemplified in the work of the ecumenical Quality in Formation Panel (QIFP). Since 1990 colleges and courses within the Church of England were subject to detailed internal inspections overseen by the House of Bishops. Increasingly this became ecumenical and in 2007 QiFP was established, drawing in the Methodist Church, the URC and the Baptist Union. QiFP has produced significant literature in the form of questionnaires and notes, which have developed over time,[49] and drawing on "best practice" in other areas, particularly the

---

45. Mayes, *Spirituality in Ministerial Formation*, 64.
46. Mayes, *Spirituality in Ministerial Formation*, 171: it is not "evangelical" language.
47. Comments made in interviews for the original DMin research.
48. Foster *et al.*, *Educating Clergy*, 100.

49. At the time of the original research there were iterations from 2008, 2010 and 2012. The 2010 and 2012 documents bring together two previously separate components, the curriculum validation process and the periodic external review. The former has its origins in the Church of England, *Education for the Church's Ministry* and its format was developed in the 1990s and articulated in *Mission and Ministry: The Churches' Validation*

The Practice of Preparation

OFSTED framework, the QiFP material influences the wider field of the practice of preparation both linguistically and conceptually.

While there is an explicit stress on the inspected institution's own understanding of the mission of God and the resulting ministry of the church, the QiFP framework is, of course, not neutral. The fact that certain questions are asked in a certain order already deeply embeds theological assumptions and the language of the questions will shape answers given. But the over-riding impression is that there is no clear and explicit understanding of formation as a shared basis and the documentation shows signs typical of the wider confusion.

First, as elsewhere, the language of education, training and formation are at times used interchangeably, to refer to the whole process of preparation and distinct aspects of it. There are clear developments within the iterations: the title of the 2010 handbook, *Quality Assurance and Enhancement in Ministerial Education* is revised in 2012 to *Quality Assurance and Enhancement in Ministerial Formation*, although its subtitle is still "a guide for inspectors and training institutions". Even with the subtle change in title, it is the language of "training" that is most commonly used in both the 2010 and 2012 versions, followed by formation and then education.[50]

Secondly, the documentation can refer to "ministerial, personal and spiritual formation"[51] with no discussion of any differences in these terms, or simply to "ministerial formation". Conceptually, the QiFP documentation suggests a practice of preparation that aims at being holistic, in that it seeks to incorporate a number of distinctive elements that draw together Foster *et al.*'s categorization of the cognitive, normative and practical, but does so in a way that is not entirely consistent.

Despite the confusion, it is nevertheless clear that there has been a trajectory over the last forty years of an emerging formation paradigm and that there is some truth in Mayes' conclusion that "this is not just a change in semantics, but represents the embracing of a new dynamic model

---

Framework for Theological Education (1999) and 2nd edition (2003.) The latter has a long history, although the form of the questionnaire as it is in the QiFP documents takes shape in the 2002 inspection handbook.

50. The 2010 version uses training 117 times, formation 76 times (including 31 references to QiFP) and education 58 times. In the 2012 version training is used 62 times (plus a further 10 references to the training of inspectors for their role), formation is used 48 times (of which 7 refer to QiFP) and education is used 36 times (plus a further two references to a candidate's previous education).

51. This was the title for Section F in the documentation.

of learning that resonates with ancient concepts and yet challenges some inherited patterns of training."[52] From a Baptist perspective, Chris Ellis echoes this conclusion while recognizing that to describe formation language as a culture shift is still contested.[53]

However, what is "new" about this model must be stated with clarity and care. In previous patterns of preparation when predominantly young men studied for university degrees in residential communities, there would have been a similar underlying concern for Christian maturity and deep spirituality, and some expectation that living in the semi-monastic community of a seminary centered upon the chapel, refectory and library would naturally shape students.[54] The experience of students may well have been that there was little, if any, explicit mention of character or spirituality, but David Russell, in 1971, speaks of "the need to wrestle with truth and be prepared to pay the price of distress and doubt in order to possess it,"[55] ideas which would be considered deeply formational. Similarly, Norman Moon reflects on the purpose of the College at Bristol, and expresses what would have been the common view:

> The primary task of a theological College is not merely to teach, certainly not to indoctrinate, nor merely to train in techniques, but to help students grow as persons, Christian men and women. For such a purpose the residential community is most valuable in itself.[56]

But the development of the formation paradigm offers three advantages. First it offers the possibility of a shared language which makes explicit what has often been assumed but left unsaid. Second, it offers a model for connecting together a variety of aspects of the practice of preparation that often remained distinct and separate. Third, it brings to the fore the integrative model of preparation be being intentional and explicit in the language used.

52. Mayes, *Spirituality in Ministerial Formation*, 72.

53. Ellis, "Being a Minister," 57.

54. Taylor, writes "having acknowledged this, in my tradition at least, we tend to leave it to look after itself. Great faith is often put in the college community . . . being forced to live with other students in training, having to maintain good relations with them, 'knocking spots' off each other, smoothing rough corners, sharing the times of doubt and faith, giving and receiving in fellowship with a common aim, these are the dynamic realities which can be trusted to mould raw material into suitable characters for ordination." (1st lecture, 14th Atlantic Seminar in Theological Education, 7).

55. Russell, "The College and its Future," 4.

56. Moon, *Education for Ministry*, 98.

The Practice of Preparation

A SHARED PRACTICE: DEVELOPMENTS IN THE BRITISH BAPTIST COLLEGES

There has been little published reflection by Baptists on the practice of preparation, with Paul Goodliff's recent book *Shaped for Service* being the exception. However, the decision by the Baptist Colleges to move to a peer review process prompted not only practical discussion but also theological reflection on our shared practice, with a paper, which I drafted, entitled *Ministerial Formation in the British Baptist Colleges: A Commitment to Shared Practice*, agreed by the Baptist Colleges' Partnership.

The possibility of such an agreed document itself points to a significant degree of shared practice and understanding, which we may also describe as structured, collaborative and creative. It is collaborative not only as this document has been explicitly developed together, but the whole way that the preparation for ministry has developed over time has been shaped by interaction between the colleges. It is structured both in terms of the way that the practice of preparation has persisted and developed historically, but also in the way more recently that documents drawn up together have become the structuring reality of preparation for ministry. Yet within this structuring and collaborative pattern there is significant space for creative development. This co-operative and structuring practice of ministerial formation among Baptists has developed over time weaving together a number of distinct aspects.[57] Six such aspects are particularly significant all of which contribute to the kind of pastoral imaginations Baptist colleges are seeking to develop in their students.

University Validated Courses

Central to the current practice of preparation is an academic course in theology, either with the college being a constituent part of a university or as a validated partner. The Baptist Union requires that all those who are accredited have studied theology at least to Diploma level (level 5 in UK qualifications).[58] While this is clearly the contemporary shared practice, historically there have been two quite distinct strands of thought.

---

57. For a more detailed exploration of these historical developments see my "How Did We End Up Here? Theological Education as Ministerial Formation in the British Baptist Colleges."

58. See Baptist Union of Great Britain, "Towards a New List: Proposals for the

Forming Ministers or Training Leaders?

An emphasis on academic education has been a long-standing tradition among Baptists. The founding of Bristol Baptist College by Edward Terrill's gift deed witnesses to this desire to provide for the education of young men for ministry by someone "well skilled in the tongues of Hebrew and Greek,"[59] and Paul Ballard traces the general impetus back to the seventeenth century and the puritan demand for an educated clergy.[60] This trajectory developed as the various colleges established greater university connections. Baptist colleges were significantly involved in the early years of the new universities in London, Bristol, Manchester and Cardiff and even Spurgeon's College, which under Spurgeon himself had been very cautious about formally recognized education, began considering a possible affiliation with London University in 1902, which was finalized in the 1930s. David Russell, General Secretary of the Baptist Union and a former college Principal, summed up the role of the colleges to produce mature men and women of God as:

> among other things this will mean the creation of an educated and cultured ministry. This has been characteristic of our Baptist theological education in the past and I hope it will continue to be ... And this in turn will mean the encouragement in our students of an open-minded search for the truth wherever it be found. [61]

Yet, intertwined from the beginning was also a strong anti-intellectual strand, for "to be destitute of learning has been esteemed a good proof of a preacher's mission from above."[62] At the dawn of the twentieth century there were fierce debates in response to the Baptist Union's desire to introduce the concept of ministerial accreditation to safeguard the use of a proposed Sustentation Fund, with the first Ministerial Recognition Committee established in 1896, and the later introduction, or imposition, of the Baptist Union examination.[63] Behind this lay both some sense of antago-

---

Restructuring of the List of Accredited Ministers of the BUGB."

59. Moon, *Education for Ministry*, 1.

60. Ballard, "The Emergence of Pastoral Studies," 9.

61. Russell, "The College and its Future," an address given on the retirement of L. G. Champion and the inauguration of W. M. S. West as President of Bristol Baptist College, 1971, (private papers in the Angus Library).

62. Nicholls, *Lights to the World: A History of Spurgeon's College 1856–1992*, 24, quoting St Andrew's Street Church Book, Cambridge, 72A.

63. Randall, English *Baptists of the Twentieth Century*, 64–68 and Sparkes, *An Accredited Ministry*.

nism between those who had trained at the Baptist colleges and those who had entered ministry through other routes, but also a distinctly mixed view of university education, with those at the heart of the Union's structures being supporters of high levels of education with others concerned that "ministers empty churches by degrees"![64] Randall suggests that at the turn of the twentieth century only eight per cent of Baptist ministers had been connected with a validated university as opposed to just a college course.[65]

Some in the early decades of the twentieth century feared that this partnership would open ministers to the influence of liberal and secular theology,[66] while others celebrated Baptist involvement in higher education.[67] More recently Stephen Pattison writes of a conservative turn in British church life with less interest in the liberal ethos of secular universities, and the financial attraction of cheaper church-centered courses.[68] Alongside the positive benefits, there has also been some recognition of the constraints of university affiliation over the years, especially those laid on the curriculum by a degree program.[69]

There are also questions about the broader educational philosophy. The founding of University College, London in 1828[70] on a distinctly utilitarian-based approach to education led the way to the forming of polytechnics which later became universities, and degrees in single, increasingly vocational, subjects. The debate from Locke onwards about the teleological end and utility of education has been settled firmly in recent years by connecting education with employment. The increase in vocational education and training particularly in UK in the 1980s, partly in response to unemployment, and the introduction of NVQs in 1986, with their stress on the development of competence and transferable skills, are clear evidence of this. More recently the government moved responsibility for higher education to the Department for Business, Innovation and Skills, although this

---

64. Randall, *English Baptists of the Twentieth Century*, quoting Ian Sellers (ed.), *Our Heritage: The Baptists of Yorkshire, Lancashire and Cheshire 1647–1987*, 128.

65. Randall, *English Baptists of the Twentieth Century*, 64.

66. Randall, *English Baptists of the Twentieth Century*, 133–36.

67. So T. R. Glover's article in *The Times*, March 1932.

68. Pattison, "Research, Resources and Threats," 144–45.

69. As early as 1967 David Russell makes this point in a paper "Theological Education in the Free Church Tradition: The British Situation" (private papers in the Angus Library).

70. Regent's Park was significantly involved in the developing of London University. See Clarke and Fiddes, *Dissenting Spirit*, 49–57.

was then reversed in 2016.[71] The adoption of the formation paradigm asks searching pedagogical questions to these validating partners about the extent to which practices should be virtue-based or utility driven.

Currently all five Baptist colleges are firmly rooted in higher education settings, which seems significantly symbolic: of a commitment to open critical enquiry; of a belief that good practice of pedagogy and theology can be found in these wider institutions; of an understanding of the relationship between the church and the wider world in which both are incorporated in God's wider purposes.

Practical Theology Methodologies

In the latter half of the twentieth century there was a growing sense of unease that such academic theology was not enough. R E Cooper's history of Regent's Park College,[72] addresses to the Baptist World Alliance by David Russell,[73] then joint Principal at Northern, and letters to the *Baptist Times*[74] all express the same concern that there was not enough practical training, teaching on spirituality or engagement with experience. Colleges seemed to some to be preparing professors not ministers. Significant changes developed which partly focused on an increased skills-based approach in the curriculum, a move perhaps from an education to a training paradigm, but was also shaped by a developing approach to the study of theology itself.

The mid-1960s saw the appointment of lecturers in Pastoral Studies, as an academic discipline in its own right, first in Birmingham and then later in Cardiff and Manchester. Paul Ballard, a Baptist minister, was appointed to teach at Cardiff in 1968, and looking back highlights a number of important contributing factors to these developments, such as the general growth of professional training in areas like administration and social welfare, the professionalization of the clergy, especially in the Church of England, and the influence of practice from other parts of the world, notably liberation

---

71. The then Education Secretary, Nicky Morgan, explicitly talked about character, stressing that a narrow focus on passing exams will not produce a well-rounded education; *Daily Telegraph*, 16th March 2015.

72. Cooper, *From Stepney to St Giles*, 128–31.

73. Russell, "Practical Training for the Ministry in Britain," (private papers in the Angus Library).

74. Gethin Abraham-Williams, *Baptist Times* 13th, 20th, 27th September, 1973.

theology and the movements of Clinical Pastoral Education and Pastoral Counselling from the United States.⁷⁵

Within wider Baptist circles, an address by David Russell in 1964 already recognized the issues involved, that the more practical side of the courses were "full of bits and pieces", and also offered clear insight into the necessary way forward.⁷⁶ He rejects the false dichotomy between theoretical and practical knowledge, between becoming professors and mere technicians who are good at the mechanics of churchmanship, arguing for an integrated approach. This is one which does not simply "apply" theology to different contexts, which recognizes the significance of the whole experience and environment and not just the course of study, and which would produce spiritual leaders able to live in the world as true interpreters of the Gospel, enabling the ministry of the Church in the world. He recognizes that British colleges may have much to learn from his American audience especially about the centrality of "field-work" and the necessity of learning through pastoral experience. Despite Russell's foresight it would be some time before these changes were realized more generally in the British context.

But when these changes happened, it was Michael Taylor again who was a significant and mediating figure. From his arrival as Principal at Northern in 1969 he took a more radical approach which played down the traditional stresses on biblical languages and systematic theology in favor of a course which strongly related theory to practice, and offered a constant dialogue between the church and contemporary culture together with an openness to other disciplines.⁷⁷ Under his leadership Northern developed their whole degree course around contextual theology. In 1975 Taylor notes how the colleges had responded in different ways to the concerns of ministers and the rise of pastoral studies. The colleges in Cardiff and Manchester had developed university diplomas in pastoral studies, Regent's had developed its own in-house course as a supplement to the University degree, and Spurgeon's was re-working its degree program to include something similar.⁷⁸ A few years later Taylor would write to his fellow Baptist ministers, that "forming a person to be such a reflective theologian rather

---

75. Ballard, "The Emergence of Pastoral Studies" 9–18. See also Taylor, 2nd lecture on "The Theology of Spiritual Formation," 3.

76. Russell, "Practical Training for the Ministry in Britain".

77. Shepherd, *The Making of a northern College*. 229–30.

78. In a paper prepared for Ecumenical Consultation on the role of Theological Colleges, (private papers in Angus Library).

than teaching a person a lot about theology is what theological education is ultimately about."[79] And significantly influenced by Northern's experiments this new way of bringing theory and practice began to shape other colleges too. Regents' Park appointed its first full-time and stipendiary Tutor in Pastoral Theology in 1981, Bruce Keeble, and one of his first actions was to visit Northern and talk with Taylor. Keeble writes[80] of his own three basic principles: the formation of the whole person, doing theology as a way of life, and beginning with experiences and letting these experiences raise questions, especially what the experience prompts us to say about God.

Ultimately this is a change in methodology. The parallel and intersecting rise of sociology and psychology, the advances in learning theory and adult education, and the influence of practical field education all combined to challenge the dominance of the deductive *Wissenschaft* model which certainly reserved a real place for practical theology, but only as the pinnacle of a deductive process derived from first principles. Practical theology is now "an academic field primarily defined by method and only secondarily by a sense of content."[81]

The Schleiermachian approach has its attractiveness in seeming to ground practice on a prior understanding of Scripture and the traditional doctrines of the church. By contrast Pattison describes theological reflection as "a critical conversation which takes place between the Christian tradition, the student's own faith presuppositions and a particular contemporary situation."[82] Practical theology has its own spectrum of the particular balance between theory and practice, but the notion of Scripture being included in a genuinely critical conversation is, certainly for some students, a challenging development.

But the Baptist colleges have all adopted the methodologies of practical theology and the practice of theological reflection now finds a place in the curriculum and in patterns of assessment. The language of ministers as essentially "reflective practitioners" is commonplace. Long essays, fieldwork reports, and portfolios have come to replace some or all of the traditional exams producing a very different educational experience and reflective practice becomes central to this sense of a structuring and co-operative practice.

---

79. Taylor, "Ministerial Training at Northern College," 6.
80. In private correspondence.
81. Ballard, *Practical Theology: Proliferation and Performance*, 61.
82. Pattison, *A Critique of Pastoral Care*, 136.

The Practice of Preparation

Practice-based Patterns

Up until the end of the 1970s preparing for ordained Baptist ministry involved three years (at least) in a residential college. Now the vast majority of Baptist ordinands are on a pattern generally referred to as "congregation-based" or "church-based", which involves a student becoming a "Minister-in-Training" in a local Baptist church, either in the role of sole pastor or as part of a wider team, living in the community of the church and travelling into a college for one or two days a week.

Once again it was Michael Taylor who led the way and in September 1978 Northern began an experiment entitled the Alternative Pattern of Training (APT). Taylor was partly influenced by developments happening around him in the Church of England, such as the North West Regional Training Scheme, but also patterns of theological education in the rest of the world: the pedagogical challenges of Freire and the critical reflective approach of liberation theology; the refusal and practical inability to privilege both full time residential training for young men and women and then full time stipendiary ministry; the desire to develop extension courses where theological education could run parallel with secular employment; the engagement of those who were already of some Christian maturity.[83]

Baptists, as well as other denominations, had discussed for some years alternative approaches to ministry and recognized the need to have other patterns alongside full-time stipendiary roles[84] but this had not yet translated into the practice of preparation for ministry. Northern's APT, the first such experiment, was alternative in a number of ways, such as the intensity of the course and the age and experience of the majority of the students, but the fundamental change it made was on the priority of the placement of each student, which was no longer the context in which the theology learnt at college was merely applied, but at least as important a place for learning and formation as the college context. Education, training and formation happened in two centers and as Taylor expressed it:

> our case study on ministerial formation suggested that the main place or agent of formation is the practice of ministry itself. Men

---

83. See Newbigin, "Theological Education in a World Perspective," 3–8.

84. Most significantly in the 1969 Baptist Union of Great Britain report *Ministry Tomorrow*.

and women become ministers by being ministers in the local congregation right from the beginning of their training.[85]

Regent's then began its congregation-based course (Regent's In-Pastorate Training) in the autumn of 1982, deeply influenced by the "two center" (college and church) pattern at Northern, with five students accepted to study in this way. Spurgeon's, although initially quite critical, declaring that the ATP had dumbed down serious scholarship and undoubtedly still wary of the associations with Taylor,[86] nevertheless began to adopt the pattern in 1985.

The congregation-based pattern drew its pedagogy significantly from the experience of fieldwork in the USA, and the emerging methods of practical theology. But more than being the basis for reflection *on* practice, it also established the methodology of reflection *in* practice. One of the distinctive aspects of current Baptist practices of preparation, enabled by a distinctive ecclesiological basis, is that these are more than placements for students, although they are seen in that way as well, but are opportunities for the genuine practice of ministry by those who have been called into ministry by local churches.

Without doubt there were also financial motives to the original developing of a congregation-based pattern, searching for sustainability in a way that college-based patterns would not provide. Increasingly for Baptists it appears that there will be little place for a more traditional college-based approach, except for those much younger candidates who have not yet had student loans, but the experience of even these students will be shaped by the rationale, methodology and experience of practice-based patterns. Baptists have begun to reflect on the extent to which the congregation-based pattern itself is sustainable, and whether sufficient local churches are willing and able to cover the significant funding of stipends, accommodation and expenses, but this current shared practice has fully embedded patterns of theological reflection in the process of preparation.

---

85. Taylor, 2nd lecture on "The Theology of Spiritual Formation." Note here the total interchangeability of formation and training.

86. See Shepherd, The *Making of a northern College*, 250. Taylor had caused significant controversy in 1971 in a sermon at the Baptist Assembly which many took to doubt the divinity of Christ.

Professional Ministry

The roots of ministerial professionalization may be traced back to the so-called clergy paradigm developed from Schleiermacher, which then was developed further by both the increasing utility of education and the growth of the professions in the twentieth century. Ballard highlights the effect that this wider professional development had on the preparation of ministers, including the dialogue between theology and other traditions such as sociology and psychology and the influence this has on the curriculum.[87]

These changes happened alongside the change in the student body of the colleges. Moving away from the residential community of almost exclusively young men, Northern's APT program was specifically designed to make preparing for ministry possible for more mature students, married with families, and this was paralleled in other colleges as the congregation-based pattern developed. By 1989 the average age of students at Spurgeon's was 32.4.[88] Increasingly they brought with them other professional training together with leadership experience in secular contexts. This was the context when Paul Beasley-Murray was Principal from 1986–1992.

A further important development here is the language of competency, key to the development of secular vocational training. In the early 1980s the language of competence is used, though sparingly, for example in *The Aims and Objectives of Ministerial Training* at Northern Baptist College, from around 1982, and Michael Taylor brings competence and professionalism together for "this ministry is a profession in that like other professions it can quite properly be expected to be competent."[89] But the more dominant language at this time would nevertheless seem to be personal qualities rather than competencies.[90] The 1998 report "Towards a New List"[91] then brings these together and talks of the three elements necessary for accrediting ministry as call, competence and character.

Competence language is taken further in the work of Bill Allen, when Tutor in Pastoral Studies at Spurgeon's College, who offers a list of seven key competencies for ministry, which in turn should shape ministerial

---

87. Ballard, *Foundations of Pastoral Studies*, 12, 16.
88. Randall, *English Baptists of the Twentieth Century*, 451.
89. Taylor, West Midlands Area Ministers Conference, Essays in Ministry 1.
90. Taylor offers 25 personal qualities in his 14th Atlantic seminar presentation, 1982.
91. Baptist Union of Great Britain, "Towards a New List".

training.[92] A few years later, partly prompted by the stimulus of the Hind Report and partly from the concerns of a new Head of Ministry, a paper went to the Baptist Union Council in August 2005 proposing a number of core competencies for accredited Baptist ministers.[93]

Within a commitment to wider ministerial formation, these core competencies, modified slightly, now feature significantly in all the Baptist colleges and have shaped the way that curricula have developed and assessment takes place. But there would seem to remain some uncertainty and hesitation about the competencies, both in terms of the language itself and in the more functional stress they bring. An on-going search for other language continued. Jim Gordon, then Principal of the Scottish Baptist College, offered a paper at the 2012 Baptist Colleges Staffs' Conference on "Ministerial Attributes"[94] as an alternative, more person-centered approach to expressing something of the hoped for pastoral imagination of those leaving college, and the consultation report of the recent Baptist Union review of formation suggested the development of core comprehensions and core virtues alongside competencies.

The *Ignite* report from 2015 led the way to the development of *Marks of Ministry*, which have a greater stress on character, and which while not replacing the competencies have become more central to an understanding and assessment of ministry. But the language of competencies, even though they are expressed in language that operates in a strongly formational way, has shaped current shared practice as part of a more professional understanding of ministry. The extent to which competencies or virtues, or marks of ministry shape the practice of preparation will in turn have an influence on the kind of pastoral imaginations being developed.

---

92. Allen, "Pathways to Leadership." Allen's seven competencies are the ability to: engage in theological reflection and application; construct a foundation of spirituality to undergird ministry; carry out mission and ministry with integrity; communicate in public and private settings; lead others; engage in effective pastoral care and support; manage self and workload in a competent way.

93. Baptist Union of Great Britain, "Patterns of Ministry among Baptists."

94. Fuller and Fleming conclude that competencies can be used in a holistic and "soft" way to refer to characteristics and attributes rather than a "hard" way about skills and knowledge, although their eight competencies might be called attributes ("Bridging the Gap," 163–78).

Ecumenical Partnerships

Currently the five Baptist colleges in England and Wales have significant though different ecumenical connections. Northern remains the most ecumenically structured, with its explicit commitment to the Lund Principle and its partnership in the Luther King House Educational Trust, with the Methodists, URC, and Unitarians. Bristol and South Wales have or have had strong bi-party links with their neighboring Anglican colleges, Trinity and St Michael's respectively. Regent's is part of the Oxford Partnership for Theological Education and Training (OPTET) with the three Anglican colleges based in and around Oxford, together with the Catholic halls. The ecumenical links of Spurgeon's have developed in the area of BAME churches which have often come from an independent Pentecostal heritage and now over half their ministerial students are from churches beyond the Baptist tradition.

This has not always been the case. Unsurprisingly, it was Michael Taylor who expressed, on his appointment as Principal, the key conviction that ministerial formation needed to be thoroughly ecumenical in its nature.[95] Taylor proceeded to begin discussions with the Congregational College, the Methodists, who moved into Brighton Grove in 1973 when Hartley Victoria College was going to be closed, and the Anglican North Western Ordination Course, resulting in, amongst other things, the Northern Federation for Training in Ministry launched in 1984.[96]

Within the wider Union at that time there were mixed views on this as a way forward. The establishment of a new and innovative ecumenical college in Birmingham in 1970, The Queens Foundation, made some Baptists at least wonder if they should be part of this process.[97] At a similar time, *The Report of An Advisory Group and Other Related Documents made available by the Baptist Theological Colleges in England and Wales* encouraged Northern Baptist College to explore ecumenical opportunities in the light of its perceived struggling context for ministerial training but seems more generally to have stressed residential training and been distinctly cool on ecumenical commitment.[98]

---

95. Shepherd, *The Making of a northern College*, 229.

96. See Shepherd, *The Making of a northern College*, 244–47, 253–54. More recently the Methodist church has pulled back from the Luther King House partnership after denominational reviews.

97. Russell, "Theological Education in the Free Church Tradition."

98. Shepherd, *The Making of a northern College*, 236–37.

The next two decades saw considerable development in the attitude of the denomination in this respect, represented most significantly by the rise of the Inter Church Process and the *Not Strangers but Pilgrims* report of 1987. The Union voted to join the new ecumenical process at the Assembly in 1989 (although a quarter of delegates were not in favor) and decisions to formally join CTE and CTBI in 1995 received larger majorities.[99]

In 1986 the Churches Together in England document *Called to be One* looked for opportunities for ministerial students to live alongside each other and explore other traditions. The response of the Baptist Union Council the following year stressed the need not just for ministerial students to know something about, but to immerse themselves in the realities of other traditions,[100] and the Union, through the then Ministry Department, joined the ecumenical inspection process in 2003.

Taylor's early and more radical convictions have become, in time, the mainstream approach, and there is a clear willingness expressed in the different college partnerships not to be isolationist, but to view the preparation for ministry within the wider context of the universal church. Yet there is clearly some range within the colleges themselves, and probably a much wider spectrum within the churches of the Union. The geographical and university contexts of the five Baptist colleges offer different kinds of ecumenical relationships, which will impact on the kind of pastoral imaginations being developed, but these are individual college developments within a shared practice of ecumenical co-operation.

Missional Concerns

While not, of course, uniquely Baptist it has often been recognized that the "missionary impulse" is both a Baptist distinctive and a key part of Baptist history and identity.[101] Yet it is also clear that the changing developments within contemporary culture over recent decades have demanded that clearer and more focused attention be paid both to the church's missional call and the context in which it works.

Spurgeon's College responded with the development, in 1990, of a specific church planting and evangelism course, alongside that for pastoral ministry, and around half the modules taught were in conjunction with

---

99. Randall, *English Baptists of the Twentieth Century*, 495.
100. See Baptist Union of Great Britain, "Partners Together," 9.
101. See Holmes, *Baptist Theology*, 141–43.

the pastoral ministry track. This particular approach lasted until the early 2000s when the two courses were integrated more fully together, but in a way which allowed some choice of modules through the course. Spurgeon's were partly reflecting on their own experience, that there was no clear correlation between the particular pathway a student chose at the beginning and the kind of ministry they exercised on leaving the college.

In 2001, the BUGB Council agreed to make some formal distinctions within ordained ministry and to add the categories of accredited youth specialists and accredited evangelists alongside that of the pastoral minister. Yet the distinction between evangelists and pastors was not entirely clear. For example, the suggested ordination service in *Gathering for Worship*, after initial shared questions on belief in God, making disciples and being a disciple offers different words for pastors and evangelists. The former are much more extensive and have some focus on word and sacrament, whereas the latter focus on being a witness and a minister of peace, love and hope, which have long been seen as part of the role of all ministers.[102] The core competencies initiated by the Ministry Department were originally the same for both pastors and evangelists, and the number of those seeking to be ordained as evangelists has been very small, anecdotally because being an accredited pastor allows an individual to act as an evangelist but accept other possibilities for wider ministry as well. With the possibility of the subdivision into other categories the Baptist Union Council closed the separate categories of ordained youth specialists and evangelists in 2018, moving (back) to one category of ordained minister.[103]

Interestingly, in the period when the Baptist Union had a distinction between pastors and evangelists, the colleges were increasingly placing greater stress on integration, so pastoral ministry and evangelism appeared as different emphases within one course, which as a whole has developed a more explicit and culturally relevant missional feel. There was at this time some resistance from colleges to the call from some for a separate church planting or pioneer course, seeking instead a greater integration of pioneering mission across all ministerial formation, alongside opportunities for some to focus more on pioneering ministry.[104]

---

102. Blyth and Ellis, *Gathering for Worship*, 125. This, also, is representative, not normative.

103. See, for example, Baptist Union of Great Britain, *Ministerial Recognition Rules* (October, 2019).

104. Based on discussions at the 2010 annual Baptist Staffs Conference.

Forming Ministers or Training Leaders?

But from 2010 the Colleges began to offer some more distinct pathways through ministerial formation, with Bristol beginning an urban mission and church planting pathway in partnership with Urban Expression, in which part of the overall course was shared with all ministerial students and part was distinct and unique. By 2020, Bristol, Northern Baptist College and Regent's Park College were offering distinct Pioneer options and Spurgeon's College was working on their own Pioneer course. There were other initiatives in this period to develop Pioneering within the Baptist Union, such as the Incarnate Network in 2007, the Pioneer Collective in 2013, Urbanlife, of which Bristol Baptist College was a partner and the host, and the development of the Light Project, an initiative in Evangelism, into the Light College and Collective which from 2020 was able to offer a route to accredited Baptist ministry, in partnership with Northern Baptist College and with academic courses validated by Chester University, that offered a strong emphasis on mission and evangelism.

One further aspect of the changing missional context is the partnership which all the colleges have had in recent years with BMS World Mission. In March / April 2008 Bristol took the first student teams abroad to India and Brazil with BMS, with the other four colleges following soon after. This reflects a more significant place for the contribution of the global church to the formation of ministers in the UK and for the significant learning and experience of BMS.

Culturally relevant, globally sensitive and alert to the need for a greater emphasis on pioneering ministry: this would seem to reflect the colleges' desire for contemporary ministerial formation and so the pastoral imagination for all ministers, in which there would also be space for a variety of particular specialisms to grow.

In summary then I suggest that the British Baptist colleges have a growing understanding of their shared practice in which they are seeking to develop a pastoral imagination in their students so that they:

- engage in open critical enquiry, drawing from the tradition of the church and the understanding of the wider world
- are reflective practitioners
- can reflect *in* practice as well as *on* practice
- are competent in a range of ministerial practices
- are ecumenically sensitive

- are missionally engaged, culturally relevant, globally sensitive and alert to the need for a greater emphasis on pioneering ministry

FORMATION OR TRAINING?

From the above review two recent historical developments have become clear. First, alongside other denominations, there has been a clear move towards using formation language to describe the practice of preparation in the Baptist colleges,[105] and second, among the Baptist colleges there has developed structuring and co-operative practices, focusing on six key aspects identified above that already shape some shared sense of the kind of pastoral imagination Baptist colleges are looking to develop in their students.

In the same way that there was no simple contrast between ministry and leadership, so again it is not possible or helpful to cast education, training and formation as opposed to each other, for the development has been towards integration not separation and there is no attempt to offer one without the other. But they are, and have been, balanced in different ways and so, in a similar way to that suggested in the previous chapter, "formation" and "training" can each represent a different *habitus*, which will in turn shape the pastoral imagination in different ways.

Within the "formation" paradigm, two concepts in particular stand out, which might be summarized as integration and integrity. Integration offers a model that unites different aspects in one process. These include the integration of separate theological disciplines, theory and practice, the church and the world, prayer and spirituality, previous life experience and current ministerial formation, pre- and post-ordination training, the individual and the community. Integrity places the student, and the student's spiritual development at the center of the process, while combining knowledge and skills. While all language here has been problematic, with Baptists moving between virtues, marks, attributes,[106] integrity describes the key element in formation that revolves around spirituality, character and maturity. Combining these aspects of integration and integrity together Foster

---

105. See the Colleges working paper, *Ministerial Formation in the British Baptist Colleges.*

106. Mayes, *Spirituality in Ministerial Formation*, 80–84, recognizes the difficulty, with character and ministerial "identity" both carrying particular theological undertones in different Christian traditions.

et al. suggest that "learning as formation is a process by which the student becomes a certain kind of thinking, feeling, acting being."[107]

On the other hand, the paradigm of "training" places the acquisition of skills center stage so that the gaining of knowledge and any development of character are in the service of the development of these skills. This does not reject the more cognitive or formational aspects but stresses the relationship in a different way. Paralleling Foster's comment above, learning as training might be thought of as a process that enables a student to act in a particular kind of way, although we must be careful not to overplay this distinction as Foster *et al.* also suggest that professional training will always have some formative element to it. Training and formation *can* stand as each offering a different *habitus*, while historically there seems to have been more of a development between these two approaches. As a structuring structure a formation or training *habitus* provides a fundamental framework within which a pastoral imagination is shaped.

Reflecting on fifteen years working as Tutor in Pastoral Studies at Regent's Park College, the ways I have worked on curricula, handbooks and other documents, the content of my teaching and my conversations with other tutors, then increasingly I too have wanted to frame my own practice as that of forming ministers. This is the *habitus* into which I have increasingly grown as a tutor rather than the more training *habitus* that was my experience as a student. This is the kind of *habitus* I argue for in this book.

Returning once more to our opening question—what do I do?—we may ponder whether this might be answered quite differently by those "trained" or those "formed" for ministry, in other words those for whom ministerial preparation has concentrated on skills to be developed and now put into practice, and those for whom ministerial preparation has concentrated more holistically on who a minister is. This, of course, might then lead to some challenge to the initial question itself: is the starting point to ask "who am I as minister for this congregation?" rather than begin with "what should I do?"

---

107. Foster *et al.*, *Educating Clergy*, 10.

4

Exploring Practice and the Pastoral Imagination

An Example of Empirical Research

I BEGAN WITH AN existential question about what a new minister might actually begin to do in ministry, that is about the practice of ministry, suggesting ministry may be seen as a structured and co-operative practice, which persists over time, and provides something of a *habitus* within which the individual minister may creatively improvise. I suggested that the way an individual minister answers this will be complex, shaped by various things, but will involve their experience of preparation for ministry, which can also be described as a structured and co-operative practice with its own *habitus*. The way these two practices are connected, I suggest, is through the concept of the "pastoral imagination", a way of seeing and interpreting the world which shapes everything a minister thinks and does, and which a college is seeking, implicitly or explicitly, to shape and develop.

By exploring a variety of literature I then argued that, although there are alternative voices, there is a *representative* voice among British Baptists which understands the practice of preparation as forming ministers, and that some shared, co-operative and structuring sense of the nature of formation which seeks to produce an overall pastoral imagination has developed.

This co-operative practice and the *representative* voice, then, both suggest that there should be some significant similarities in the practice of preparation within the British Baptist colleges and the particular pastoral imaginations they are each seeking to develop. Yet the different contexts, histories and the popular belief in the differences between the colleges suggest that there might be some important differences as well. Rather than relying on either the *representative* voice seen in some shared documents, or popular and historic stereotypes my aim in the empirical research undertaken was to test the co-operative practice and *representative* voice that has emerged from the literature against the actual practice of each college, offering an opportunity to further refine and triangulate the co-operative practice and *representative* voice. I, therefore, asked two fundamental empirical research questions.

- What is the pastoral imagination which the Baptist colleges individually are seeking to inculcate in their students?
- Is there a particular combination of practices and elements of a pastoral imagination that could be considered distinctly Baptist?

The first question considered what is distinct to each of the five colleges and aimed to move beyond the anecdotal to a more secure empirically based understanding of the unique nature of each of the five colleges. It explored, with an in-depth analysis, the five Baptist Colleges which are: Regent's Park College, Oxford; Spurgeon's College, London; Bristol Baptist College; Northern Baptist Learning Community, Manchester; South Wales Baptist College, Cardiff. These are the five Baptist Colleges in England and Wales which are at the heart of the Baptist Union of Great Britain,[1] and which have expressed their commitment to a degree of shared practice.[2] There is an important sense of completeness to the research as all the Baptist colleges in membership with the Baptist Union were included.

The second question considered what might be shared by the Baptist colleges but be different from other approaches to the practice of preparation, seeking to understand whether there is anything that can be considered distinctly Baptist. It explored this by considering the results of research into the Baptist colleges alongside data from a similar in-depth analysis of five non-Baptist colleges or courses, chosen to represent breadth and variety.

---

1. Y Coleg Gwyn (North Wales Baptist College), Bangor, The Scottish Baptist College and the Irish Baptist College are also in membership of the Baptist Union of Great Britain, but are more connected to other Unions, ie Baptist Union of Wales, Baptist Union of Scotland and the Association of Baptist Churches in Ireland.

2. For example, the Colleges' Partnership Meeting, the annual Baptist Staff's Conference and regular Principals' meetings.

These included residential colleges and non-residential courses, institutions from a single denomination, those which are ecumenical or non-denominational, and from a breadth of churchmanship. The sample is not large enough to make valid comments on the practice of preparation in other denominations, or in independent colleges, or in courses rather than residential colleges, which are all valid and important areas of research in themselves. Rather this second set of data offered a representative sample used to help explore further the particular emphases of the five Baptist colleges.

RESEARCH METHODS

As set out in chapter 1 this was a piece of practitioner research in which I sought to generate knowledge, as a basis for further reflection on my own role and practice and then offered to the wider community both within and beyond the Baptist Union. The "four voices" of Cameron *et al.* provide the overall methodological framework and my aim in this empirical research was to establish the particular *operant* and *espoused* voices of the different institutions through an analysis of documents from the five Baptist colleges and the five non-Baptist institutions and a series of semi-structured interviews. There were a number of methodological and ethical issues that raised in the development and conduct of the empirical research which are worth considering further.

I approached the research as both a participant and as an observer, and as both an insider and an outsider. Knott explores the connection between these two and proposes a continuum rather than simple alternatives.[3] Overall I am an "insider", in that I am researching an overall area in which I am deeply involved as a participant. I am a tutor of one of the Baptist colleges, involved in both denominational structures and collaborative ecumenical teaching. I have significant relationships with the other Baptist colleges, but I am an "outsider" to their particular institutional life, and this is true to a much greater degree with the non-Baptist institutions.

The very particular nature of the empirical research, in which both the researcher and the interviewee are theological tutors engaged in the practice of preparation created an expectation that an interview would be a shared conversation in theological reflection, one of the core elements identified by Cameron *et al.*[4] Further, although I initiated the conversations those

---

3. Knott, "Insider / Outsider Perspectives," 262.
4. Cameron *et al.*, *Talking about God in* Practice, 23.

interviewed have a clear and significant interest in the development of the research, and generally appreciated the opportunity to reflect with someone else on a central part of their role. The nature of these interviews suggests that the data gathered here will already be theologically rich and able to contribute to a developed understanding of theology as well as practice.

Drawing further on the literature, and the insider-outsider issue, I recognize my own non-neutrality in the research project. I adopt the wider and more general hermeneutical approach of Gadamer which does not seek some imagined neutrality, but recognizes the involvement of any researcher, with his or her prejudices, as a prerequisite to understanding,[5] together with Silverman's warning that always "facts are impregnated with our assumptions."[6] More than this I came to the empirical research with particular views formed over time about both the practice of ministry and the practice of preparation and which I have already begun to articulate. The research thus demands a significant degree of reflexivity to recognize what I bring to the research, how my views shape the conduct of the research project and how my views change and develop through the process, but the data will always be shaped to some degree by my own perspective.

Of the nine institutions involved in the process I only experienced defensiveness in one institution, which was much more guarded about the release of internal documents that could be considered at all sensitive, and seemed a little more concerned about presenting an institutional line than engaging in shared conversation, perhaps sensitive to previous questioning within inspection processes. Whereas interviewing those with whom I had strong relationships would have been unavoidably shaped through the lens of friendship, these individuals were also the most open with their documentation, allowing a greater insight into the institution. Here insider-outsider relationships played out in a particular way. I am aware, for example, of responding much more positively to interviews marked by an openness and vulnerability that developed shared theological reflection rather than those that seemed more defensive.

The other Baptist Colleges were willing to engage in this project on the basis that the institutions were named; given that there are only five colleges, all of which are involved in the study, it would be impossible to prevent incidental information identifying a particular institution. However, since five non-Baptist institutions have been chosen from a larger number of

---

5. See Swinton and Mowat, *Practical Theology*, 110–16.
6. Silverman, *Interpreting Qualitative Data*, 11.

colleges and courses involved in the preparation for ministry, it is possible to offer some degree of anonymity. Institutions were invited to participate in this research project on the basis that as far as possible anonymity would be protected, and so these institutions are simple listed as A, B, C, D and E.

Despite the good institutional and personal relationships involved, there is an inevitable and unavoidable element of the "market" involved in the preparation of Baptist ministers, shaped particularly strongly within a Baptist ecclesiology. Individuals who sense a call to ministry are commended by the local church and Association and are free to apply to whichever college they choose. For Baptists this "market" extends beyond the five Baptist colleges and may include non-denominational colleges and ecumenical courses, which a significant minority of Baptist ministers attend. There may be advice given by current ministers as well as traditional church connections with a particular college, but with the significant financial burden often falling on the individual student, their own choice becomes paramount.

As a researcher I also bring a variety of commitments to the project. I have a clear instinct for the college in which I work to appear in the best light, as do others in the research. For me it is this aspect that has been more dominant and it has made being critical of other Baptist colleges harder. Within the non-Baptist institutions I had a much wider range of relationships, knowing one of those interviewed well, two of them to a degree and meeting two others for the first time in the process. I am equally aware that within a much wider range of theology and churchmanship represented I warm more naturally to some institutions than others, as well as respond to the degrees of openness in different ways, and this affects both the content of the interviews and the analysis of all the documents.

A final ethical issue involved the conduct of the interviews themselves. The interviewees were asked and all agreed to the conversations being recorded, with the recordings then transcribed. The feel of the interviews as shared conversations was aided by the lack of any power in-balance between interviewer and interviewee.[7] All those interviewed held significant responsibility in their institutions, being very well qualified academically and with significant experience in the preparation of ministers.

---

7. Silverman, *Interpreting Qualitative Data*, 144.

DISCERNING THE ESPOUSED VOICE

I sought to establish the *espoused* voice the other four Baptist colleges and the five non-Baptist institutions are seeking to develop in their students by combining a document analysis together with an interview of the person in the institution most connected with the practice of preparation. The document analysis centered on submissions by the colleges to the inspection process, QiFP inspection reports, handbooks, brochures, strategic plans and websites. Some of these documents are in, indeed intended for, the public domain, as part of a college's promotion of its approach to preparation for ministry and others are private confidential documents kindly supplied by the colleges.

These documents were mainly examined on the basis of an ethnographically shaped narrative analysis,[8] exploring the way that such texts "depict reality,"[9] recognizing that different texts may have different authors, are written for a variety of different contexts, purposes and readerships, but which together build up a narrative of the institution. This was combined with a certain amount of content analysis,[10] in which, for example, the frequency of the use of specific language, especially formation, training and education, was counted in documents. While holding some hermeneutic of suspicion that documents cannot necessarily be "firm evidence of what they report",[11] my assumption was that the nature of these documents, as primary sources produced for clear and specific purposes, suggests a high level of confidence in their reliability,[12] that is, the internal documents, those produced for an inspection and those produced to communicate with the public reliably reflect the actual understanding of the college, and that an inspection report reliably reflects the opinions of that team of inspectors.

After an initial document analysis I arranged an interview as a second source of gathering data, normally, with one key representative whose responsibilities meant that they were able to offer an authentic, valid and significant insight into the theological understandings currently shaping the practice of preparation in that institution, aware that principals and

---

8. Silverman, *Interpreting Qualitative Data*, 164.
9. Silverman, *Interpreting Qualitative Data*, 168.
10. Silverman, *Interpreting Qualitative Data*, 159.
11. Coffey and Atkinson "Analyzing Documentary Realities," 58.
12. See Bell, *Doing Your Research Project*, 119.

tutors have had significant impact on the way current ministers understand their role.

In two of the Baptist colleges it was the principal and in one it was the vice-principal who subsequently became principal. In the fourth Baptist college I interviewed both co-principals, since they shared equally responsibility for ministerial preparation and this is part of the college's self-identity, together with the president of the wider ecumenical partnership, a Baptist minister, since the majority of the curriculum is shared ecumenically and overseen by the partnership, significant documents had come from the partnership, and without such an interview the same overall ground might not be covered. In the non-Baptist institutions, two of those interviewed were the principal, two were a vice-principal with particular responsibility for the preparation of ministers and one was a pastoral tutor, who again carried the significant responsibility for the practice of preparation.

These interviews were recorded and the transcripts then became documents that were analyzed in a similar way to the other sources, building on Gummesson's emphasis that there is a "continuous flow of data" between documents and interviews rather than a significant distinction.[13] Conducting in-depth interviews after the initial data analysis provided a process of triangulation.[14] Given the assumption that both the document sources and interviews would be the result of considered theological reflection, my expectation was that the process of triangulation would result more in confirmation than challenge. Taken as a whole, the breadth and depth of the research together with appropriate reflection and analysis of all the gathered information suggested that the process offers some viable and credible conclusions.[15]

One of the challenges of the research decision to interview, normally, just one person in each institution was the possible, even likely, difference of opinion between staff. In one way this contrasts with the document analysis, which sought to be comprehensive by considering all the documents available, whereas the interviews sought one perspective. But the triangulation of interviews with college documents, suggests that while there is clearly the danger that distinct voices in each institution are not heard, there can be some confidence in the representative nature of interviewing one individual. It would have been possible to develop the research further by deepening

---

13. Gummesson, *Qualitative Methods in Management Research*, 126–27.
14. Bell, *Doing Your Research Project*, 118.
15. See Bell, *Doing Your Research Project*, 119–20.

the participant observation of each institution and interviewing a much wider group of people. This would certainly have given a more in-depth and nuanced picture of each college and could be a future piece of work.

Given the respective roles and existing relationships, the interviews were conducted as "a guided or focused interview,"[16] which were wide-ranging, relatively unstructured, but were always "a conversation with a purpose."[17] This approach allowed the maximum space for the conversation to be shaped by the interviewee. The nature of the interviews draws on what Silverman describes as an emotionalist approach with some elements of constructionism.[18] That is, I understood the interviews to give authentic insight into the experiences and understandings of the interviewee, while recognizing that the shared conversation might generate a certain amount of mutually constructed meaning.

The first question in the interview asked interviewees to suggest the key words that they hoped would describe students when they leave the college. It would have been possible, as an alternative, to have used a method of a card sort or a repertory grid, so that those interviewed could choose from a selection of words I had chosen. While this may have had some advantages in comparing answers, the open interviews allowed tutors, themselves practical theologians, the maximum space to develop answers in their own language.

The interviews then focused first on a number of open questions, which explored key ideas around ordination, leadership and the professional nature of ministry, and the language and understanding of the practice of preparation.[19] Finally, the interviews explored a number of more specific questions emerging from the document analysis, seeking points of clarification or expansion.

DISCERNING THE OPERANT VOICE

Alongside an *espoused* understanding expressed in the documents and interviews sits the *operant* voice expressed in the actual practice of preparation. The aim of this aspect of the research was to establish as clearly

---

16. Bell, *Doing Your Research Project*, 65.

17. Bell, *Doing Your Research Project*, 164, quoting Dexter, *Elite and Specialised Interviewing*, 123.

18. Silverman, *Interpreting Qualitative Data*, 118.

19. Appendix 1 contains the list of the core questions used in all the interviews.

as possible the actual practice of each institution so that the *operant* voice might confirm or challenge the *espoused* position. This data, itself rooted in practice, will enable a clearer conversation between theory and practice.

Following Eisner, the wider practice of preparation may be thought about in terms of explicit, implicit and null curriculum.[20] The null curriculum is a helpful concept in that it alerts us to what might be absent from a particular curriculum and raises questions about choices made for inclusion, but it is also philosophically problematic. There is something instinctively ambiguous about the definition of something that is absent, for something can only be deemed "missing" from a curriculum on the basis of a prior framework that is already established as educationally valuable.[21] My intention here was to compare the curricula of the colleges to each other rather than to any separate normative curriculum and so I focused on exploring the explicit and implicit curricula of each of the different institutions, highlighting certain aspects that are absent or have a reduced significance compared to the other institutions. But there were still questions as to how best to identify an explicit and implicit curriculum.

The Explicit Curriculum

The explicit curriculum is that which an institution professes to teach and is found in guides, texts and courses.[22] From the handbooks, module details, timetables and interviews I sought to establish the explicit curriculum that each college considers to be compulsory for its ordinands. The central methodological challenge was to provide a clear and fair way to compare the different curricula. I approached the task by dividing the overall curriculum into a number of different areas and establishing the percentage of the curriculum that could be located in each of these areas.

There is no objective way of dividing the curriculum and, therefore, an inevitable degree of arbitrariness in the choice of these categories ensues. Although all the institutions divide the curriculum into different modules, shaped by the need to account for teaching hours, credit and as the basis for assignments, they do so in different ways, using different pedagogical approaches in their choices. In any examination of these different curricula

---

20. Eisner, *The Educational Imagination*, 87.

21. For further discussion of the usefulness and ambiguity of the null curriculum see Flinders, Noddings and Thornton, "The Null Curriculum."

22. Eisner, *The Educational Imagination*, 88.

it is necessary to impose categories, which meant dividing some modules that an institution kept as a whole.

It would have been possible to use a basic Schleiermachian model with four subject areas, and when the data is arranged in this way it does itself produce interesting results. But practical theology is too wide a category and the detail too important for all the material in this area to be grouped together. Working instead with the various sub-divisions the different institutions used and developing the categories as further documents were read, the following emerged from the research as the final list of curriculum areas, which has more sub-divisions than any single institution uses but which offers the most detailed data:

- Bible
- Doctrine
- History
- Ethics
- Mission
- Worship / Preaching
- Pastoral Care
- Spirituality / Personal Development
- Leadership
- Baptist Identity
- Theological Reflection
- Placement
- Quiet Days / Retreats
- Tutorials
- Other
- Student Choice

While all the colleges offer a number of different pathways for ordinands depending on previous qualifications and experience, the curricula compared here are those offered to a ministerial student without any previous theological study before embarking on an undergraduate course. This offers the best comparison of those elements that an individual college desired to include without needing to build on previous academic curricula.

Exploring Practice and the Pastoral Imagination

I allocated the curricula to these different areas on a percentage basis of contact hours, thus avoiding the differences between overall contact hours amongst the colleges.[23] In order to focus on how the pastoral imagination is intentionally developed by the college, I included those aspects of the curriculum that are compulsory and gathered under student choice those which are optional.

The Implicit Curriculum

The implicit curriculum is that which is beyond the clearly specified modules, which Eisner suggests centers on values and culture, is often unintentional and is because institutions, in his case schools, "are the kind of places they are."[24] I chose to concentrate an exploration of the implicit curriculum on the corporate worship of each institution, because this emerged from the documentation of the different institutions as of significant importance and also because there was clear documentation on the way that each institution sought to develop this area of its life. This offered an insightful, though limited, perspective into each institution, and is based again on documentary analysis and interviews. This is one of the more limited areas of the research and a more thorough immersion into an institution through extended participant observation would create significantly more data about the implicit curriculum, including a "feel" of the worship in each institution. This lay beyond the scope of my research, but would be helpful further research in its own right.

In gathering information about the corporate worship of the different colleges, recognizing the variations of different pathways, I applied the same criteria of an ordinand taking an undergraduate course and, again, I focused on the corporate worship that ministerial students are expected to attend, rather than that which is optional. Consistent with the approach that seeks to explore the intentions of the colleges, this aspect of the research made no attempt to measure actual participation or student response to collective worship. Exploring the range of corporate worship within the various institutions, six categories clearly emerged from the varying practice:

---

23. Such differences, themselves part of operant practice, are discussed in chapters five and six.

24. Eisner, *The Educational Imagination*, 93.

- Shorter services of morning or evening prayer
- Longer services of the Word
- Eucharistic services
- Shared ecumenical services
- Informal prayer in small groups
- Retreats / Quiet days

Discerning a Representative Voice

I have already reflected on the *representative* voice of the Baptist Union concerning the practices of ministry and preparation for ministry through a literature analysis, but alongside this, there was a further "guided and focused" interview, with the then team leader of the Ministries Team within the Baptist Union, Revd Dr Paul Goodliff. Matters relating to ministry, and especially those related to ministerial accreditation, are one of the most centralized aspects of British Baptist life[25] and so Goodliff acted primarily as a representative of the then position in the wider Union. Somewhat different to the other interviews this was more akin to an "expert interview", used as a "parallel" and "complementary method"[26] to the other interviews, able to gather information within the field and to offer both connections and contrast to the other interviews. Given the very particular nature of this interview, which was to clarify recent developments and explore the theological understandings of ministry explicitly and implicitly held within the wider Union, there was no question of anonymity in the final thesis. However, noting that Goodliff's own research was, and is, in a similar area, the extent to which those in office within the Union are reflecting their own theological views or those of the Union, at least as agreed in Council and Executive, remains an open question.

---

25. This desire for a Union wider accredited ministry was reaffirmed by the recent Baptist Union of Great Britain *Ignite* report.

26. See Flick, *An Introduction to Qualitative Research*, 168.

CONCLUSION

Building on the methodology of exploring theology in four voices through participant observation, I have set out in this chapter the research methods and choices used in discerning the *espoused* and *operant* voices within the different institutions and in further refining the *representative* voice of the Baptist Union. The results of this empirical research are set out and explored in the following chapters. In chapter 5 the *espoused* voice of the other four Baptist colleges is presented and analyzed and then the *operant* voice of the five Baptist colleges, including Regent's Park is discussed. In chapter 6 the *espoused* and *operant* voices from the five non-Baptist institutions are considered.

5

Discerning a Pastoral Imagination
Some Findings Among Baptist Colleges

THE FIRST RESEARCH QUESTION I set out to explore was this: what is the pastoral imagination which the Baptist colleges individually are seeking to inculcate in their students?

What I offer in this chapter is a summary of my research findings in which I describe the pastoral imagination that I discerned in the other four Baptist Colleges, by setting out first their *espoused* theologies, based on document analysis and interviews[1] and then their *operant* theologies based on the curriculum and patterns of worship. The advantage and disadvantage of this empirical approach is that is offers something of a snapshot of a college, which hopefully offers a clear and accurate insight into the *espoused* and *operant* theologies of the college at the time when the research took place (2013–2015), but which may, of course, have changed since then. Undoubtedly changes in staff in some of the colleges since 2015 will have led to some changes and new developments, but if our thesis that ministerial formation is a practice that persists over time, is shared with others and acts as a structuring structure then we would expect innovation to occur within a particular tradition. So this would suggest that insights gained at one particular time can be helpful in the ongoing life of an institution.

---

1. For clarity of reading here the more detailed references back to interviews have been removed.

ESPOUSED THEOLOGIES

Northern Baptist College (NBC)

Northern Baptist College[2] was formed in 1964 by the amalgamation of two independent colleges, Manchester College and Rawdon. It is a founding member of the Luther King House Educational Trust (LKH) combining Baptist, Methodist, URC and Unitarian traditions. The partnership is explicitly founded on the Lund Principle, first embedded in the charter for the Northern Federation for Training in Ministry in 1984 which then developed into LKH.

NBC used the language of formation, education and training in a variety of contexts often inter-changeably. Both the *Memorandum of Association* of LKH[3] and the *Mission Statement of NBLC*[4] defined the principal work in terms of "theological education". The language of training was disliked, because of too great an association with a set of skills, and the language of formation, although preferred to training, was tainted by its use elsewhere. NBC strongly rejected ideas that the process of preparation for ministry was about conformation to a particular model; rather it was about starting with individuals who grow and develop uniquely. It drew on the meaning of education as "to lead out", as the linguistic and pedagogical basis for this, with the banking model of education specifically rejected and a Freirean approach to learning, which both valued the contributions of the learner and was alert to political and justice issues, specifically embraced.[5] Their commitment to one-to-one tutorials was in line with this approach.

NBC launched its BA in contextual theology in 1994, when it became an affiliated institution able to develop its own degree program, more fully integrating the placement experience, paying attention to the particular and specific nature of the context within a framework that is wholeheartedly committed to the methodology of practical theology, and with a commitment to contextual learning along Freirean lines.

---

2. During the time of the research it had changed its name to Northern Baptist Learning Community, but has subsequently changed its name back to Northern Baptist College.

3. "The advancement of education in areas of Christian faith, practice and dialogue . . ."

4. "The NBLC is a widely accessible resource for mission through theological education, equally available to the whole people of God across the whole constituency of the Midlands and the North."

5. LKH inspection submission, 4.

Forming Ministers or Training Leaders?

The QiFP Report (2012) suggested that contextualization was "a thread running through the whole learning process,"[6] although the journey to such contextual integration was at times difficult,[7] and this was expressed as part of the core ethos of the College. This involved the centrality of students being "rooted" in communities, with whom and from whom they learn, shaped by a collaborative understanding of ministry.

Although there was some concern about possible connotations of formation language NBC was deeply committed to a formation paradigm that held together integration, integrity and contextualization. Within this understanding of the practice of preparation the pastoral imagination that NBC sought to develop might be described as:

Ecumenical: NBC had deliberately chosen not to be without its ecumenical partners or the other students who attend through LKH's Open College. This was intended as a deeply formational experience, which shaped ecumenical awareness. The majority of the curriculum was shared together with just one separate session of "college time" each week. The strong ecumenical context brought struggles as well as benefits, for example feeling the need to work against a very strongly ontological view of ordination and some understandings of formation within wider ecumenical partners. But NBC was committed to the belief that "formation in an ecumenical context makes a huge contribution to the development of denomination-specific identity."[8]

Reflective: The QiFP inspection report stressed the centrality of reflection,[9] which was affirmed strongly in interviews. The first module taught was on theological reflection with an assignment involving facilitating theological reflection with a group in their placement.[10] But there was also a strong "reflexive" element, with expectations that students will have questioned assumptions and been through a process of deconstruction and reconstruction, aware of patterns of faith development.

Global: The combination of language used in the interviews and documents which touched on missional concerns and identified an outward

---

6. QiFP *Inspection Report Luther King House*, 35.

7. The interviewees offered a frank reflection on some of the struggles of the journey, which offered a different perspective to the much more positive version in the more official history, in Shepherd, *The Making of a northern College*.

8. QiFP *Inspection Report Luther King House*, 7.

9. QiFP *Inspection Report Luther King House*, 35.

10. Module descriptor for BA401 "Learning Together Theologically."

looking aspect may be best summarized as "global". This was expressed as the desire to see ministers as global citizens particularly sensitized to issues of justice, drawing on the language of liberation theology, and expressed both in LKH's teaching and commitment to diversity. This global / liberation stress derived from and supported a Freirean approach to education.

Collaborative: NBC had the desire to "shape patterns of discipleship which are essentially participatory,"[11] offering an explicit model of ministry that was deeply collaborative, eschewing disabling hierarchies and seeking to empower others. Such a desire was reflected in the collaborative governance of LKH itself and in the development of co-principals in NBC. The language of leadership and professionalism was used sparingly, generally sidelined because of implicit connotations. A variety of leadership styles were taught because "they need to know what the other styles are in order to critique them" while the collaborative style was unashamedly affirmed as being truly Baptist. Further this is also expressed in gender terms with the model of the sole heroic leader cast in male terms being replaced by the collaborative, consultative "more female" approach to leadership. This seems one of the few areas in which the college staff would look to inculcate a particular understanding of ministry.

Spurgeon's College

Spurgeon's College was founded in 1856 as The Pastor's College with the explicit aim of preparing ministers for Baptist churches. This remains at the core of its vision, although it has diversified considerably, offering counselling courses, on-line theology courses, and expanding the number of independent ministerial students, who now outnumber those who are accredited BUGB students. In particular Spurgeon's reflects its South London setting, drawing significantly from London based Pentecostal BAME churches, and from the newer charismatic streams.

Spurgeon's understood the process of preparation to involve education, training and formation, but the language of training dominated in its documentation. Three of the five aims of the college, set out in their strategic plan (2010–13), refer to training while one refers to continually improving levels of education, formation and learning, and the person who oversees the preparation of Baptist ministers had the title "Director of Training", which has subsequently changed to "Director of Ministerial Formation and

11. LKH inspection submission, 3.

Training". Formation, training and education were used interchangeably, as in the college's inspection submission in 2011, and with some degree of inconsistency.[12] But drawing explicitly on the work of Foster *et. al.* the document also prioritized formation and the college seemed to be moving towards an increasing use of formation language, so that "the overall aim is to practice the presence of God and grow in spiritual leadership."[13]

The practice of preparation sought to integrate the three aspects of knowledge, skills and character—frequently using the three-circle Venn diagram[14]—together with a clear desire to integrate theory and practice,[15] with the BTh and BD drawing on the methodologies of practical theology and theological reflection.

Spurgeon's has embraced, to some degree, the language of formation and is also committed to the ideas of integration and integrity that are at its heart. There was, though, also a clear commitment to the concept of "training" as an important aspect of the practice of preparation and Spurgeon's sought to hold together both training and formation. It seems significant that a number of Spurgeon's Principals have placed a greater stress on the leadership paradigm, especially Paul Beasley-Murray.

The documentation as a whole explicitly affirmed an espoused pastoral imagination by using a variety of different adjectives: their inspection submission centered on being "orthodox, evangelical, radical, missional and ecumenical,[16] developing ministers who are grounded in the life of faith, rooted in Scripture and the Free Church tradition, able to relate faith effectively to contemporary culture, competent, winsome and an effective witness to Christ;[17] an internal document, on the other hand, described the college's core activity as "the training of attractive and evangelical ministers"[18] and that it sought to "prepare confident, competent and credible leaders."[19] Drawing together these with all the other evidence, the pastoral imagination that Spurgeon's sought to develop might be described as:

12. Inspection submission (2011), 19.
13. Inspection submission, 22.
14. Inspection submission, 20, 24.
15. Inspection submission, 35.
16. Inspection submission, 12.
17. Inspection submission, 17.
18. *Models and Patterns of Training at Spurgeon's College*, 2.
19. *Models and Patterns*, 3.

Discerning a Pastoral Imagination

Evangelical: understood in a broad sense, this was a key descriptor within their *Mission Statement,* one of five areas of common concern, and was deeply rooted in the college's history. Spurgeon's has developed its own set of key elements of ministry, which parallels the BUGB core competencies and a comparison reveals more clearly espoused evangelical concerns: communicating the Gospel faithfully and persuasively, guarding its truth, having the intellectual ability to interpret faith accurately and defend it against misrepresentation and hostile criticism.[20] It does therefore seem significant that the word "evangelical" was not used at all in the interview, perhaps to avoid appearing type-cast, although it remains central to the college's espoused pastoral imagination as set out in its documentation.

Missional: this featured significantly in the *Mission Statement*, as the first of five areas of concern. Ministry was understood as "highly missional", with the college seeking to prepare "missionary ministers"[21] and "desiring to embed mission in all training,"[22] although this perspective was slightly tempered by the *Supervisors Pack for College-based Students* in which the template for reporting was dominated by more "pastoral" aspects of ministry such as worship, preaching and pastoral care, rather than mission.

Spiritual: In the interview the central description of the college was as a discipling institution, concerned with preparing ministers as a form of "specialized discipleship", so that amid developing skills and understanding there was a core element of growth in spiritual and personal awareness. The particular version of the three-circle model always appeared in Spurgeon's documentation with spirituality at the overlapping center. Spiritual also included the language of being attractive, credible, and winsome, because there was an authentic and deep spirituality woven through all ministerial practice.

Professional: The core, shared formational activity was described as "Professional Ministerial Practice", and professional language was found in learning outcomes for the BTh and BD, the *Strategic Plan* and generally through the documentation. The interview confirmed this is language that was positively embraced and welcomed. It was reflected in the repeated desire to develop competent ministers. Linked with this, the language of leadership featured strongly in the documentation. With the variety of their student body, "leader" may be a more helpful generic term than "minister". Leadership was understood as communal service not the exercise of

---

20. Inspection submission, 16
21. Inspection submission, 15.
22. QiFP *Inspection Report Spurgeon's College*, p. 10.

dominion,[23] which the staff sought to model in the day-to-day life of the college. Professional would also seem to be a key word of self-description of the college, reflected in its desire to be a "progressive and competent evangelical institution."[24]

Bristol Baptist College

Bristol Baptist College has also diversified in recent years developing an expertise in youth, community and children and families' workers, as well offering theological education to independent students alongside the core activity of preparing ministers. The college has traditionally taught academic awards from Bristol University, although in 2014, with its very strong partnership with Trinity College, it joined the Common Awards.

The documentation used a mixture of formation, training and education language and the composite nature of some documents, for example, the *Student Handbook*, suggests how the language has developed, with ministerial training being gradually replaced with the language of ministerial formation.[25] The reworked aims and objectives, agreed by the college council in 2012, described the purpose of the college as to "share in the mission of God in the world through the formation of . . . women and men for different forms of Christian ministry." Wider documentation and the interview concur that there was a preference for understanding the whole practice of preparation as one of formation, of which education and training are aspects. The documents expressed the importance of integration both in terms of the connection between learning, skills and character and between theory and practice through practice-based learning.[26]

The college has expressed clearly and succinctly its pastoral imagination as the formation of "competent, passionate, spirit-filled and evangelical" ministers. This is a deliberate modernization of the historic description of the pastoral imagination expressed by Caleb Evans in a sermon on the death of his father Hugh Evans, the Principal of the college, in 1781 "as not merely to form substantial scholars but as far as in him lay he was desirous of being made an instrument in God's hand of forming them, able,

---

23. Inspection submission, 14.

24. *Spurgeon's College Strategic Plan.*

25. The Aims and Objectives refer to the formation of ministers and the training of children's, community and other church workers.

26. Inspection submission, 2–13.

Discerning a Pastoral Imagination

evangelical, lively, zealous ministers of the Gospel."[27] Although these words are part of the tradition and were warmly embraced, some of the emphasis actually seemed to lie elsewhere. For example, the college willingly used the language of "competent", shaped by its commitment to work within the then BUGB framework of competencies, while at the same time seeking to move beyond that, and so lessening its significance, giving a greater place to the language of values and character. The pastoral imagination that Bristol sought to develop might, therefore, be described as:

Missional: The inspection submission articulated the missional challenge as a major concern and the central responsibility for ministers as making disciples and helping to sustain the discipleship of others.[28] This advocated a holistic view of mission, drawing on the five marks of mission[29] while recognizing that Baptists have historically tended to stress those more concerned with proclamation and conversion.[30] The college has developed in recent years a more explicitly mission-focused version of its course and mission features as one of its distinct three cross-curricula themes.

Evangelical: This is a word that appeared in both the historic and contemporary list of adjectives, but was always understood with a lower case "e". It was understood to refer to the authority of the Bible, "something very significant for Baptists", and "biblical" was the second of the cross-curricula themes. The underlying foundational competence was "the indwelling of the Christian story and the ability to communicate it with others," from which all others flow.

Leading collaboratively: The college, in its documentation, willingly embraced the language of leadership. It prepared women and men for pastoral and missional leadership,[31] described the role of pastors on the accredited list as the "ministry of pastoral leadership"[32] and the college's overall vision was to train Christian leaders of healthy growing churches.[33] Discipleship and leadership was also the third of the three cross-curricula

---

27. Quoted in Ellis, "Being a Minister," 57.

28. Inspection submission, 1.

29. These originate in the global Anglican context but have been embraced more widely. See Walls and Ross, *Mission in the 21st Century: Exploring the Five Marks of Global Mission*.

30. Inspection submission, 2.

31. Inspection submission, 1.

32. Inspection submission, 8.

33. *Student Handbook*, 30.

themes. The language of leadership was carefully nuanced and understood as servant leadership, expressed as oversight that empowers and enables others.[34] Such collaborative leadership was modeled in the collegiality of the college and the insistence on shared common space and meals between students and staff. The *Student Handbook* on occasion positively embraced the language of professional, while the Principal was much more cautious, stressing instead the importance of spirituality and character. Ministers were "disciples who make disciples and help sustain the discipleship of others" and hold "power in order to hold the ring so that others can exercise their gifts in non-competitive ways."

South Wales Baptist College

South Wales Baptist College (SWBC) relates to both the Baptist Unions of Great Britain and of Wales. Its bilingual heritage gives the college a particular context, which is also shaped by their independent students, its then significant partnership with St Michael's Anglican College, before St Michael's reconstituted itself in a different way, and its close connection with Cardiff University, where some lectures are taught across a whole range of students.

There was a clear commitment to an integrated approach, drawing on the same three-circle diagram and increasingly articulating that the whole of the experience contributes to the whole of the process of preparation and to the three strands within it. Their documents also revealed a clear development of language, with some older, seemingly composite, documents using the language of training very heavily.[35] The more recent documents, confirmed in interview, showed a much greater use of and commitment to formation as the overarching description, which included elements of training and education. The new document *Ministerial Formation at SWBC* highlighted four components, one of which was pastoral training, the others being personal and spiritual development, biblical and theological studies and a placement.

---

34. Inspection submission, 6–7; the Principal expressed his own preference for the term "oversight" to the language of word and sacrament as this allows for greater missional diversity, and understood this, more unusually, as a shared oversight of the whole Union which is focused in a specific local context.

35. For example, the *Church Based Training* booklet, *A Reflection and Evaluation of the Strategic Plan*, the *College Handbook* and the *Student Handbook* combine the language of training and formation.

This integrated approach was reflected in the BTh, whose *Programme Specifications* stress that the whole course was one of critical theological reflection, drawing on the methodologies of practical theology and on other disciplines such as psychology and sociology. This was perhaps shaped by the significant place Cardiff University has had in the development of practical theology. While the degree was deeply contextual there were still some elements of the whole process of formation which did not yet find a place in the BTh. Such future development was the clear intention and the recent addition of a level 4 module on preaching is an example.

A new document, *Equipping for Ministry and Mission at South Wales Baptist College*, expressed a pastoral imagination as missional, reflective, rooted, global and holy. Drawing on this, wider documentation and recent developments at SWBC the emphasis of the pastoral imagination that SWBC sought to develop might be described as:

Missional: All ministry was connected with mission, and this is a crucial example of how a pastoral imagination has become more explicit. Some of the older documents around placements give much more space and emphasis to pastoral rather than mission activity. The current espoused pastoral imagination seemed more explicitly mission focused.

Reflective: The college was committed to reflective practice as the primary theological method, recognizing that "evangelical activists" often "do not find it easy to reflect on practice."[36] One of the significant opportunities of the context of SWBC in the specific bilingual and increasingly devolved Wales was a very specific context to reflect upon. Again there are hints of the way this was developing, for an older document, *Guidelines for Term-time Student Placement*, suggests that the placement was where the theoretical input of College is worked out in practice, suggesting a more "applied" model rather than an integrated one, but in other ways there was a clear commitment to practical theology.

Global: Recognizing that "the centre of gravity of world Christianity has moved south of the equator"[37] the need for ministers who are global in their understanding and commitment had recently received greater emphasis, as indicated by the connection that SWBC had made with BMS World Mission. The hope was expressed that this would become increasingly embedded in the course, supported by a new module on "Majority

---

36. *Equipping for Ministry and Mission at SWBC*, 4.
37. *Equipping for Ministry and Mission at SWBC*, 5.

World Voices", drawing on the then Principal's previous experience of partnering in theological education with seminaries in Ghana.

SOME REFLECTIONS

While one college claimed it "has developed its own distinctive values and models of training"[38] another suggested that the "desire to provide a process which encourages personal formation as gospel practitioners is reflected in the integrated model of theological formation which undergirds the courses in all of the Baptist colleges."[39] The reality combines both.

The Practice of Preparation

Exploring the practice of preparation of the other four Baptist colleges, two issues come to the fore.

First, there is strong evidence of a developing shared understanding and description of the practice of preparation as one of formation, evidenced both by the language itself and the way the who process of preparation is understood and explained. There is also strong evidence that this has been a more gradual development rather than a sudden change. Several of the foundational documents in the colleges clearly appeared to be composite, developed over time, perhaps another example of the shared *habitus* of the practice of preparation. But there are also clear developments within the tradition, towards embracing formation language. This is confirmed by my own experience of inheriting a set of documents which I have worked with and developed rather than beginning completely afresh. I too have gradually reworked these documents so that formation language and ideas have become more prominent, while the language of training has decreased.

But it appears to be a developing understanding rather than one that is completely settled. Formation was the language that was used most significantly in all the interviews, but not in all the documentation. The college websites contained more references to ministerial formation than they did five years previously, but this was not consistent or complete, with some colleges more strongly embracing this language (eg Regent's Park and Bristol). On the other hand, the Baptist Union website's material at the time

---

38. *Models and Patterns of Training at Spurgeon's College*, 2.
39. *Equipping for Ministry and Mission at SWBC*, 2.

strongly deployed training language. It is of course more than simply the use of language—NBC was probably the most hesitant about the language itself, but with the strongest commitment to the underlying ideas of formation—but the language we use is important.

Further, this has also been something of a shared journey. From the visits in the early 1980s of Bruce Keeble to Michael Taylor to Peter Stevenson's explicit drawing on Spurgeon's documents after appointment as Principal at SWBC there are clear individual connections. In addition, the colleges have acted as a community of practice, with ideas and developments flowing between them. The yearly Staffs' Conference, meetings of the Principals, as well as other informal links have helped develop a shared practice. This shared journey is most clearly expressed in the document *Ministerial Formation in the British Baptist Colleges: A Commitment to Shared Practice.*

Formation, then, has then gradually developed as the clearest *habitus* of the practice of preparation for British Baptists. If there is a structured and structuring structure which is shared by the colleges and which seeks integration and integrity as key aspects, then it is expressed as formation. But within a commitment to the integration of the three aspects represented by being, knowing and doing, there is also space for creative improvisation so that the three aspects might be given different weight or emphases in a different college. In pictorial form, the three circles may in fact be different sizes—the research showed a greater stress at Spurgeon's on training, for example, and this might enlarge their "doing" circle.

But the language itself has not been universally embraced. The most recent Baptist Union document on ministry, *The Ignite Report*, was clearly moving in this direction in the way it understood the practice of preparation, but the Baptist Union website at the time used almost entirely the language of training. Is it the case that language is understood differently by different people, or is there a tendency to implicitly incline to language that is most familiar, or is there an intentional use of training language as most likely to communicate to others beyond the world of college life? My suggestion is that there is work still to be done here as colleges and as a Union to develop further a shared language and a shared understanding of the practice of formation.

Second, there have been clear developments in the way that all the colleges have moved away from a more traditional academic approach to theology and have developed courses shaped by the methodologies of practical theology. Northern Baptist College was the first to launch a fully contextual degree and others have followed in that direction to varying degrees. Alongside the commitment to contextualization, the integration of theory and practice and theological reflection, there have been developments to ensure that all the different aspects of the curriculum are integrated into the validated program, rather than standing as a separate pastoral studies strand, and an increasing commitment that the whole of the wider curriculum delivers the whole of formation. "Academic" modules, for example, do not simply offer knowledge, but these are also understood to shape character and spirituality. This is in distinction to Foster *et al.*, who seem to divide the whole into different apprenticeships accomplished by distinct aspects of the whole curriculum.[40]

Again, within this co-operative practice there are some practical differences, shaped by pedagogical and educational distinctions. Baptist colleges reflect the spectrum and diversity within practical theology about the way that theory and practice mutually influence each other. Northern Baptist College, for example, expresses the most distinct educational philosophy drawing on Freirean and wider liberation theology models, gives most space to the way that practice can shape theory, and pays the most attention at the beginning to the practice of theological reflection.

My own experience at Regent's fit into this same pattern of development. The Oxford University BTh, first developed in the mid-1990s, as an alternative to the traditional BA, was still shaped around the classic fourfold sub-divisions of theology, although with the different aspects taught contemporaneously not sequentially, with methodologies of theological reflection limited to certain papers. The reworking of the BTh in 2014 offered some scope for further developments and aspects of practical theology methodologies are now in an increasing range of papers, but within an overall degree that still retains a more traditional shape of biblical studies, historical and systematic theology and practical theology. As colleges continue to develop their courses, an open and important question focuses on both the desirability and practical possibilities of a fully contextual degree, recognizing that all the colleges work within different Higher Education contexts.

---

40. Foster *et al.*, *Educating Clergy*, 7–8.

The Pastoral Imagination

In terms of the pastoral imagination that each college seeks to develop there is also considerable overlap. Almost all of the adjectives above would be embraced by all the colleges, but given differing emphases. There would be very broad agreement that a shared pastoral imagination should be missional, reflective, contextual, spiritual, ecumenically sensitive, collaborative, and rooted in the Scriptural witness and the tradition of the church, particularly as expressed among Baptists. Evangelical would be more contested, because of concerns it may carry a very narrow meaning. Spurgeon's adopt this language most fully in its documentation, although I have already noted significant hesitancy in the interview to use this terminology. Where evangelical is taken in its broad meaning, of a commitment to the importance of Scripture, the place of conversion and baptism, and the missional nature of the church, as expressed, for example, in the Declaration of Principle, it would find broad assent.

Within a shared pastoral imagination it is Northern Baptist College which seemed to offer the most distinct emphases, being the most ecumenically committed, the most collaborative in their approach to ministry, understood partly in gendered terms, and the most committed to seeing the practices of both preparation and ministry through the lens of liberation theology and the quest for global justice.

There are also genuine differences in the way that professional language is adopted, which connects with understandings of leadership. It would appear that the five colleges would broadly assent to what was described in chapter two as the dialectical model of ministry rather than to the leadership paradigm. Where leadership language is used it is with a sense of collaboration and service. But again within a broader agreement there are important differences. Spurgeon's most readily adopted leadership and professional language, and sought to teach a range of views of leadership, so that students can develop their own understanding, but also recognized that the breadth of their student body will shape these discussions. NBC was the most collaborative in its approach to ministry, seeking to stress and inculcate a particular approach as Baptist, and so mitigate ecumenical influence at this point. Within a spectrum NBC offered the strongest espoused view of a collaborative ministry and the dialectical model, while Spurgeon's seems to show the greatest influence of the leadership paradigm.

These findings do seem to confirm the way that the historical *habitus* of a college acts as a structured as well as a structuring structure. The legacy of Michael Taylor has actually shaped all colleges, but the distinct ecumenical and liberation stress at NBC corresponds most closely to his work, where there is, as expected, the strongest legacy. Equally the greater stress on leadership and professionalism that marked the work of former Principals at Spurgeon's, especially Paul Beasley-Murray and Michael Quicke, correlate with a greater continuing stress on these aspects of formation. The desire of Bristol to faithfully rework the pastoral imagination as expressed by Hugh Evans points to a willing embrace of that historical structuring.

The pastoral imagination here has been deliberately described using adjectives—which adjectives are the most appropriate in describing ministry—rather than trying to define the noun "ministry". The research specifically did not focus on differences expressed in functional, ontological or sacramental understandings of ministry and there are certainly different views among tutors about the nature of ordination. But these adjectival descriptions carry their own embedded theology and so shape the meaning of the noun, some, perhaps, more so than others. To describe ministers as missional, or collaborative or professional not only describes the way that ministers might shape their own practice but also suggests quite strongly something about the very essence of that practice. Or, in other words, being missional, or collaborative or professional cannot be purely functional but does carry ontological undertones.

The Context

Alongside the understanding of the practice of preparation and the distinct pastoral imagination, a third important issue, shaped by and also influencing the other two aspects, is the specific context of each college. In fact, it is the context of each of the five Baptist colleges, shaped historically, strategically and theologically, that appears most distinct. This confirms the research of Foster et al. who suggest five factors which influence theological education, the first being campus setting and the fifth including the diversity of the student body.[41]

The colleges work within their own structured structures and these have affected location, validation and the constituency to which a college most immediately connects. One striking example is the decision of Regent's Park to move to Oxford in the 1920s, so that a Baptist presence would increase the Free Church contribution to one of the two historic

---

41. Foster et al., *Educating Clergy*, 43–58.

universities and so the college, and the Baptist Union, could benefit from all the resources and status of Oxford University.[42] This decision has shaped Regent's on-going approach to formation. Whereas in the past one fundamental aspect of the shared context would have been full-time residential communities predominantly for Baptist ordinands, financially it has not been possible for any college to survive in this mode, resulting in a variety of strategic decisions about buildings, expanding student numbers and partnerships with other colleges.

The move to create the partnership around Luther King House is driven most clearly by explicit theological convictions, but financial considerations and geographical contingencies played a part in a move that was otherwise theologically shaped. The presence of Anglican colleges in Bristol, Cardiff and Oxford have led to varying degrees of partnership within ministerial formation, and the changing nature of church life and ethnic make-up in London has led to a distinct and increasingly varied context for Spurgeon's.

These contexts are partly chosen and partly contingent. All five contexts have become increasingly ecumenical, although this has shaped the pastoral imagination most significantly at NBC. All five contexts have a range of other students who are not Baptist ordinands, although the context at Regent's Park is the broadest. All five contexts welcome independent students, although the number and diversity at Spurgeon's seems to be the most significant in shaping the whole college. The contexts of the colleges offer ministerial students different experiences of formation, and this seems to be one of the most significant ways in which the five colleges remain distinct.

This has also been one of the major underlying issues within various reviews of ministry. Financial concerns have meant that there have been, and no doubt will continue to be, voices calling for the amalgamation of some or even all the colleges, for Baptist ordinands to be formed all together in one central location, or for ministerial formation to be devolved to Association Partnerships, perhaps without university validated courses. Yet context is of theological significance, particularly in terms of ecumenical relationships, and any discussions within the Baptist Union must pay close attention to the desired contexts of formation.

---

42. See Clarke and Fiddes, *Dissenting Spirit*, 104–10. Regent's Park College almost moved to Cambridge in 1922, before it moved to Oxford in 1927 with the Governing Body voting to which of the two historical universities they should relocate.

OPERANT THEOLOGIES

The Explicit Curriculum

Chapter 4 set out the way that explicit curriculum would be considered based on set contact hours for different subjects. The tables, below, show the results when the curricula of the five Baptist Colleges were assessed by these criteria—recognizing again that this is a snapshot taken in 2014/15 and that curricula are always developing. Once again, there are some significant overall similarities but there are also some real differences.

	Spurgeon's BTh		Spurgeon's BD		Bristol—Pastor		Bristol—Mission	
	Hours	%	Hours	%	Hours	%	Hours	%
Bible	120.5	15.4%	186.5	19.2%	123.5	13.5%	93.5	10%
Doctrine and Ethics	89.25	11.4%	100.25	10.3%	67	7.3%	57	6%
History	44	5.6%	44	4.5%	20	2%	20	2%
Ethics								
Mission	83.25	10.6%	83.25	8.6%	110.5	12%	150.5	16%
Preaching / Worship	42.25	5.4%	42.25	4.3%	75	8%	75	8%
Pastoral Care	80.25	10.2%	80.25	8.3%	68	7%	68	7%
Spirituality / Personal Development	37	4.7%	37	3.8%	76	8%	76	8%

Discerning a Pastoral Imagination

	Spurgeon's BTh		Spurgeon's BD		Bristol—Pastor		Bristol—Mission	
	Hours	%	Hours	%	Hours	%	Hours	%
Leadership	49.25	6.3%	49.25	5.1%	12	1%	12	1%
Baptist Identity	37	4.7%	48	4.9%	30	3%	30	3%
Theological Reflection	6.25	0.8%	6.25	0.6%	72	8%	72	8%
Placement					70	7.66%	70	7.66%
Quiet Days / Prayer Groups	102	13.0%	102	10.5%	75	8.2%	75	8.2%
Tutorials								
Other	2.5	0.3%	2.5	0.3%	35	3.83%	35	3.83%
Student Choice	91	11.6%	190	19.6%	80	9%	80	9%
Totals	784.5	100%	971.5	100%	914	100%	914	100%

Forming Ministers or Training Leaders?

	SWBC		NBC		RPC—DTPS	
	Hours	%	Hours	%	Hours	%
Bible	78.5	11.4%	73.5	12.3%	89.5	12.3%
Doctrine and Ethics	87.25	12.6%	8	14.7%	45.5	6.2%
History	24	3.5%	4	5.7%	13	1.8%
Ethics			2	2.0%	16	2.2%
Mission	73.25	10.6%	78	13.1%	31.5	18.0%
Preaching / Worship	28.75	4.2%	61.5	10.3%	92	12.6%
Pastoral Care	24.25	3.5%	52.5	8.8%	77.75	10.7%
Spirituality / Personal Development	70.75	10.2%	43.5	7.3%	30.5	4.2%
Leadership	24	3.5%	15	2.5%	17.5	2.4%
Baptist Identity	20.25	2.9%	28	4.7%	40	5.5%
Theological Reflection	48	7.0%	27	4.5%	37.75	5.2%
Placement						
Quiet Days / Prayer Groups	85	12.3%	36	6.0%	15	10.3%

	SWBC		NBC		RPC—DTPS	
	Hours	%	Hours	%	Hours	%
Tutorials			39	6.5%	15	2.1%
Other	6.25	0.91%	9	1.51%	21	2.9%
Student Choice	120	17.4%		0.0%	28	3.8%
Totals	690.25	100.0%	597	100.0%	730	100.0%

If sub-divided within a traditional scheme of Biblical, historical, systematic and practical theology, then it is significant how the majority of all the courses can be accounted for by practical theology. The figures for biblical, historical and systematic theology might increase in recognition that sessions on mission, preaching and pastoral care will contain doctrinal and biblical input, but it is also significant that such input is shaped explicitly by the concerns of practice. Such a rebalancing towards practical theology and an integrated approach has happened across the colleges and reflects the *espoused* theology of integration discussed above.

In particular the concern for mission, expressed in both the *representative* voice and in the *espoused* approaches shared by all the colleges, is confirmed by its place in the curricula. In all the colleges it was given the most time amongst the areas more explicitly connected to practice, and was one of the highest three subjects in all colleges.

The two columns from Spurgeon's raise the important issue of college-based (BD) and congregation-based (BTh) patterns of formation, which transcend colleges. Spurgeon's college-based BD students had more contact hours than the BTh, and all of the additional hours center on the more traditional subjects of Biblical studies and doctrine. More strikingly still, the Spurgeon's college-based BD course offered 32% of the curriculum on Biblical studies, doctrine and history, compared to only 18% on the Bristol Mission congregation-based course. There is clearly scope for some further work here to examine the way that the more contextually shaped degrees do, or do not, include clear biblical and doctrinal material in mission and pastoral focused sessions.

Further, the two pathways with the most student choice were the residential courses at Spurgeon's and SWBC. Congregation-based courses which have to deliver the teaching in a more restricted time-period necessarily involve the restriction of choice, although there is still some limited choice in some contexts. My own experience is that the pressures on teaching have continued over recent years and at Regent's Park space for student choice has subsequently decreased. This reduces opportunity both for student-led learning and for space where students can begin to explore particular specialties and interests, but this is balanced by what is deliverable in any context. Within the whole patterns of college-based and congregation-based formation, then, the balance between the three elements of knowledge, skills and character is arranged differently. We would expect that those who are congregation-based will have significant time devoted to the practice of ministry and so developing skills, and that those who are college-based have greater time for academic study, for this is part of the rationale for the courses. What is of particular interest is that the greater space for academic study is focused on more traditional subjects.

Not only do the majority of Baptist ordinands now prepare through congregation-based patterns, it would appear that increasing pressures on these patterns are likely to result in students being in college for less time. There is clear evidence here that the majority of Baptist ordinands, while engaging increasingly in the practice of the ministry, will have had significantly less time to study the more traditional subjects of Biblical studies, doctrine and history, with a very limited possibility of becoming proficient in a biblical language, and less chance to pursue particular interests. The latter may be compensated for by students pursuing study at Masters' level, but the pressure on curricula and limited contact hours will not decrease and so the detail of formation pathways remains an important discussion.

There were also some important differences between the colleges. The courses were constructed in slightly different ways. Bristol was the only college to give formal credit for engaging in a placement, although the experiences of placements were built on in other colleges; Northern and Regent's Park were the two colleges that gave a significant place to tutorials. There was also a considerable variety in the contact hours of different colleges, with the highest overall contact hours offered by Spurgeon's college-based route.⁴³ These differences might be shaped by regulations of validating universities and by pragmatic issues of time and money, but there are also pedagogical influences at play.⁴⁴

All the colleges were committed to theological reflection as a core aspect of the whole curriculum, but include it in different ways. Spurgeon's sought to integrate theological reflection into all its areas and so it appeared to have a very low figure. Yet the other colleges sought to do this as well, in addition to setting aside time for teaching and practice, and this suggests some difference of approach. A more detailed examination of pedagogical practices across the whole curriculum would be needed to be more certain, but these figures suggest that theological reflection had significantly less space at Spurgeon's.

Regent's offered the most time to both preaching and worship and also pastoral care within the formal curriculum, with the least contact time devoted to spirituality and personal development. By contrast SWBC gave the most time to spirituality and personal development in the formal curriculum and the least time to both preaching / worship and pastoral care. Again, further exploration may help decide whether these differences in the explicit curriculum do give a greater element of training in the skills of preaching, leading worship and pastoral care at Regent's Park and greater emphasis on formation at SWBC, or whether these are balanced by other aspects of the wider experience.

The Implicit Curriculum

Chapter 4 also set out the way that patterns of worship would be explored and the table below sets out the number of occasions different kinds of worship took place over a year, again the figures coming from 2014/15.

---

43. Spurgeon's worked on 24 contact hours per 10 credits, although in practice taught 22 hours plus a reading week. Bristol had 20 contact hours per 10 credits at level 4 and 10 contact hours per 10 credits at levels 5 and 6. NBLC and SWBC had 12 contact hours per 10 credits and at Regent's 10 contact hours for the equivalent of 10 credits was required by University regulations.

44. "Contact hours" and their definition, has been a significant issue for universities and students in recent years. See, for example, work from the QAA, http://www.qaa.ac.uk/en/Publications/Documents/contact-hours.pdf.

Forming Ministers or Training Leaders?

Patterns of Worship	Spurgeon's	Bristol	NBLC	SWBC	Regent's
Short services	30	56		63	34
Longer services of Word	24	3	12	17	20
Eucharistic services	4	16	12	4	6
Ecumenical services		4	all	1	2
Retreat days	3	3	2	2	1
Prayer Groups	24	22		20	22

In all the colleges formation happens in the wider context of corporate worship, which is an important integrative element and key aspect of the implicit curriculum, although the nature of corporate worship has changed with the move away from the semi-monastic models of a residential community. Once again, behind the figures, there are key aspects of a shared practice. All the colleges had one central weekly worship service in term time for all ministerial students, which were supplemented in most colleges by shorter "daily prayers", which students attended on those days when they are in college, together with occasional retreat days. Differences emerge particularly around the balance between Eucharistic and non-Eucharistic services and the ecumenical experience of worship. The figures for Bristol and SWBC for shorter services are higher as their pattern was two shorter services plus a longer service each week, compared to one of each for Spurgeon's and Regent's.

NBC appears the most distinct with only one longer service each week, which was always ecumenical, with no other services or prayer groups. This clearly offered the most ecumenical experience, but also both the least "Baptist" and also the least opportunity for corporate worship to shape formation. This obviously raises issues about how worship is deemed to be "Baptist". Spurgeon's worship, for example, reflecting the variety of the student body, often had a more Pentecostal and BAME flavor alongside patterns that might be considered more Baptist. The implicit curriculum is significant in shaping the experience of preparation, but the less frequent time in college puts greater emphasis on the local congregation as a context for liturgical formation.

CONCLUSION

My first empirical research question was: what is the pastoral imagination which the Baptist colleges individually are seeking to inculcate in their students?

In this chapter I have answered this question by outlining the pastoral imagination of the other four Baptist colleges, expressed by both *espoused* and *operant* theologies, and I have suggested that there is both a significant degree of shared practice as well as important differences of approach. I would suggest that the following are important features of a shared approach:

- Ministry should be understood in strongly missional terms, and there is also some important shared understanding of ministry as collaborative and dialectical.
- There is some clear agreement that the practice of preparation is best understood as formation, which involves integration, integrity and contextualization, even with diversity of language
- The colleges have been on a shared journey of developing more contextual degrees shaped around the methodologies of practical theology.

I would suggest that the following are important areas where there is a diversity of approach:

- Within a broader understanding of collaborative ministry understandings of leadership and the professional nature of ministry vary, leading to differently shaped pastoral imaginations.

- Within a broader approach of formation, the emphasis on more cognitive aspects of education, more practical aspects of training and then spiritual and character development vary.
- The context, histories and traditions of the colleges act as important structuring structures, shaping the experience of students, perhaps more so than any differences in curriculum

I would suggest that the following are important considerations for the colleges and Baptist Union to continue to consider:

- What language is best used to describe the process of preparation that is intended to be formational so that it can both be a shared approach amongst those involved in ministerial formation and communicate clearly with those not, and not yet, within the orbit of the work of the colleges?
- With increasing pressure on time available for colleges to engage with students, with the assumption that college-based students will continue at very low numbers, and with the many demands on curriculum time, how might both the explicit and implicit curricula be best shaped so that it can enable this process of formation?

6

Discerning a Pastoral Imagination
Some Findings Among non-Baptist Institutions

THE SECOND QUESTION I set out to explore was this: is there a particular combination of practices and elements of a pastoral imagination that could be considered distinctly Baptist?

What I offer in this chapter is a summary of my research findings in which I describe the pastoral imagination that I discerned in five non-Baptist colleges and courses, by setting out first their *espoused* theologies, based on document analysis and interviews[1] and then their *operant* theologies based on the curriculum and patterns of worship. The research again took place between 2013 and 2015 and offers a snapshot in time, and the purpose of this element to the research was to offer some empirical evidence from beyond Baptist colleges to help understand the work of these colleges better. Reflection on the research then is focused on how these findings help us discern a Baptist approach to the practice of preparation.

---

1. Again, for clarity of reading here the more detailed references back to interviews have been removed.

ESPOUSED THEOLOGIES

Institution A

Institution A is a single denomination, principally full-time, residential college whose core activity has been the preparing of candidates within that denomination. It is set within a wider university context and is part of a strong ecumenical partnership.

Different language for the practice of preparation was used interchangeably. Training was used quite extensively in a variety of documents, and in the institution's most recent submission to QiFP it is by far the dominant language. Elsewhere, in a published lecture by the Principal, the language of theological education was by far the most frequent. There is evidence—the appearance of training and formation language in distinct clusters—that some documents may have been composite, drawn together from different sources and adapted over time. There is also evidence that as an institution it has moved from a more training paradigm—one document rejects a utilitarian view of education—and would now embrace the understanding of formation as a holistic overarching description even if Institution A is not always consistent with language. Their handbook was shaped around the language of ministerial formation and new trust deeds set out the institution's aims as including "training in theology and formation for ministries." This was confirmed in the interview with the Principal who would want "to use all three words, but make formation king." Such language has the inherent danger of suggesting a "sausage machine mentality", but helpfully stresses that there is a tradition to inhabit.

Whereas the word "minister" was explicitly used to describe those who are ordained and lay, with no distinction, the Principal's lecture used the language of "leader" throughout. The recent inspection submission referred to leaders in a number of key places and the website suggested that their vision was to train church leaders. On the other hand, professional language was mainly avoided,[2] accepted as an adjective but not as a noun.

The documentation pointed to an espoused pastoral imagination, but different documents offered different lists! The website pointed to six areas, the general handbook four areas, the tutorial handbook four different key objectives, the inspection submission seven suggestions under "curriculum

---

2. The inspection submission describes one of the strengths of the Institution as a strong academic team "committed to developing . . . the appropriate professionalization of pastoral theology" (inspection submission. 17).

for education and formation", together with six areas of development given by wider denominational documents. Drawing on this document analysis and an interview with the Principal, the pastoral imagination that Institution A sought to develop might be described as:

Wise: The institution aimed "to produce wise . . . leaders who know how to step back from situations, to read, to think and to seek God's Word in the words and actions of all kinds of people and places,"[3] and this was reflected in other documents. Such wisdom was explicitly understood in practical terms, drawing on the term phronesis, the key to which is the ability to integrate theory and practice within personal integrity and maturity, so that being a reflective and reflexive practitioner is a key aspect of being wise. Yet Institution A clearly valued its very strong academic heritage and the importance of being within a rigorous community of scholarship,[4] and was keen to offer more "traditional" subjects such as biblical languages alongside practical theology, so that the wider Christian tradition might contribute to the development of wisdom.

Prayerful: This was the first response in the interview, understood not in a narrowly pious or individual sense, but used to express spiritual maturity, serious discipleship and living out of a shared and corporate tradition. As a "residential community of prayer and scholarship"[5] shared worship remained a significant feature of the institution's common life and is "an intentional tool of formation."[6]

Ecumenical: The institution was part of a wider ecumenical partnership, and was committed to forming people who are rooted in their particular denomination but thoroughly ecumenically shaped and committed. Much of the learning happened in an ecumenical setting, including academic content and shared life and worship, and the particular and specific context of an ecumenical partnership had been hugely important for the formation of ministers. Thus, this had been very positively embraced in the pastoral imagination. Yet being ecumenically aware and sensitive had also helped ordinands to feel competent and confident to be ministers in their own tradition.

---

3. Inspection submission, 21.
4. Inspection submission, 4.
5. Inspection submission, 5.
6. Inspection submission, 5.

Institution B

Institution B is a non-denominational college, whose students come from a broad evangelical background and which has a residential community at its heart, although it has diversified to include study through block weeks, at other satellite campuses, and on a part-time basis. It has a strong evangelical self-understanding with a commitment to Scripture and mission. Institution B has the status of collaborative partner with its validating university, through whom it offers undergraduate and postgraduate degrees.

The language of training dominated in all the documentation, and was clearly Institution B's self-understanding of its work, which might be summarized as training effective Christian leaders. The language of formation was in fact avoided, used only once in a quote from the QAA Theology and Religious Studies Benchmark statement,[7] which may also reflect a more general uncertainty among an evangelical constituency about language with a Catholic origin. However, the institution's commitment to a holistic approach to education and training was stressed repeatedly, combining and integrating spiritual, practical, academic (or intellectual) and relational aspects. The end of year *Supervisor's Report* concentrated more on character, relationships and self-awareness than on skills. Understanding this to be a life-long process, Institution B sought to avoid the impression that it can fully educate or train someone in three years.

Institution B was committed to practice, and to practice-based learning, and students were expected to learn both in, and by reflecting on, practice. The degree program was not fully contextual, but all modules were included in the validated degree and the desire was that practice connected somewhere to every module and all aspects of the course.[8] There was a strong sense that integration was understood in quite applied terms—applied theology is the description of the course—in which the theory is worked out in practice rather than a more critical conversation between theory and practice, although further email correspondence revealed a range of opinions within the institution.

This stress on training was linked to a particular emphasis on the employability of students, as the college invited current professionals into meet students and advertised possible employment opportunities, but also partly shaped by the QAA self-evaluation process. With such an

---

7. QAA Self-Evaluation Document, 14.
8. QAA Self-Evaluation, 66–67.

emphasis on training and employability Institution B seemed to fit happily into current higher education practices which have a strong utilitarian focus, tempered with its own stress on holistic growth and maturity. Professional language was used frequently and positively, as students develop professional competencies, tutors share their professional experience and practice, and with an MA course explicitly conceived as continuing professional development.[9] Institution B did not use the language of "ministers", which may be shaped by its particular historical tradition, and offered no particular understanding of ordained ministry. The preferred language was that of practitioners or leaders.

Drawing on the document analysis and an interview with one of the vice-Principals, the pastoral imagination that Institution B sought to develop might be described as:

Growing in maturity: Institution B's strategic plan started with "growth as disciples" and in the interview developing Christian character was stressed as the most significant hope for students. In recognition of the great breadth of age and initial maturity of the student body such growth might be summarized as growth in maturity. The exact nature of this growth was not spelt out in detail, although a consultation with a group of professional advisors drawn together produced a list of twenty qualities they hoped to identify in graduating students. This consultation process led to qualities such as emotional intelligence being given a higher place, and self-understanding was a major theme developed within the course.

Effective: Institution B understood its primary role as equipping students to be effective practitioners,[10] and being equipped with tools to be effective Christian leaders was the second point of the strategic plan. The stress throughout was on applied theology, as faith was worked out on the ground, alongside the development of character and key skills.

Professional: Professional language was warmly embraced with a desire that leaving students could obtain employment and flourish in those settings. The *Programme Specifications* for the BA included the "demonstration of excellent professional approaches and skills", and the second-year course contained specific sessions on writing CVs and being interviewed. The fact that Institution B teaches youth and community work and is accredited by the National Youth Agency, drawing on a strongly utilitarian and professional language, influenced the general approach of the college.

9. QAA Self-Evaluation, 26, 30, 66–67.
10. QAA Self-Evaluation, 4.

Institution C

Institution C is a part-time non-residential ecumenical course, drawing students from a number of denominations. Students work via distance learning, in local groups, in supervised ministry practice and gather for short regular residential blocks. The majority of students exit with a Foundation Degree, which can be topped up post-ordination to a BA.

It offered a fully contextual and integrated course, combining together Biblical studies, doctrine and practical theology in all their modules, and issues of integration and critical theological reflection were foundational to the course. There was no student choice in the course, which was designed around an explicit theological journey. Placement work was significant and was set within a clear missiological understanding. The overall explicit curriculum was wider than the validated modules with residential weeks providing teaching which undergirded, expanded and complemented the distance learning rather than always being directly related to a distinct module, while also giving significant time for both corporate worship and time in small groups.

Rooted historically in a commitment to education and training, the aims of Institution C were now expressed in terms of education, training and formation, which both represented the three distinct strands,[11] but were also used to describe the whole process of preparation. The language of training dominated in the documents, and in the inspection submission and the very detailed *Student Handbook* training appeared significantly more than the other two term combined,[12] although, like other institutions, it seemed to be increasingly embracing formation language, normally used with a number of qualifying adjectives, such as personal, ministerial and spiritual. There was again some evidence of composite and developing documents: the inspection submission included three pages taken from an earlier document that offered an "articulate and inspiring vision"[13] employing only formation language.

Professional and leadership language was embraced to some degree, for Institution C offered "professional training for public ministry which

---

11. *Programmes Handbook*, 7, 29.

12. In the *Programmes Handbook*, training is used 218 times, compared to formation (37 times) and education (48 times). Although "initial ministerial education" is set up as the normative language "initial ministerial training" actually occurs four times as often.

13. QiFP *Inspection Report*, 28.

Discerning a Pastoral Imagination

meets the criteria of sponsoring churches."[14] But in other ways this was undercut in the interview, which tended to avoid both leadership and professional language. A representative approach to ordained ministry, concerned for the ministry of all, was generally stressed, although it was interesting that the curriculum approval process asked that the self-description "training for public ministry" be expanded to "training for public, ordained and eucharistic ministry"[15]—and alerts us to the fact that a pastoral imagination in a particular institution may also be shaped from outside.

Institution C sought, in its own words, to be theological, doxological, missiological, contextual, ecumenical and collaborative. Changes in denominational practices meant that its ecumenical nature was under threat, and although being directed towards God's world was part of its orientation[16] it did not actually seem to feature strongly. Drawing on this document analysis and an interview with the Principal, the pastoral imagination that Institution C sought to develop might be described as:

Reflective: Foundational to the way the whole course has been designed was critical reflection worked out through a contextual degree and in assessment portfolios. The aims of the course included developing reflective practitioners "marked by wisdom, empathy and compassion" who understand the importance of context[17] and who can "connect thought and practice in rigorous, creative and prayerful ways."[18] Alongside this the course sought to engender an ongoing desire to learn and grow rather than any sense of completion. A distinctive feature of the overall course was the Local Learning Group, made up of people beyond the course, in which the students themselves led reflective learning on the module being studied.

Mature in Christ: This was the key answer offered in interview, which was expressed in strongly psychological terms as part of wider human development, as personality and character issues were resolved, but within a relationship with God that provided "a fundamental confidence." Its aim was that "ministerial development and spiritual formation are fully mainstreamed"[19] in all its different modules.

---

14. *Programmes Handbook*, 7.
15. *Inspection submission*, 12.
16. *Programmes Handbook*, 5–6.
17. *Programmes Handbook*, 7.
18. *Programmes Handbook*, 36.
19. *Programmes Handbook*, 5.

Institution D

Institution D is a denominational residential college, which has expanded in recent years to include a broader student base and wider educational pathways. Within the evangelical tradition and with a strong reformed heritage it has an explicit theologically conservative standpoint. It works with a validating university partner offering Foundation Degrees, Honors Degrees and a variety of postgraduate courses. Until 2014 the college had combined a degree with its own unaccredited certificate in ministry but this was now being fully integrated into the degree programs.

Institution D also drew on the varied language of education, training and formation in which information, skills and spiritual depth form a coherent whole.[20] In the documentation the language of training was the most dominant[21] whereas the interview used training and formation more evenly, with just the concern that formation might carry particular meanings from the denominational center. The *Programme Specifications* highlighted skills, although this might be shaped by the QAA framework. The development of Christian character was stressed, information must go together with formation and transformation,[22] often employing the language of Christian graces; throughout the course "personal formation is a constant focus"[23] with an emphasis on "character, competence, chemistry and conviction."[24] There were times when aspects of character were described in quite strongly cognitive terms, so maturity was based on seeing the Bible as a whole and understanding how the different aspects of theology build on each other,[25] and students were encouraged to "grow in the intellectual graces of truthfulness, humility, charity, rigor and godliness,"[26] but the interview offered a more holistic view of formation into the image of Christ.

The reshaped course explicitly included theological reflection for the first time, which was treated as a discrete area generally linked with

---

20. *Prospectus*, 6.

21. The *Prospectus*, for example, uses training 22 times, formation 4 times and education once.

22. *Strategic Plan*, 4.

23. *Learning Pathways Brochure*.

24. *Aims for Students at Institution D (handout)*.

25. *Prospectus*, 6.

26. *BA Programme Specifications*, 1.

placements, and models that apply biblical truth rather than develop critical conversations seem preferred as students "trace through from a specific area of systematic or historical theology to its practical implications,"[27] and integration as a whole is principally found within Scripture.[28] The theme of integration was important, including the way that the whole of the broad curriculum contributed to the whole process of preparation, and the recent development of the Foundation Degree as practice-based learning has been a significant change.

Drawing on this document analysis and an interview with one of the vice-Principals, the pastoral imagination that Institution D sought to develop might be described as:

Christlike: This was the first answer in the interview and was used a number of times. It linked to the commitment of Institution D to a formation process, even when sending churches would rather the students simply gain knowledge. This was supported by the various references in the *Prospectus* to the expectation that the experience will be positively transformative for students.

Biblically literate: The integrating aspect of Scripture meant "to understand it in depth,"[29] pedagogically combining a complete over-view, in-depth study of key biblical books and biblical language study.[30] The mission statement of Institution D was described as "equipping people to serve with a grasp of God's revealed truth that is adaptable, deep, broad and integrated."[31] In the published stories of former students now in ministry the greatest gratitude for the college course was for Biblical insight and doctrinal truth.[32]

Effective as preachers: Within its reformed heritage it saw preaching as something unique and the foundational ministry of the church's life, thereby "enabling missionary congregations by pastoring through teaching". It was therefore the central, although not only, ministry task for which students needed training. Behind such a conviction was the foundational place of Scripture and Biblical studies, reflected in all the college's documents.

---

27. BA Programme Specifications, 2.
28. Strategic Plan, 6.
29. Prospectus, 4.
30. Prospectus, 5.
31. Strategic Plan, 4.
32. The Inspection Report comments that students are seen by others as good preachers and communicators, 28.

Adaptable: The college's mission statement used four adjectives to describe the "grasp of God's revealed truth" the first of which was adaptable and this "distinguishes the college's programs".[33] Based on an understanding that culture was in significant flux, those who are being prepared for a lifetime of ministry would need to adapt their practice several times during their future ministry to respond to changing culture. The undergraduate course deliberately began with a module on culture, the college had developed a significant cross-cultural strand, and modules on apologetics and world religions were both compulsory.[34]

Institution E

Institution E is a single denomination college that embraces both a residential community and those preparing for ministry on a part-time non-residential basis. It relates to two universities and had some limited ecumenical partnerships.

Language of education, training and formation was used in the documentation both interchangeably and with some inconsistency. The *Formational Handbook* actually used the language of training more than twice as often,[35] although this was partly explained by the inclusion of denominational documents in appendices where training language dominated. Generally training described the overall preparation in which the formational aspect was a key element.[36] However, other evidence suggests that the college is working more within a formational paradigm. *Information for Supervisors* and the *Placement and Practical Theology Handbook*[37] gave templates for reports on students which were significantly weighted towards formational rather than training issues and the interview confirmed formation would be the preferred overall descriptor.

Formation was described as "academic, personal, liturgical, ministerial and spiritual"[38] and within this, liturgical formation seemed to be a

33. *Strategic Plan*, 4.
34. *Learning Pathways*.
35. Training is used 71 times, formation 31 times, and education once.
36. *Formational Handbook*, 3. The *Guide to Foundation Degree* and the *Guide to MA* use training language predominantly.
37. *Information for Supervisors: Long Summer Placement*, 7–10; *Placement and Practical Theology Handbook*, 29–30.
38. *Formational Handbook*, 2.

Discerning a Pastoral Imagination

significant aspect of the overall preparation, for worship "transforms us as we grow into the image and likeness of God"[39] and "provides the overarching context for all our learning and being together."[40]

For Institution E methodologies of critical theological reflection were fundamental, together with the integration of education, training and formation into a whole. One reason for retaining formation as an element of the whole was that "it would be entirely inappropriate to treat such honest self-reflection as an academic exercise."[41] Placements were central and "the crucial aspect of every placement . . . is the critical theological reflection which stimulates authentic integration."[42] This integration was not in academic achievement or ministerial skills but understood as a "growth in wisdom, habit of life, and representative role."[43] The most recent inspection report also recognized the distinct way that the two validating universities handled integration, with one being rather frustratingly more fragmented.[44]

The process of preparation was part of a lifelong commitment of discipleship, and was both "a more intense awareness of the spiritual journey we share with all Christian disciples,"[45] while also something distinct. Some documents spoke of the "transition"[46] from being a lay member of the church to being ordained, made more complicated by the breadth of churchmanship in the college. Alongside this, one of the key areas of learning from a placement was described with professional language.[47]

Drawing on the document analysis and an interview with the Director of Pastoral Studies, the pastoral imagination that Institution E sought to develop might be described as:

Reflective: at the heart of the espoused understanding was the desire for ministers to be reflective practitioners, something which was more than a skill but became "habitually part of their understanding and approach to ministry". Reflective presentations on placements, which explicitly drew on tools like journaling, critical incident reports and verbatim reports, were

39. *Worship Handbook*, 4.
40. *Ministry Course Worship Handbook*, 3.
41. *Formation Handbook*, 4.
42. *Placement and Practical Theology Handbook*, 3.
43. *Formational Handbook*, 5.
44. QiFP *Inspection Report*, 31.
45. *Formational Handbook*, 10.
46. *Second and Final Year Placements: Information for Supervisors*, 1.
47. *Placement and Practical Theology Handbook*, 20.

seen as central.[48] Such reflection involved a significant degree of reflexive practice as "formational theology on the course will focus very largely on personal reflection"[49] expressed in self-awareness and self-assessment.

Spiritual: the espoused place of worship in the institution's life, together with the quiet days, a retreat in daily life and the role of spiritual directors suggested that the spiritual growth of students is a key aspect of Institution E's understanding. Although the language of training dominated the website, there was also the stress there on ministerial and spiritual formation,[50] and denominational expectations are interpreted not in academic achievement or ministerial skills, but growth in wisdom and habit of life.[51] There was a sense ministerial formation was understood within a virtue ethic framework.

Integrated: Not only was the wider practice of formation "much more demanding and far more enriching than a purely academic course of study,"[52] Institution E placed significant expectation on the individual to be able to integrate the various aspects of the process of preparation for themselves as part of personal growth towards maturity.

SOME REFLECTIONS

The sample of five other institutions is a comparatively small percentage of the total number of such colleges and courses in England and Wales, but it does contain some significant degree of breadth. It is interesting, therefore, and potentially significant, that many of the same issues that we observed in the previous chapter, around the language and understanding of the practice of preparation, the nature of the pastoral imagination and the importance of context, come to the fore again here.

The Practice of Preparation

First, there was a clear sense that all the Institutions had a foundational understanding of their practice as being holistic and integrated, concerned not simply for knowledge or skills but also for character development.

---

48. *Information for Supervisors: Long Summer Placements.*
49. *Formational Handbook*, 4.
50. *Formational Handbook*, 3.
51. *Formational Handbook*, 3.
52. *Formational Handbook*, 3.

Discerning a Pastoral Imagination

This integration was expressed in different ways, and to different degrees, but all five institutions offered holistic courses combining elements often designated as education, training and formation and also sought ways to connect theory and practice together. The Baptist colleges are clearly part of this much broader understanding of the practice of preparation which I have suggested is most clearly named as formation. We recognized earlier that this was not a new concept for Baptists, and no doubt for others too, because living in college with others would be formative, even if the greater espoused stress was on theological education. But there is now clearly a much greater espoused stress on a holistic process of preparation for ministry or Christian leadership, suggesting that this kind of *habitus* and practice is shared much more widely.

Second, the same diversity and confusion of language noted among the Baptist colleges existed in these institutions as well. Three of the institutions seem clearly on a similar journey and, while training language still dominated documents, were moving towards describing the whole practice of preparation as formation. In these institutions there was also similar evidence of the gradual development of formation language with an analysis of the documents showing them to be composite and developed over time. Although in Institution C the most strongly formative language came from a slightly older document inserted into the handbook, which alerts us again to the fact that this has not been a steady progression, the general move in these institutions was towards formation language. In the other two institutions formation language clearly was used ambivalently or avoided, despite a more holistic stress. Part of this seemed more a matter of language, and one likely correlation is that the two more conservative and explicitly evangelical institutions had more reservations about the language of formation, perhaps seen as too ecumenical or Catholic, and preferred the language of training.

Thirdly, though, and in a similar way to the Baptist colleges, there were important variances and distinctions within the practices of these institutions. So, in terms of the integration of theory and practice all five institutions now included theological reflection, but this was practiced in different ways. Again, in the two more conservative institutions theological reflection seemed to be used in a more "applied" way, in which theory was worked out, even if the conversation began with practice, and for Institution D this was a very recent addition, still on the fringe of the curriculum. In other institutions, especially C and E, theological reflection was both central to the whole curriculum and understood as a critical conversation between theory and practice. Similarly, the understanding of the relationship between the different aspects of the curriculum and the whole process of preparation varied, with some institutions explicitly intending that all aspects of the whole curriculum promoted education, training and formation, whereas others expressing some frustration about the lack of an overarching unity between learning and formation through academic modules, community life and placements.

Overall, there seems to have been a greater variety among the other five institutions in their espoused understandings of their work than among the Baptist colleges, which would be as expected. This would suggest, again as expected, that the Baptist colleges are part of a wider development among those engaged in the practice of preparation both towards the formation paradigm and towards a strongly integrative understanding of this process based on methodologies of practical theology. But it does also seem that within the broader range of institutions here the Baptist colleges are generally at the forefront of these developments, adopting formation language, developing patterns of integration and reflecting on how the whole of the broad curriculum provides the whole experience of formation.

The Pastoral Imagination

In reflecting on the pastoral imaginations that these institutions were seeking to develop, there was, again as expected, some significant areas of overlap with each other and with the Baptist colleges. But there were also important points of difference. For example, the stress on effective preaching in Institution D was stronger than in any of the Baptist colleges, all of which would have been concerned with preaching, and was equally in contrast with the recognition in Institution E that their students might be preaching for the very first time as part of their first year summer placement.[53] Within a broader holistic approach shared by all institutions, the two most clearly evangelical institutions both seemed to have a stronger activist element that stressed the development of skills. Picturing this visually, the "skills" circle in our Venn diagram would appear to be larger in institutions B and D than the others; on the other hand for Institution A, though certainly not discounting skills, it would appear to be the smallest circle.

53. *Information for Supervisors: Long Summer Placement*, p. 2.

Similarly, while all of the institutions would want to be preparing those who would be outward looking and engaging with the world, the concept of being missional seemed to appear much less than among the Baptist colleges, and even in those institutions in which the language was used more (Institutions B and D), it was not such an emphasis as to clearly be a part of the pastoral imaginations the institutions were seeking to inculcate. The other institutions certainly recognized and responded, in different ways, to the current context of the church, but there is a clear suggestion that for the Baptist colleges this had a stronger place. Two of the Baptist colleges have stressed the importance of a global influence on ministry, shaped by experience and in one case an explicit liberation emphasis. Such an emphasis was not found in these other institutions.

There was again diversity in the use of professional and leadership language, which was used to some degree by all five institutions, although more cautiously in some than others. So, for example, professional language was most strongly embraced by Institution B but was used much more cautiously by Institutions A, C and E, especially by those interviewed. Yet the patterns were not always clear. Institution A, for example, developed leadership language in its documentation alongside a wide-ranging use of the language of ministry but was very cautious about professional language. There does seem to be an attractive reason to use leadership language in a non-denominational setting where students come from many traditions and where it can be embraced as a helpful generic term and thereby avoiding the theological complexities of ministerial language. There were clearly ways in which leadership language and paradigm are positively embraced, but also the possibility that what appeared more generic leadership language may fill the vacuum where there is no, or no agreed, or a contested understanding of ministry. In some settings leadership language may offer what appears to be a more neutral possibility free from some of the long-standing ecclesial debates, although bringing its own cultural shaping.

The Context

One of the features which distinguished the five institutions from each other and from the five Baptist colleges was again context: the inspection report for one of the institutions, for example, comments on problems resulting from a residential community of mainly intelligent, competitive young men. A number of aspects relating to context help develop our reflections on the Baptist colleges further.

First, two of the institutions had an explicit ecumenical context, and this aspect featured most strongly in their pastoral imaginations. But impending changes for Institution C confirm the fragility of such partnerships, as well as their importance. These ecumenical partnerships may, again, result from a mixture of historic, pragmatic and intentional reasons but underline the significance this has for the pastoral imagination. It challenges the Baptist colleges about the intentionality of their current contexts.

Secondly, four of the five institutions continued a strong residential pattern and stressed, in different ways, the importance of the gathered community. I have noted the way that the Baptist colleges, by contrast, have all developed more dispersed communities based on congregation-based patterns of formation and some of the issues this has raised, and there is little prospect that residential ministerial formation for Baptists beyond a very small number would be possible, even if desirable.

Thirdly, while congregation-based patterns dominate, the Baptist colleges have had a shared commitment that formation cannot be achieved through on-line study. Such a position receives some challenge from Institution C, which is by no means restricted to on-line modules, but it does mean that the overall time that the wider formational community gather together is much more limited. Baptist colleges had already begun to rethink patterns of formation that might both draw on developing technology and result in less time physically together for students, and the Covid-19 pandemic pushed all such institutions very quickly into an entirely on-line mode of delivery. It is too early to say what exactly the longer term impact of this will be for colleges preparing ministers as it is for any other aspect of society, but this experience has certainly created a greater familiarity with on-line learning and it will be very surprising if this does not feature more strongly in the future patterns of ministerial formation.

Fourthly, these five institutions had a variety of university settings, and I suggested above that the strongly utilitarian ethos of modern universities and the QAA framework is a factor that shaped the overall context of an institution. This may resonate with wider concerns of a college, as it seems to with Institution B, or be an aspect a college explicitly works against. On the other hand, these institutions have also developed Foundation Degrees in theology, partly attractive for being two-year courses, which have an explicit practice-based element to them. Such contexts clearly are not neutral and this raises fundamental questions about a theology of higher education, the place of ministerial formation in the modern university and what those institutions engaging in ministerial formation have to offer the wider university.

OPERANT THEOLOGIES

The Explicit Curriculum

Chapter 4 set out the way that explicit curriculum would be considered based on set contact hours for different subjects. The tables below set out the results when the curricula of the five non-Baptist institutions were assessed as set out in chapter four and in a similar way to the Baptist colleges—recognizing again that this is a snapshot taken in 2014/15 and that curricula are always developing

	Institution A FdA		Institution A BTh		Institution B		Institution C	
	Hours	%	Hours	%	Hours	%	Hours	%
Bible	102	20.4%	62	11.5%	180	22.3%	124	28%
Doctrine and Ethics	42	8.4%	32	5.9%	60	7.4%	53	12%
History	20	4.0%	30	5.6%	15	2%	18.5	4%
Ethics							11	2.4%
Mission	27	5.4%	7	1.3%	85	11%	44	10%
Preaching / Worship	42	8.4%	42	7.8%	40	5%	68.25	15%

Forming Ministers or Training Leaders?

	Institution A FdA		Institution A BTh		Institution B		Institution C	
	Hours	%	Hours	%	Hours	%	Hours	%
Pastoral Care	51.5	10.3%	41.5	7.7%	20	2%	22.25	5%
Spirituality / Personal Development	37.5	7.5%	47.5	8.8%	50	6%	39	9%
Leadership	12	2.4%	12	2.2%	80	10%	5.75	1%
Denominational Identity	64	12.8%	64	11.9%	8	1%	20.75	5%
Theological Reflection	20	4.0%	40	7.4%	70	9%	8	2%
Placement							7	1.55%
Quiet Days / Prayer Groups					66	8.2%	18	4.0%
Tutorials	16	3.2%	16	3.0%	13	1.6%		
Other							9	2.00%
Student Choice	65	13.0%	145	26.9%	120	15%	2	0%
Totals	499	100%	539	100%	807	100%	450.5	100%

Discerning a Pastoral Imagination

	Institution D		Institution E FdA		Institution E BTh	
	Hours	%	Hours	%	Hours	%
Bible	272	28.2%	89	16.3%	112.75	19.7%
Doctrine and Ethics	76	7.9%	48	8.8%	50	8.7%
History	63	6.5%	18	3.3%	13	2.3%
Ethics	30	3.1%	23	4.2%	23	4.0%
Mission	51	5.3%	28	5.1%	33	5.8%
Preaching / Worship	55	5.7%	92	16.8%	92	16.1%
Pastoral Care	39	4.0%	69	12.6%	69	12.1%
Spirituality / Personal Development	17	1.8%	20	3.7%	20	3.5%
Leadership	23	2.4%	4	0.7%	4	0.7%
Denominational Identity	10	1.0%	12	2.2%	12	2.1%
Theological Reflection	10	1.0%	26.75	4.9%	26.75	4.7%
Placement						
Quiet Days / Prayer Groups	72	7.5%	45	8.2%	45	7.9%

Forming Ministers or Training Leaders?

	Institution D		Institution E FdA		Institution E BTh	
	Hours	%	Hours	%	Hours	%
Tutorials						
Other		0.00%				
Student Choice	247	25.6%	72	13.2%	72	12.6%
Totals	965	100%	546.75	100.0%	572.5	100.0%

A number of reflections can be made of similarities and differences between the five institutions themselves and then with the five Baptist colleges. In the majority of the categories the highest or lowest figures, and occasionally both, were recorded by the non-Baptist institutions, and in the remaining areas they are virtually identical. It is not surprising that, given the greater diversity of theology and church practice, there was a wider spectrum of curricula, in which the Baptist colleges were located in a narrower range. This would support the notion of a more shared Baptist approach to ministerial formation. But within this general observation there were some significant aspects of Baptist practice which stand out.

First, we noted that the average for Biblical studies, history and systematic theology in the Baptist Colleges was around 23% of the curriculum, although this figure may increase a little further when student choice is included. Among the five non-Baptist institutions the average for these subjects was around 33%, again probably increasing with student choice, with the highest figures being above 40%. More specifically, Biblical studies averaged at 13.3% among the Baptist colleges compared to 21% in non-Baptist institutions. Three of the four non-Baptist institutions, which were residential colleges, are also quite strongly committed to the teaching of biblical languages. The most obvious conclusion is that the Baptist colleges simply taught less of these three traditional subjects, and that is certainly true of biblical languages given the time needed in both class and private study. It may be that the Baptist colleges taught them in a different way, where the focus and starting point was within the realm of practical theology, and further research could explore this, but this is still unlikely to equate to the percentages at the non-Baptist institutions. One clear conclusion is that those who have left Baptist colleges could be less biblically and theologically literate.

Second, and by contrast, the Baptist colleges seemed particularly committed to the place of mission in the curriculum, since its percentage was significantly more in the Baptist colleges (12.7%) than the non-Baptist institutions (6%). So a further suggestion from the figures is that the Baptist colleges have placed a stronger emphasis on the need for ministers to be formed in missional ways.

Thirdly, in three of the non-Baptist institutions (A, C and E) there was a significant combination of worship and preaching, pastoral care, and denominational identity (25%-32%), which, by contrast, have figures of only 8% and 11% in Institutions B and D respectively. It is perhaps to be expected that the two single denomination colleges and an ecumenical course where the focus is strongly on ordained ministry should have high figures. Equally, as a non-denominational college with a much broader range of students it is not surprising that Institution B had the lowest figures for these areas, and instead had the highest figures for leadership which correlates with its espoused theology that was expressed much more in generic leadership terms than in ministry. The figures for Institution D are more surprising, given a much stronger espoused pastoral imagination centered on preaching, but a lower figure on preaching is supplemented by a much higher figure for biblical studies—the stress appears to be on hermeneutics not homiletics. For the Baptist colleges the combined figures for teaching in worship, preaching, pastoral care and denominational identity were located around the middle of the whole range, suggesting these elements remain important but not as strongly stressed, lending further support to a Baptist stress on more missional aspects of practice.

Fourthly, the issue of pathways and pedagogical preferences was again highlighted by contact hours and student choice. There was among these institutions an even greater spread of contact hours with Institution C, a part-time course that utilizes on-line courses that are expensive to set up and develop, offering less than half the contact hours of Institution D, a more traditional residential community. In a similar contrast there was virtually no choice in Institution C's carefully constructed part-time non-residential course, compared to real choice in almost a third of the course at Institution D (although the choices are limited, shaped by the arrangement of modules within streams). Of the five non-Baptist institutions it is Institution C that had most similarity to the non-residential pattern of formation undertaken by most Baptist ordinands. It highlights again some of the consequences of the kind of pathways on offer.

Finally, the combined figures for spirituality / personal development together with quiet days / prayer groups are higher for the five Baptist colleges than for the other Institutions, but these figures need to be treated with some caution. Whereas Institution C is non-residential, and has one of the higher figures, the other non-Baptist Institutions are residential communities which all place a significant, though differing emphasis on both the formational nature of the community and a particular pattern of shared worship, which is considered below. What this may reveal is that among the Baptist colleges, which are predominantly non-residential, spirituality and personal development are written more into the curriculum whereas they remain assumptions of community life in other institutions.

The Implicit Curriculum

The table below sets out the number of occasions different kinds of worship took place over a year at the five non-Baptist institutions, as set out in chapter 4, with the figures once more coming from 2014/15.

Patterns of Worship	A	B	C	D	E
Short services	48	15	30	27	162
Longer services of Word	18	25	1	81	46
Eucharistic services	24	3	9	27	43

Discerning a Pastoral Imagination

Patterns of Worship	A	B	C	D	E
Ecumenical services	12		all		2
Retreat days			1		9
Prayer Groups	24	27	9	27	27

The most striking aspect of the above figures is the variation between institutions. Some differences are explained by overall patterns of formation, for example residential or dispersed communities, but more fundamentally the differences seem based on theological approaches tied closely to wider ecclesial understandings. These figures also suggest some strong correlations between the pastoral imaginations of the institutions and their patterns of worship. So, for example, higher figures for ecumenical worship in Institution A reflect its setting and the high level of preaching in the shared worship of Institution D clearly reflects its pastoral imagination. A little more tentatively we might surmise that the comparatively low figures for Institution B, given it is a residential college, also correlates to a pastoral imagination that retains a strong skills-based professional approach.

CONCLUSION

The second empirical research question I sought to answer was: is there a particular combination of practices and elements of a pastoral imagination that could be considered distinctly Baptist?

I have suggested in this chapter that Baptists have been part of a shared process of development, for example in the adoption of the emerging formation paradigm, share concerns with other institutions, for example integration and integrity, but also have some particular emphases. The Baptist colleges appear to occupy a narrow section of a wider spectrum of approaches to the practice of preparation, as might be expected for colleges that share a denominational history. The Baptist colleges, with others, also appear at the forefront of developments in the developing practice of preparation within this formation paradigm.

The data that has emerged in this chapter also suggests a number of areas that contribute together to a distinctive Baptist approach. The Baptist colleges have a greater overall commitment to congregation-based pathways, although other denominations are increasingly developing these, have an explicitly missionally orientated curriculum, develop a collaborative approach to ministry and share, with others, a commitment to the methodologies of practical theology.

But the empirical research has also raised significant questions and challenges that the Baptist colleges will need to reflect on further and will be discussed later in this book:

- the place of biblical studies, biblical languages and systematic theology in the curriculum to ensure ongoing high levels of biblical and theological literacy;
- the differences between the experiences of congregation-based and college-based ordinands, especially with the increasing pressure on time in college;
- the importance of developing an intentional practice of formation in two centers (college and church) for all students;
- the context of each college and the way that this is intentionally chosen as well as contingently shaped;
- the importance and place of liturgical formation and the wider implicit curriculum in what are generally non-residential settings.

7

Towards a Theology of Formation for Baptists

WE SAW EARLIER THAT a recent Baptist Union document suggested that the practice of preparation for ministry is "a complex mix that is generally referred to as 'formation'".[1] A more careful study of what has been written by Baptists and of the practice of the Baptist colleges suggest it would be more accurate to say that this practice is understood to be a complex mix that is increasingly referred to as formation. We have seen that the use of language is not consistent, although the underlying idea of a more holistic approach is foundational, and I have argued that both the language and wider paradigm of formation is the most appropriate and helpful way to understand this whole practice and so should be intentionally embraced.

But, although there has been this development both in language and practice, there has been, up to now, little sustained attempt to offer a theology of the practice of preparation among and for British Baptists. The temptation has been to seek more pragmatic solutions rather than to commit to the more sustained work of theological reflection. Paul Goodliff's recent book, *Shaped for Service*, is the exception and an important and helpful contribution that considers ministerial formation from a virtue ethics perspective. This chapter offers a further contribution to the development of a rigorous theology of ministerial formation which emerges partly from a process of empirical research. This research, set out in chapters 5 and 6, revealed similarities and differences both between the five Baptist colleges

---

1. Baptist Union of Great Britain, *Patterns of Ministry Among Baptists*, 11.

themselves and between the Baptist colleges collectively and a sample of non-Baptist institutions. A theology of ministerial formation will need to respond to these similarities and differences and, therefore, what I offer here is not a Baptist theology of ministerial formation, as if totally distinct, but a theology of ministerial formation for Baptists.

Through the book I have been arguing for and utilizing an understanding of practice that balanced structure and agency and the individual and the corporate, and have suggested that this should be seen as something structured, cooperative and creative. This is true of the practice of ministry and also for the practice of the preparation for ministry, which structures the practice of ministry through the development of a pastoral imagination. I, therefore, seek to offer here a theology of the practice of preparation that is structured by the tradition from which it has emerged, co-operative in the way it has been developed with others, yet having room for creative improvisation.

The book is also set within an overall methodological framework adapted from Cameron *et al.*'s "four voices". The previous chapters have sought to identify these voices more clearly: so chapters 2 and 3 sought to discern a *representative* voice around the practices of ministry and preparation through engaging with the work of Baptists writers and with documents that have at times agreed through denominational structures; and then chapters 5 and 6 established the *espoused* and *operant* voices discerned through a process of empirical research. This then is the moment to begin to bring these voices together and to add to them the fourth voice, the *formal* voice of the academy.

The voice of the academy is itself diverse and could be heard in a number of ways, but the dialogue partner chosen in particular to be part of the conversation as a *formal* voice is Paul Fiddes. Fiddes is a leading Baptist theologian and himself a former Principal of a Baptist College. Fiddes has written extensively on issues of Baptist theology and history, but more importantly for this conversation has combined this with a desire to explore such issues within a rigorous and thorough trinitarian doctrine of God. Engaging with a doctrine of God will be one way of ensuring that a turn simply to the pragmatic is avoided and any understanding of ministerial formation has sufficient theological depth. What I argue for here is a theology of the practice of preparation for Baptists, understood as ministerial formation, which will be structured, co-operative and creative, and firmly rooted in the trinitarian doctrine of God.² To do this I offer six interweaving emphases: theological, ecclesial, biblical, missional, pedagogical and personal.

FORMATION AS PARTICIPATION: A THEOLOGICAL EMPHASIS

I have suggested that the preparation for ministry understood as formation includes more traditional aspects of academic knowledge and skills-based training in a holistic approach that integrates these different aspects in an overall growth in Christ-like character and maturity. This overall aim pre-dates the language of formation, but the formation paradigm has both made this explicit and also given attention to what practices of preparation will particularly help in this process of formation. At the heart then of formation is a process of growth and development as part of Christian discipleship.

Fiddes helps us take this forward by offering a profound theological vision based on the language and concept of participation. Convinced that the language of imitation or even contemplation is not sufficient theologically, epistemologically, or pastorally,³ compelling human beings to strive after and copy the impossible model of trinitarian relationships, Fiddes explores the gracious way that our lives are drawn into these trinitarian relationships. Thus our lives and human communities do not merely shape themselves in response to a trinitarian pattern, but are shaped by participation in the very trinitarian pattern itself. Formation, then with its growth in maturity is ultimately the gracious work of God.

One of the most striking metaphors through which Fiddes develops his trinitarian theology is that of the divine dance, bringing together two distinct patterns—a circle dance and a progressive dance.⁴ The metaphor of the circle dance, Fiddes argues, encapsulates the best of the Western trinitarian tradition, which lays stress on "the equality, mutuality and reciprocity

---

2. There is not a unique Baptist position, or an approach taken by all Baptists. Mayes, *Spirituality in Ministerial Formation*, suggests that the Anglican and Roman Catholic approach has tended to be Christological rather than trinitarian, 82, but Ward explores trinitarian thinking and theological education more fully, *Lifelong Learning*, 75–79.

3. Fiddes, *Participating in God*, 28–30, 38. Fiddes argues that, in contrast to the strongly objectifying enlightenment approach, God is known through an epistemology of participation.

4. Fiddes, *Participating in God*, 34–46. Fiddes himself understands the trinitarian persons as "subsistent relations" but suggests that the theme of participation does not depend on the acceptance of this basis.

of the three persons."[5] But not only are trinitarian relationships marked by mutuality and reciprocity, they are also truly *ecstatic*, that is they are "self-transcending in communication with others, especially in the movement of love"[6] so that Father, Son and Spirit live in the constant openness to each other in which true identity is found.

Such an ecstatic trinitarian theology becomes the theological foundation for the way human persons exist and are formed in community. Such a concept offers a dynamic picture of what it means to become more "Christ-like", as we are drawn to participate in what is like "a willing response of a son to a father, becoming co-actors and co-narrators with his 'Yes. Amen' to the Father's purpose,"[7] and are transformed by that participation. Here is formation that is not simply based on greater human effort but on an openness to the gracious work of God.

Although not explicitly dealing with *ministerial* formation, Fiddes' ideas here address two concerns we have encountered about both the experience and language of formation among those who would otherwise embrace the formation paradigm: that entering a process of ministerial formation may lead to the loss of the self and what is unique to the individual, together with the fear that formation is in reality conformity to a particular, centralized, view of ministry. Fiddes calls for a "balance between a proper self-centring, which is not a destructive self-centredness, and formation through our social relationships"[8] and insists that an "openness to others will not mean conformity to the human other, which would be a loss of one's own will, but conformity to the Christ we meet in and through the other."[9] These ideas strengthen the way that formation should be understood in an holistic sense, in the growth of the individual in community, which happens in this dialectic between self-centering and openness to the other.

Yet we need to push Fiddes here and reflect further on who the "others" might be through whom we might meet Christ and so be conformed to his likeness. The empirical research has suggested very clearly that context, whether intentional or contingent, has a significant impact on ministerial formation and the kind of pastoral imagination being encouraged. These

---

5. Fiddes, *Participating in God*, 77.
6. Fiddes, *Participating in God*, 22.
7. Fiddes, *Participating in God*, 53.
8. Fiddes, *Participating in God*, 52.
9. Fiddes, *Participating in God*, 53.

"others", through whom we are formed, cannot remain theoretical but are always encountered in particularity and in context.

Part of the context will be an institution's distinct tradition and Astley helps take this discussion forward as he contrasts and combines aspects of what he describes as formative and critical education.[10] All education has a formative element because there is no community or tradition which is neutral and value free but belongs in a particular tradition in which those preparing for ministry are developing and being shaped; that is all education is both structured, through the tradition, and structuring itself in the passing on of the church's values, beliefs and practices. Astley suggests that such formation is a "proper—indeed essential—dimension of *any* education that wishes to call itself Christian."[11]

Therefore, if our learning to be a Christian is always mediated in this way, we must insist that generic categories such as ministerial formation are not sufficient. The wider structuring Christian faith is always expressed and mediated in particular traditions so formation is always into a distinct community with its particular values, beliefs and practices. This would suggest that there must then be a distinctive *Baptist* formative education, not wholly different from others but shaped co-operatively by a *particular* tradition, in the same way as there will be, for example, a distinctive Methodist formation. That elements of this Baptist approach exist was confirmed by the empirical research.

Alongside being formed within a particular community, critical education engages in reflective analysis and evaluation of the church's self-understanding and tradition in the light of the individual's own experience. This places much more emphasis on the freedom and creativity of both a college, to improvise within the tradition, and of an individual student within the process of formation. This again helps defend the notion of formation from that of conformation, and insists that the educative process must begin with individual students, drawing out from them their understanding and creating space in which they can develop and grow in their own understanding.

This itself is a more demanding process for students than simply receiving a tradition and the ability to develop such patterns of critical engagement and reflection is neither an automatic given nor a learnt skill. It is, as Passmore and MacIntyre both suggest something much more deeply embedded

---

10. See Astley, *Philosophy of Christian Religious Education*, chapter 5.

11 Astley, *Learning in the* Way, 38.

in character.[12] As such cultivating this ability is actually part of the process of formation itself, in which students are encouraged and enabled to develop in this tradition of critical thinking.[13] I suggested in chapter 3 that grounding their work in university validated courses has been a key historic commitment of Baptist approaches to the practice of preparation, despite some continuing internal opposition. This insistence, which produces graduates, is more than providing some kind of comparable status in ministry to other denominations, although this has surely been one factor, but also provides a key aspect of a wider context for developing critical thinking. To forego these validated courses would, it seems to me, have a strongly detrimental effect on the whole experience of ministerial formation.

This wider university context also shapes the context of ministerial formation and so the "others", through whom we are conformed to Christ. Here Baptists ordinands encounter others from the Baptist tradition, those from the wider church and those within the wider university so that the experience is both formative, within the Baptist tradition as part of the universal church, and critical, reflecting carefully on this very tradition.

Baptist ministerial formation then is to be located in the formation of the whole people of God which happens in community in the negotiation of the self in relation to others, in response to the gracious invitation of God through which we are drawn to participate in the community of God's trinitarian life. It happens in a community that is both shaped by and lives a Baptist tradition, but is open to others, from the universal church and the wider university context, so that the critical and reflective skills can be developed.

Revisiting the practice of preparation in the light of this theology of participation, what is required is the kind of "space" that is shaped by the Baptist tradition, is open to others and to critical reflection, avoiding the pressure towards too narrow a kind of conformity yet allowing room for and encouraging formation to be based on participation in God's trinitarian life. The empirical research suggests a number of ways that such "space" may be encouraged.

Such space has a liturgical aspect, expressed in more formal acts of prayer and worship and, shaped by the Baptist tradition as the structuring structure, will include particular Baptist ways of responding to God's gracious invitation in worship. With the changing pathways in Baptist colleges and the dominance of congregation-based patterns, liturgical formation like

---

12. See Astley, *Philosophy of Christian Religious Education*, 84–86.
13. See Wood, "Theological Enquiry and Theological Education."

Towards a Theology of Formation for Baptists

the whole process of formation, must be understood in two centers: college and local congregation. This presents a number of challenges. Given the limited time in college, there will also be the temptation to allow worship to be squeezed out by more time in the classroom. An understanding of formation as participation will need to safeguard sufficient time for a rhythm of Baptist worship shared by the group of tutors and students as a community. With the congregation-based pattern the liturgical formation of a gathered and dispersed community, building on the models of Iona and the Northumbria Community, may offer an important way forward. Equally, more explicit attention will need to be given to the way that a local congregation acts as a community of formation and the recognition that the local congregation is not only a space for exercising ministry but also for ministerial formation in the midst of a particular Baptist worshipping community.

Such space also has an educational aspect. We would expect those preparing for ministry within Baptist churches to be shaped by their engagement, in an explicit curriculum, with Baptist history, principles, and ecclesiology. Yet our empirical research also suggests a growing understanding that the whole of the broad curriculum is involved in shaping the whole of the student. So participation in the life of God happens not only in the formal liturgical settings, but in the breadth of the explicit and implicit curriculum, and engaging in Greek or church history can and should be moments of participation. The whole of the curriculum providing the whole of formation needs to shape the pedagogical approach of tutors.

Such space, finally, has a relational aspect. Fiddes offers a vision of formation, which is both self-centering and also ecstatic in its openness to others. Colleges have stressed that inter-student relationships are as important as those between staff and students and when these work well formation happens apace. But there are also situations when relationships within a particular group of students struggle, when there is limited openness to the other, or when relationships become destructive and individuals seek their fulfilment at the expense of, rather than in cooperation with, others. One of the great challenges is to help create and facilitate the most helpful and appropriate broad learning environment, in which formation can be encouraged. In this respect the specific practices of college staff, in both teaching and in community, become important in helping to create a relational space that is both self-centering and ecstatic.[14]

---

14. See suggestions made in Smith and Smith (eds), *Teaching and Christian Practices* and Jones and Paulsell, *The Scope of our Art*.

FORMATION AS DISCIPLESHIP: AN ECCLESIAL EMPHASIS

In chapter 2 I proposed that, for Baptists, ministry must always be understood in dialectical terms, in which the few and the many stand in creative tension. Such an approach was confirmed to some degree in the empirical research in that while there is some variety between Baptist colleges and clear overlap with the other institutions, there are aspects of a distinctive approach.

Overall the Baptist colleges seem to be working within a dialectical framework supporting the *habitus* of ministry more than that of leadership, although there was a variety of approaches to the use of professional and leadership language, from warm embrace to reluctant adoption. In addition, there does seem to be some distinction between the Baptist colleges and the other institutions, which both collectively make more of leadership language and make less, ecclesiologically, of such a dialectic between the few and the many. There is thus some supporting evidence for our assertion that the dialectical model is the most authentic Baptist understanding of ministry and that, despite the influence of the leadership paradigm, it shapes the work of the colleges, although to different degrees.

I also discussed in chapter 2 the contribution of Fiddes to these discussions and in particular his championing of this dialectical approach. For Fiddes this is more than an ecclesial emphasis; rather it is rooted in his trinitarian understanding of God as he argues for a trinitarian picture of God, which avoids oppression, dominance and hierarchy, thereby challenging both political and ecclesial monarchianism.[15]

Fiddes discusses such a position in critical dialogue with both Jürgen Moltmann and Miroslav Volf, and it is Volf, shaped by his own Free Church tradition, who offers the most comprehensive trinitarian ecclesiology, and insists we must reject the "pyramidal dominance of the one" and "the hierarchical bipolarity between the one and the many," and embrace instead "a polycentric and symmetrical reciprocity of the many,"[16] that is the Trinity as a community of free and equal persons.[17]

Such a view has certainly been a strong part of the structured Baptist tradition. So a previous report to the Council of the Baptist Union of Great

---

15. Fiddes, *Participating in God*, 62–108.

16. Volf, *After Our Likeness*, 217.

17. One of Fiddes' criticisms of Volf is that Volf relies too much on the church shaping its life in correspondence to God rather than through participating in God's gracious trinitarian relationships. See, *Participating in God*, 48–49.

Britain, concerned with organizational developments around ministry begins by insisting that:

> The Persons of the Trinity are co-equal and mutually interdependent one on the other. It is not simply in the distinct Persons but in the nature of their relationship that the Trinity consists.[18]

A Baptist approach to ministerial formation will insist that it is held within an understanding of the wider shared discipleship of the whole people of God who participate in and so reflect the mutuality of trinitarian relationships, creating "space" for formative and critical education. And so a Baptist approach to this balance between the formative and the critical would include this dialectic between the few and the many. Such an approach will have a number of clear implications for the practice of preparation.

First it suggests that the process is rightly described as *ministerial* formation, rather than leadership training or formation, because the dialectical model insists that the same language be used for both the "few" and the "many", although this demands a greater clarity of expression and understanding. All are involved in ministry and the whole congregation exercises oversight over its corporate life but some are called to exercise ministry and oversight in a particular representative way.

Ministerial formation is deeply connected to Christian formation, which is also deeply connected to wider human formation. An Irenaean model of anthropology is helpful at this point, which recognizes that the process of growth is part of our God-given human nature.[19] Christian formation is then understood as this human process of growth being explicitly orientated as growth into the image of Christ. And ministerial formation, for Baptists, is not something distinct from such Christian formation, intending to shape ministers in ways that others are not, as suggested within some other traditions,[20] but a particularly intentional and intensive aspect of Christian formation or "specialized discipleship."[21] In the same way that all discipleship includes aspects best described as education and training, so such elements are also integrated into ministerial formation.

---

18. Baptist Union of Great Britain, *Transforming Superintendency*, 9.

19. For recent relevant trends in psychology and neurobiology, see Brown, Dahl and Reuschling, *Becoming Whole and Holy*, 4.

20. So Worthen, "A Model of Ministerial Formation," 41, and Angela Shier-Jones, *The Making of Ministry*, 27–31.

21. This phrase arose from the empirical research interviews.

Second, it suggests that it would also be better to avoid the language of "professional" within a Baptist understanding of ministry and formation. While professional language itself can be carefully nuanced and although the intended emphasis of professional may be on the way that the practice of ministry is accomplished—that is, well, thoroughly, competently, not in a slapdash way—an unavoidable aspect of professional language is the implied distinction and separation between those who are professional and those who are not. In fact this is the very point of the language, for one clear element in the development of the professions was, after all, to be able to demarcate clearly who belonged "in" the profession and so who did not. Yet such a total distinction undercuts a dialectical model of ministry that proposes a fundamental connection between the few and the many.

Thirdly, while the title "Minister-in-Training" continues to be used for those currently engaged in the process of preparation, especially on a congregation-based model,[22] it would seem more consistent to use the alternative title "Minister-in-Formation". While the implication that formation is complete on leaving college would need to be avoided, as would any suggestion that a new minister is trained in everything, the title "Minister-in-Formation" would both connect to the view expressed above that the whole process is now generally known as formation, and help connect the particular formation of ministers to the wider formation of the people of God. This would be strengthened if the on-going development, while drawing on the best of secular models of CPD, supervision and coaching, were to be understood as Continuing Ministerial Formation, based on mutual accountability and growth in Christ, rather than simply professional practice.

Fourthly, since, for Baptists, the local church remains the foundational expression of the formative community, it could be argued that recent practices of ministerial formation which have moved away from a pattern of withdrawal from the local church into a separate residential community, even if partly financially driven, have regained a more Baptist approach by explicitly involving the local congregation in the formation process in a dialectical way. Not only do "ministers-in-training" exercise ministry in a local congregation; that local congregation becomes the central site in which formation happens both in an initial stage of preparation for ministry and in lifelong formation, in such a way that the local congregation

---

22. Paul Goodliff, then Head of Ministry at the Baptist Union defended the title in an interview on the basis that the most significant aspect of college is training whereas formation is the "broader horizon" that precedes and proceeds from college.

Towards a Theology of Formation for Baptists

contributes to the formation process. This offers significant challenges to the way a college and a number of local congregations partner together, and to the way that a minister and congregation understand their relationship together, but this does seem an approach that resonates deeply with a Baptist ecclesial vision.

FORMATION AS COVENANT: A BIBLICAL EMPHASIS

I rehearsed, in chapter 3, the narrative of the key developments in the 1980s that decisively moved Baptist colleges from residential communities to a more dispersed congregation-based approach. While practice-based learning provided a strong educational impetus, financial pressures were present from the very beginning and have since intensified. While this congregation-based pattern is certainly not unique to Baptists, I have suggested from the empirical evidence that its dominance as a pathway for ministerial formation, in contrast to some other traditions, makes it currently a distinctive Baptist emphasis particularly suited to a Baptist ecclesiology.

Ministerial formation now happens in two centers, with students part of two distinct communities, but the relationship between the student and these two centers needs further development and clearer expression. One way of doing this is to draw on the language and theology of covenant, which is rooted biblically and is part of the structured and structuring historic and contemporary Baptist tradition.[23] Alongside the theological insights of participation and dialectic, covenant language has also been central to Fiddes' work. In discussing the various biblical covenants, especially the distinction between the Mosaic and Davidic covenants, Fiddes points out how both, although different, are firmly rooted in the divine initiative and both open up ways of response.[24] One of the unique and insightful developments that early Baptists made, he suggests, is the way that they explicitly linked the horizontal church covenants they wrote with the vertical covenant God had initiated with human beings. Human covenants are not simply statements of commitment, but are a response to and a participation in God's divine initiative.

---

23. See, Baptist Union of Great Britain, *Covenant 21* and the desire to develop covenant theology within the *Ignite* project.

24. Fiddes, *Tracks and Traces*, 74–76.

Fiddes suggests that a key aspect of the covenant made between churches is the possibilities it opens up for discovery.[25] While a local congregation sits under the Lordship of Christ and in response to that Lordship assumes responsibility for its life and mission it does not do so independently, but seeks to discover the mind of Christ through covenant relationships with others. Building on the comments above on a relational space, formation happens through encountering Christ in covenantal interaction with others. Fiddes develops this further by connecting the covenant of being God's people with the wider covenant God creates with all living things, within God's trinitarian story, arguing that our covenant relationships need to broaden, open both ecumenically to the whole of the Christian family and beyond to the whole of God's created world. He relates this specifically to a vision for higher education[26] and argues that theological education—and offers the British Baptist colleges as examples—should not happen by withdrawing from surrounding culture as if Christians were simply an alternative society, but should "live vulnerably on the boundaries"[27] in a whole world where Christ is Lord. Such covenant theology offers a number of insights and possibilities for ministerial formation.

First, within the college community the necessary distinction between tutor and student, in which the former is called to assess and commend the latter, must be negotiated within the context of covenant relationships understood within a lifelong journey of formation. This takes us deeper into this relational space, one that is created, intentionally, or otherwise, by the practices of the tutors involved and the way they navigate these relationships.

One way that this could happen is through the affirmation of a specific covenant that is written by a college community, as has happened for example at South Wales Baptist College, weaving together commitments that are made to each other within the theology of the divine covenant of grace. Such a covenant will find ways of incorporating historic elements, as part of the structured and structuring habitus of formation within a college as well as expressing the creative vision and commitment of a new re-forming of the community. Such a covenant will want to express, amongst other things, the sense of hospitality offered to each other in the light of God's welcome, the desire to go out in love, and the willingness to work at the right kind of self-centering in the midst of open relationships. It would be

---

25. Fiddes, *Tracks and Traces*, 55–56.
26. Fiddes, "Christianity, Culture and Education."
27. Fiddes, "Christianity, Culture and Education," 18.

an interesting exercise to produce a college covenant and re-write it, say every three years, so that all students are involved once.

Second, within the context of a local congregation where the student is also called to be a minister (in formation) there is a further delicate negotiation in which the student offers ministry to the church as one whose call has been affirmed and who has been welcomed as God's gift, but also as one willingly shaped by the local congregation in their own growth in ministry. Such a pattern is, of course, already based on the dialectical model of ministry we have argued as distinctly Baptist and this further stress on covenant in fact helps to see how such a dialectic can be held theologically and practically. Without denying the complexity of negotiating human relationships in which a congregation may feel empowered to dominate a "student", or a student consider this to be their opportunity to have their own way, it offers an important context for formation in a particularly Baptist approach to ministry.

Thirdly, there is the crucial connection between these two different contexts and centers. While the churches that welcome such "ministers-in-training" are often called placement churches, that language, though functional, seems inadequate to express the kind of commitment between college and church. There is the need to balance the real exercising of ministry by students, who are paid a half stipend and live in the context of the church, with the college understanding that they are full-time students, with the college having some oversight of their work. Better would be to describe them as "partner churches" and explicitly explore the way that this partnership can be expressed and developed in covenantal terms. The relationship between colleges and these churches within the one process of ministerial formation remains one of the critical aspects that has not been fully developed.

Fourthly, Fiddes' arguments suggest that in ministerial formation the relational space must intentionally move beyond the Baptist tradition and engage with the universal church, within a wider understanding of covenant. The empirical research has made clear the different ways that all the Baptist colleges do engage in ministerial formation in a wider ecumenical setting and two in particular include a global perspective in the pastoral imagination they encourage, and I suggested in chapter 3 that two of the key espoused shared commitments of the colleges were to be ecumenically sensitive and missionally, indeed globally, engaged evidenced by relations with overseas partners such as BMS World Mission.

Forming Ministers or Training Leaders?

Such espoused and operant commitments are strengthened further by the breadth and depth of this understanding of covenant, so that formation is not limited geographically but includes opportunities for hearing the voice of the universal church. Engaging in the empirical research highlighted the sometimes fragile nature of ecumenical partners, subject, for example, to denominational decisions beyond the institutions' control, and the way that financial considerations continue to make overseas visits challenging. But these are more than pragmatic issues and raise challenging questions about the breadth of our covenantal theology and the kind of space that we envisage formation inhabiting, particularly with the worldwide Baptist church and the wider universal church.

Fifthly, we have already seen how the centrality of relationships with universities are a further part of current shared practice, either as integral members or as validating partners, and Baptists here share a common pattern with the other historic denominations. The nature of the universities themselves has changed, together with the "space" offered for the study of theology, and in some cases the very presence in contemporary universities may feel sometimes uncomfortable, like "living vulnerably on the boundaries."

It would be possible to conceive of a pattern of formation in which all Baptist ordinands come together for shared teaching in a program agreed by the Baptist Union but disconnected from both university and ecumenical partners, and such possibilities have been mooted. This may reduce significantly the cost of ministerial formation, partly by removing university fees and partly by centralizing the current five dispersed colleges. Again, financial pressures may shape the theology of formation that ought rather to be understood in covenantal terms. The empirical research has revealed the importance of context, and any centralized approach is liable to reduce any kind of covenantal relationships with ecumenical partners, with a broader contextual student body and with secular universities.[28] This would be to the detriment of the experience of formation.

FORMATION AS HOSPITALITY: A MISSIONAL EMPHASIS

One of the clear aspects of the empirical research, expressed in both the *espoused* and *operant* voices, was the way that the pastoral imagination

---

28. A piece of empirical research which explores the effects of Common Awards in replacing local, perhaps more committed, validating arrangements with one national validating body would be important and helpful.

Towards a Theology of Formation for Baptists

that the Baptist colleges are seeking cooperatively to inculcate is one that is strongly missional. This is not unique, but is a distinct emphasis. Again such empirical findings clearly reinforce one of the key conclusions of the discussion of the practice of preparation in chapter 3.

Returning to the kind of trinitarian theology espoused by Fiddes, fundamental to this understanding of God is the sending of the Son and the pouring out of the Spirit, with the temporal "sendings" corresponding to the eternal generation of the Son and procession of the Spirit, pointing us to a God whose nature is fundamentally characterized by going out to others in love. In developing the metaphor of the dance, Fiddes suggests that the two patterns of circle and progressive dance may help to ameliorate each other, the circle dance mitigating against a tendency towards hierarchy in the eastern pattern while the progressive dance opens up the western tradition to ensure that the circle dance does not mean that God is closed and self-sufficient. As in a progressive dance, other dancers are always being brought into the patterns, so God opens the divine dance so that human partners can be brought in.[29] God does not want to be God without us.[30]

This approach clearly owes much to the theology of the *missio Dei*, which has become increasingly influential over the last fifty years, understanding the mission of the church to have its origin and very existence in participating in the mission of God. God is a missionary God, and "mission is not primarily an activity of the church but an attribute of God."[31] In a significant internal document on the nature of ministry, Baptists share such a perspective that "the God to whom the Bible bears witness is always 'going out' in love to others."[32] Mission, insists Fiddes, is not an imitation of, but a participation in this self-giving of God,[33] which shapes our shared life, and so mission will be at the heart of ministry, which will enable and model such "going out in love."

Alongside the metaphor of the dance, a further metaphor that has been used widely in recent theology to express this missiological approach is that of hospitality. The church is a community which makes room for the other as an embodied sign of this process of divine reconciliation[34] and in

---

29. Fiddes, *Participating in God*, 78.
30. See Karl Barth's doctrine of election in *Church Dogmatics* II/2, 36–75.
31. Bosch, *Transforming Mission*, 390.
32. Baptist Union of Great Britain, *Transforming Superintendency*, 9.
33. Fiddes, *Tracks and Traces*, 251.
34 See Pohl, *Making Room, Recovering Hospitality as a Christian Tradition*;

this way the metaphor has already been applied to theological education.[35] In addition, Henri Nouwen, proposing that hospitality is creating a free "space" where the stranger can enter, writes that "hospitality is not to change people, but to offer them space where change can take place,"[36] that change being intrinsically the work of God. Resonating with our earlier discussion on participating in God, this offers an additional and deep connection between the practice of ministry and the practice of preparation based on a deeper connection still with the practice of God who welcomes us: hospitable ministry that creates space for others in mission is formed by hospitable colleges that create a relational and missional space for students and staff.

The language of hospitality offers a creative way of pursuing a theology of ministerial formation for Baptists that takes into account a trinitarian vision of God alongside the missional stress within the practice of the Baptist colleges. The offer of grace and the subsequent sense of belonging are vital "if we want to foster that . . . vulnerability, openness to judgment, and responsiveness which are the core virtues of learning."[37] This then also raises questions about a number of aspects of the practice of the colleges.

One of the concerns I have expressed through this book is to integrate together an understanding of the practice of ministry with the practice of preparation. I discussed, in chapter 3, the way that British Baptists from the beginning of this century have tried to adapt the accredited list of ministers in the light of changing culture and need, first creating in 2001 a distinction between those who are ordained as pastors, youth specialists and evangelists, before merging these together again. The fact that only seventeen evangelists were listed in the 2012 Register of Nationally Accredited Ministers[38] together with anecdotal evidence that those coming to our colleges are tending to opt for recognition as pastors for the sake of expediency, helped prompt the more recent changes.

Yet the debate continues between more "pastoral" and more "mission", or particularly "pioneering" approaches, and these titles tend to be

---

Bretherton, *Hospitality as Holiness*.

35. See, Newman, "Who's Home Cooking? Hospitality, Christian Identity and Higher Education"; Hütter, 'Hospitality and Truth.

36. Nouwen, *Reaching Out*, 68–69.

37. Higton, *Vulnerable Learning*, 15.

38. The Baptist Union Directory (2012), 145; twenty-eight are listed as Youth Specialists.

used antithetically. While those who are called by God for ministry will be gifted in different ways, and there will be some significant differences in their practices, the distinction between those called to a more pastoral role (pastors) and a more missional role (pioneers) is not altogether helpful. It is as if, to draw on the dance metaphor again, some churches are only interested in a circle dance and some only in a progressive one. Recognizing the strengths and weaknesses of both circle and progressive patterns in trinitarian terms, this must also be true for churches and disciples who participate within these trinitarian movements—all pastoral work is seeking to go out in love to others, and all mission seeks to enable individuals to grow in their participation within God. It therefore seems time in both our language and structures to reassert that all sharing in the ministry of Christ, as churches and as ministers, is deeply missional and deeply pastoral, and to have just one category of ordained ministry.

Moving from this to the practice of preparation, one of the issues facing colleges in recent years is to the extent that there is one overarching approach to ministerial formation within which there can be different emphases, or distinct courses around, for example, urban mission or pioneering. One factor in this will of course be publicity and what courses in their name or emphases, will be attractive to potential students. Yet it is also important that the whole curriculum for any course on ministerial formation is understood as both missional and pastoral in an integrative way. The metaphor of hospitality offers a creative way of combining these emphases in which space for the other is created in all aspects of church life.

The metaphor of hospitality also helps integrate the two central contexts of a congregation engaged in mission and a college engaged in reflection. Hospitality will always seek to give full attention to the other, expressed in the inter-human relationships within and between staff and students and in the voices heard through placements, study and culture. We might conclude that the *direction* of ministerial formation is always outward looking, so that the call of the church to participate in God's going out in love is echoed in our colleges, in their going out in hospitality.

FORMATION AS INTEGRATION: A PEDAGOGICAL EMPHASIS

I argued that one key aspect to the overall formation *habitus* was that of integration. The empirical research showed there were some differences between institutions in the nuanced way that integration was understood and practiced, but it was clearly an important issue in the *espoused, operant* and *representative* voices. Integration has appeared in a number of ways. It happens between those aspects of the practice of preparation that were normally named as education, training and formation. It happens in the integration of theory and practice: all the colleges are committed to theological reflection, *in* practice and *on* practice, as a key aspect of shared understanding of formation, although there is a spectrum of how colleges have embraced this "turn to practice".[39] There is then the integration in the way that the whole of the curriculum is understood to contribute to all the varying aspects of formation, rather than expecting academic modules simply to teach knowledge and restricting formation to shared worship and community life. And, especially for the Baptist colleges there is the integration of the few and the many, in that all are called to a holistic, integrated journey of discipleship, and it is the responsibility of the church to preach, preside at the sacraments and offer pastoral care, but that some are called to do these things in a particular representative way.

I suggested earlier that at the very heart of Fiddes' doctrine of God is the notion of our participation in God's trinitarian life, which is not static but itself dynamic, ecstatic and self-transcending in the movement of love. Although language which Fiddes himself does not use, God's trinitarian life could be described as a constant and dynamic integration of Father, Son and Spirit as one God. I also pointed out the way that Fiddes explores one aspect of human formation as the integration of a proper self-centeredness with a vulnerable self-giving. If both God's own life and our own fundamental human development can be described in integrative terms, then this provides a strong theological basis for these pedagogical developments.

Although the concept of integration is both significant and varied, the exact description of this integration has not been clear. If, for example, we want to reserve formation language for the practice of preparation as a whole, how might we describe the third circle alongside education and training? Chris Ellis suggests it would be best described as "devotional practices" and the three circles together described as a "ministerial way of being."[40] This has some connection with the model at Spurgeon's which puts spirituality, understood in a broad sense, at the center, but uses "character" instead of "devotional practices". Bristol Baptist College's version

---

39. Graham, Walton and Ward, *Theological Reflection: Methods*, 194–96.
40. Ellis, "Being a Minister," 60–61.

Towards a Theology of Formation for Baptists

of the three circle diagram is similar, except that it combines spirituality and character in the third circle and uses oversight as the integrative word, which offers more emphasis on a ministry *habitus* than the original diagram from Allen which speaks consistently of church leadership.

Ellis' suggestion has the advantage of creating a clear, distinct and bounded third strand and would encourage colleges to help students focus more intensively on this aspect of discipleship. It also meets Mayes' challenge that spiritual practices, especially prayer, have been squeezed out of formation.[41] Formation would then be described as education, training and the development in spiritual disciplines. An alternative would be to keep the language of character but to give it a clearer meaning by approaching it in a consciously psychological way. In this case formation as a whole would be described as education, training and development in self-awareness, and paying more explicit attention to self-awareness may help provide a focus around which the development of character can be evaluated.

Both propositions have some attraction as they help concretize what otherwise can remain nebulous. So, while the three circles diagram allows for a clearer overlapping center, it is perhaps time to develop that pattern into four interweaving strands: gaining knowledge, developing skills, deepening spiritual practices and growing in self-awareness. Such an interweaving pattern describes a formation *habitus*, which is structured, drawing significantly on a Baptist tradition, could be agreed co-operatively, while also allowing space for creativity and improvisation. For different individuals at different times, the stress on individual strands may be different. Equally, within a commitment to shared practice different colleges may offer an experience of formation that balances the strands in different ways.

A second issue in the exact nature of integration, again prompted by the empirical research, concerns the particular influence that theory and practice exert on each other. We saw in the different institutions a diversity of approaches to relating theory and practice, from the kind of a "critical conversation"[42] proposed by Pattison in which there is space for change in all three of the conversation partners to a more "applied" model. The empirical evidence also suggested a narrower spectrum among the Baptist colleges, with collectively a greater commitment to methods of theological reflection. Yet this integration is not straight forward. Questions around this methodology of integration are deeply rooted in some of the popular

---

41. Mayes, *Spirituality in Ministerial Formation*, 3.
42. Pattison, *A Critique of Pastoral Care*, 136.

concerns about academic theology, which questions everything, and from where some of the historic stereotypical understanding of the Baptist colleges emerges. Alongside the adoption of the methodologies of practical theology, part of the structured and structuring Baptist tradition has always been a stress on the importance of the biblical witness as a source of authority, thus the term "evangelical" in some of the pastoral imaginations. One of the key areas of integration then for Baptist colleges will be between this historic and contemporary commitment to scripture alongside engaging in theological reflection in such a way as to allow this process to challenge and change particular hermeneutical positions. To label colleges as "evangelical" or "liberal" on account of the way this integration happens simply lacks the necessary nuance of trying to accurately describe practice. What is at stake is not the commitment either to Scripture or practical theology methodologies but the precise way they may be integrated in the work of a college or even of a particular tutor.

FORMATION AS GROWTH IN VIRTUE: A PERSONAL EMPHASIS

Alongside integration, the second key aspect of the formation *habitus* that I developed at the end of chapter 3 was integrity, which also then emerged through the empirical research in a whole variety of ways. Corresponding to the pedagogical developments within the practice of preparation is the more personal aspect of those who are in the process of being formed. I suggested that the desire, in the recent *Ignite* report, to replace the language of "competencies", against which ministry is evaluated, with *Marks of Ministry* is evidence of the growing place integrity has in the *representative*, and indeed, *normative* voice, and corresponds to the move away from a more functional view of ministry.[43]

Whereas various different words were used within the institutions to describe the pastoral imaginations that they were seeking to develop, a significant number—spiritual, growing in maturity, wise, mature in Christ, prayerful—focused in different ways on this personal development in spirituality and virtue. Understanding ministerial formation as a process of growth in virtue requires a significant openness to the process, to others and to God that is marked by vulnerability and risk-taking.

---

43. Goodliff, *Ministry, Sacrament and Representation*, 146–49.

Towards a Theology of Formation for Baptists

At Regent's Park, both at interviews and at the very beginning of the course, reference has often been made to probably the earliest book on pastoral theology in English, George Herbert's *The Country Parson*, which places this same need for growth in virtue at the heart of preparation and refers to those at university in a preparatory way:

> whose aim and labour must be not only to get knowledge, but to subdue and mortifie all lusts and affections: and not to think, that when they have read the Fathers, or Schoolmen, a Minister is made, and the thing done. The greatest and hardest preparation is within.[44]

Returning to Fiddes once more, one of his earlier and most distinctive theological contributions, *The Creative Suffering of* God,[45] traces this vulnerable openness back into the very life of God. The very particularity of the birth of Jesus expresses God's commitment to creation not only in this unique moment, but also as the climax of God's covenant history with the people of Israel. And this particularity is the "going out" of God in vulnerability, in which God gives Godself away in love, encountering negativity and death, while remaining true to who God is eternally.[46] These concepts of covenant and willing vulnerability, in which God is genuinely open to the world, are not the kind of kenotic theology in which God *becomes* vulnerable on the cross. Rather the very possibility of the cross is based in the eternal covenant and vulnerability within the Trinity between Father, Son and Spirit and is the very basis for God's risky "going out in love" to the world, and including us in God's trinitarian life.

David Cunningham has developed trinitarian thinking in a similar pattern, and in a way that resonates particularly with this discussion he connects together trinitarian virtues and practices. He understands virtues as those "dispositions that *God has by nature* and in which *we participate by grace*" and "as gifts, these virtues are not forced upon us; but we can allow them to form us, and thus allow God to take us up into the divine life."[47] For us, Cunningham suggests, it is not simply virtues that lead to practice, rather:

---

44. Herbert, *The Country Parson and Selected Poems*, 13.
45. Fiddes, *The Creative Suffering of God*.
46. Fiddes, *Participation In God*, especially 170–86.
47. Cunningham, *These Three are One*, 123.

elements of the *triune* character of God . . . are present in our development of specifically *triune* habits. In this way our lives can take on a triune character as well, conforming more closely to the image of God in which we were created.[48]

Fiddes' trinitarian theology describes the *willing* vulnerability of God, in which nothing is imposed on God, but God freely and graciously opens the divine life to the world.[49] Human life will, of course, sit in a somewhat different tension between that which the individual freely chooses and that which is imposed from without, that is between what is structured and creative, but the process of ministerial formation will require participating in those practices which involve risk-taking and willing vulnerability, the opening up of life to others, through which this trinitarian virtue will be shaped. This further shapes the whole way we must understood the practice of ministry and so the practice of preparation.

The change from the language of *Competencies to Marks of Ministry* reflects a shift in the understanding of the *habitus* of ministry, a shift that has a strong theological rationale. The trinitarian theology outlined by Fiddes and Cunningham stresses the way that human virtues are formed through participation by grace in God's life and that engaging in trinitarian practices will lead to the development of trinitarian virtues. Whether the language of attributes, qualities or marks is used, a virtue inspired rather than competence driven approach is rooted more firmly in this trinitarian theology. Such virtues will, according to our dialectical theology, be Christian virtues, rather than any sense of priestly character, which those called to ministry seek in particular intentional and intensive ways.

With regard to the practice of preparation, Astley offers three metaphors for the wider process of education: as a production line in which the "teacher" does something *to* the learner, as gardening in which the "teacher" does something *for* the learner and as a journey in which the "teacher" does something *with* the learner. Understanding formation as growth in virtue, in which the teacher and students are both engaged in their own formation, the only kind of metaphor that is applicable is Astley's "journey".[50] Astley himself quotes Dykstra:

> Everything is not all decided in advance, and what happens in my learning will make a difference to her. She is willing to become my

48. Cunningham, *These Three are One*, 125.
49. For more discussion of this see my *A Cry In the Darkness*.
50. Astley, *Learning in the Way*, 40.

equal and to be vulnerable to what takes place. I see in her face that my own learning moves her, and that she is committed to me and my learning over the long haul.[51]

But even in this sense of ministerial formation as a journey, the process not only involves a willing risk-taking but can also *impose* a certain vulnerability on those who respond to God's call, placing people in a threatening, if affirming, context. A change of employment, housing and schools, a potential drop in income and being launched into an unfamiliar setting are all significant challenges. Perhaps one of the greatest challenges for many is the return to study with the need to write essays and sit exams, in which an identity as a "student" replaces a very different employment and life-situation. This itself can be hard and feel both threatening and de-skilling and a key challenge in ministerial formation is to enable students to willingly embrace that which is already, to a degree, imposed.

This then has significant implications for the liturgical, educational and relational "space" created in a college context, which seeks to encourage growth in virtue in a context that enables risk-taking and vulnerability. This will impact the relationships which staff develop and model where the necessary asymmetrical relationship of staff and students is challenged by an alternative mutuality and openness, for styles of teaching, that do not hide behind unquestionable expertise but open up a common journey of learning, and for the way that our Baptist colleges relate together in a community of practice. The recent development of a peer review process, for example, reflects something of this risk and vulnerability.

CONCLUSION

Building on an understanding of a Baptist *habitus* of ministry, categorized as a dialectical model, and a shared Baptist approach to preparation for ministry, best understood as formation, and using the *formal* voice of the academy to add depth to the *representative*, *espoused* and *operant* voices, I have offered here a theology of ministerial formation for Baptists. I have suggested how it is structured and structuring, cooperative and creative, distinctly Baptist but part of the broader understanding of the church and based on a trinitarian theology of participation and vulnerability. I offer this as a theology that emerges from the tradition and can shape future practice, both at Regent's Park, in the wider denomination, and beyond.

51. Dykstra, *Vision and Character*, 104.

8

Towards a Pastoral Imagination

"WHAT SHOULD I DO, now, first?" This was the existential question of a new minister with which I began. I have suggested that the answer to this question will be shaped by many things, including the minister's context and personality, but it will be particularly shaped by the pastoral imagination a college is seeking to inculcate during the process of preparation. It has been shown that college principals and tutors have significantly influenced the theological understanding of students,[1] and so we can expect this also to be true for the pastoral imagination. It does not mean that all students will be shaped in the same way and the same degree, but that we can expect the kind of pastoral imagination that a college is seeking to inculcate will have some impact on those who come as students. In any college a more implicit pastoral imagination might already be at work, but there would be distinct value in a clear and explicit description of the intended pastoral imagination, which in turn will influence and shape pedagogical practice. But what "pastoral imagination"?

In chapters 5 and 6 I attempted to identify the pastoral imagination that the other Baptist colleges and a sample of non-Baptist institutions were actually seeking to develop in their students. This was based on both the *espoused* self-understanding and also the *operant* practice of the institution in their explicit and implicit curricula. This empirical research afforded me the opportunity to recognize the pastoral imagination that has been implicitly at the heart of our practice of preparation, but also to stand back and

---

1. See Goodliff, *Ministry, Sacrament and Representation*.

reformulate this more explicitly. In chapter 7, I developed a theology of ministerial formation deeply rooted in an understanding of the nature of God and Baptist theology set down in conversation particularly with Paul Fiddes.

In this chapter I propose an *espoused* pastoral imagination that builds on the empirical research and theological understanding set out in the previous chapter and which I personally would look to shape the work of a college and its students, and then I suggest ways that this pastoral imagination might be embedded in practice, so that an assessment of operant practice might lead back to this same pastoral imagination. In order to give this clear focus, and in the same way as I sought those key words that were descriptive of other colleges and courses, here I offer three words that for me express best this pastoral imagination. The three areas highlighted are not intended to be radically new ideas, but emerge out of the co-operative and structured practice of preparation for ministry among Baptist and others which has continued over time. But it does seek to give both clarity and theological depth to issues that sometimes have remained too implicit.

A PASTORAL IMAGINATION

Reflective (and Reflexive)

This may be considered to have a focus on the way that a minister as a disciple relates to her or himself before God. Reflective is unlikely to be a surprising choice as theological reflection has been shown to be increasingly at the heart of a common practice of preparation and central to the developing understanding of ministers as reflective practitioners. But theological reflection as an activity deeply resonates with our understanding of ministerial formation as a practice: it is a fundamentally integrative activity, bringing together different aspects within the whole experience of formation which I have suggested is a fundamental pedagogical approach, as well as being structured, cooperative and creative.

Reflection is, first, integrative in that it enables the relating of theory and practice together in contextual ways, but is even more so when it is understood to be much more than a task or a skill. John Swinton expresses this well in suggesting that:

> theological reflection might be best understood as a virtue which contributes to the development of Christian character which in turn enables approaches to exploring the Christian tradition

which are faithful and transformative both to the theologian and to the particular situations and experiences she is examining.[2]

This understanding of reflection as a virtue also then intertwines the qualities of being reflective and reflexive, that is being deeply self-aware. One aim of ministerial formation is to develop reflective and reflexive ministers in such a way that this becomes not just a task to be fulfilled but a fundamental aspect of their *habitus*. Swinton suggests that one of the outcomes of theological reflection is the development of Christian character in what might be seen as a virtuous circle, in which reflection as a virtue helps develop other Christian virtues. One of the fundamental questions then in reflection is always what is happening to me in this experience so that reflection is always reflexive. We might note at this point, that there are a number of aspects of the Baptist Union's recent development of *Marks of Ministry*[3] which tie into this in significant ways. These talk about the need for reflective self-aware ministers, rooted in Scripture, a resident theologian, and growing in maturity. The *Core Competencies* include an understanding of the Christian faith and especially the Baptist tradition.

Theological reflection is also integrative in that it brings together the three registers of theology that Rowan Williams, for example, describes as "celebratory, communicative and critical."[4] While the whole process of ministerial formation may have a significant focus on critical theology and for many introduces this for the first time in the explicit curriculum, the wider experience of formation includes elements of the celebratory in worship and preaching, and the communicative in the sharing of life and faith. Theological reflection is one of those moments in the whole process that seeks to bring these registers into clear conversation.

Yet, it appears while such reflection has inspired and enthused some, it has been difficult for many students, who have struggled to grasp both its overall purpose and appropriate practices.[5] While a necessary part of the pastoral imagination it may not always be an easy aspect to develop. One aspect of the difficulty experienced can be the need for this significant degree of self-awareness. Those who already struggle with their self-awareness may be able to develop theological reflection but in a way that

---

2. Swinton, "Is theological reflection a technique or a virtue?"
3. Available at https://www.baptist.org.uk/Articles/565399/Marks_of_Ministry.aspx.
4. Williams, *On Christian Theology*, xiii.
5. See Graham, Walton and Ward, *Theological Reflection*, 6–7.

is not always *reflexive* which limits the way reflection acts as and develops virtue and character.

Theological reflection is then a structured practice, not that there is a model to follow, although that too can be helpful, but because its fundamental purpose is to engage intentionally, faithfully and critically with the theological tradition which is part of the structuring structures of faith. Another difficulty some students encounter is to make reflection truly *theological*, as opposed to being based on experience, individual ideas or self-awareness. Good theological reflection demands engagement with all the resources of the Christian tradition in order to respond in the present context.

One of the significant areas of reflection about ministerial formation and education in recent years has been about the kind of knowledge that is involved, with a turn towards an understanding of wisdom that has its roots in both the Biblical narrative and Aristotelian ethics.[6] Rejecting both the *Scientia* approach at the heart of the Enlightenment and the *Wischenshaft* approach of technical and professional learning there has been a desire to embrace the approaches embodied in the language of *phronesis* (the practical wisdom of Aristotle), *sapientia* (the knowledge not about God but of God) and also *paideia* (the development of the whole person as the basis of Christian education). Reflection as a practice helps integrate these different aspects of knowledge, in which the best of what might sometimes be termed "academic" knowledge is brought to the service of practice, spirituality and virtue. Goodliff, quoting Daniel Treier's understanding of the early church, looks for an approach to ministerial formation that is "in hot pursuit of *sapientia* (wisdom), a kind of knowledge with teleology: the formation of virtue in the people of God."[7] How is such wisdom pursued? Partly at least through the practice and virtue of theological reflection.

Theological reflection is also best understood as a collaborative practice, especially in the context of ministry, and this will be explored further below. Our original understanding of practice was partly drawn from Dykstra and Bass who argued that a practice needed to be a "sustained, co-operative pattern of human activity that is big enough, rich enough, and complex enough to address some fundamental feature of human existence."[8] Reflection must be a co-operative venture, and there are two ways of understanding this. First, engaging with the tradition is part of this

---

6. See Goodliff, *Shaped for Service* and Leach "*Is Wisdom the Principal Thing?*"
7. Goodliff, *Shaped for Service*, 73–74, quoting Treier, *Virtue and the Voice of God*, 3.
8. Dykstra and Bass, "A Theological Understanding," 27.

co-operation, on the basis that our desire is not to use the theologians of the past for our own ends but to listen carefully and pay attention to what they have to say so that our own work might develop together with them. This highlights the importance of historical and systematic theology as key resources for reflection. Second, engaging with those around us is how this co-operation develops. One of the criticisms of theological reflection is that it can be an isolated and individual practice, and including reflection in university assessments can add to that sense. At its best reflection is something that draws on the collective wisdom of the community and part of the necessary skill and virtue of theological reflection is being able to facilitate this reflection with others.

Reflection, finally, is also a creative activity, not bound by the tradition simply to repeat what has been done in the past but always open to improvise and develop in new ways and in so doing the wider structuring structures themselves develop. Reflection then is deeply responsive to the changing culture and context, always willing to engage the new, but not simply in a pragmatic way on the basis of what has worked elsewhere, but drawing on the depths of theological resources. Elaine Graham, for example, has argued that what we need is a model of practical wisdom which is both "indwelt" and "constructed",[9] that is one that is structured from the tradition but reinterpreted creatively in each context.

Collaborative

This might have a focus on the way that a minister, as a disciple, relates to others, especially in the church, before God. Central to my argument is that a dialectical approach to ministry, in which ministry and oversight are exercised by the whole congregation but also by a "few" set aside by the church, is both the representative Baptist understanding and also the most appropriate theological position. While the notion of collaborative ministry is of course not peculiarly Baptist,[10] I suggested that there remains a particular Baptist understanding of ministry, in this dialectical model, which is particularly well expressed in the language of collaboration. This is more than structural polity and I have argued that this is rooted deeply in an understanding of the nature of God and also Baptist understandings of the nature of the church. This stress appears in a number of ways in the

9. Graham, *Transforming Practice*, 95.
10. See, for example, Pickard, *Theological Foundations for Collaborative Ministry*.

pastoral imaginations of the Baptist colleges and being collaborative also appears explicitly in the recent Baptist Union *Marks of Ministry*.

Understanding that all formation is contextual, within a tradition, the practice of preparation at a Baptist college must be necessarily and unashamedly a process of Baptist formation, that is students and tutors are working within a structuring structure that is owned, recognized and celebrated. This will certainly have elements of "ecumenical formation" and will share much with those preparing for ministry in other traditions, but it will also be distinct, and this collaborative approach arising from a dialectical understanding of ministry is central to a Baptist distinctive.

It is generally recognized that an aspect of our current "post denominational" and consumer age is the willingness of Christians to choose the most suitable local church regardless of its denominational links, leading to many within Baptist congregations who have been formed in particular practices and understandings in a whole variety of church traditions. Anecdotally the consequence of this has been the increasing numbers of students coming to college to prepare for ministry with much less Baptist experience than in the past, and often in Baptist churches that have struggled with their own understanding of ecclesiology.

This prompts a further, though more tangential issue, which is the practice of accepting onto the Register of Nationally Accredited Ministers those who have not prepared for ministry in a Baptist college. A course on Baptist history and principles is mandatory, and the Residential Selection Conference can insist a candidate engage in further formation, although this seems to be understood more generally in terms of character, maturity and spirituality. Yet this does not seem sufficient. Given our previous arguments for integrated formation which cannot be a-contextual, a course of study which can be taken by distance learning may provide some helpful information but can never be Baptist formation, which can only happen in a Baptist context, however ecumenically that context is shaped. New patterns of teaching Baptist History and Principles that demand much greater engagement with both a college and with other Baptists is certainly a positive development. But as a denomination we should be looking to ensure that all those who are accredited as ministers have been truly formed in a Baptist context, although this may raise ecclesiological tensions between the local church that calls a minister and the wider Union that accredits.

Forming Ministers or Training Leaders?

Hospitable

This might have a focus on the way that a minister relates to the wider world before God. Rooted in an understanding of God who is deeply committed to the whole of creation as the partner of divine love, and who opens the divine life to welcome the other into God's trinitarian community, I suggested in the previous chapter that hospitality is a metaphor that takes us deep into the being and action of God. It has been used as a metaphor that encompasses the church's participation in the mission of God,[11] combines this with an approach to pastoral care and the value of the other,[12] and has also been used to describe the nature of theological education.[13] To describe a minister, or disciple, as hospitable, means participating in the hospitality of God, of being committed to the whole world in a missional sense, but not simply as a function to perform but as an essential part of one's character or disposition—it is a virtue as well as a practice—and of having a vulnerable and pastoral openness to others. As a World Council of Churches document puts it:

> God's hospitality calls us to move beyond binary notions of culturally dominant groups as hosts, and migrant and minority peoples as guests. Instead, in God's hospitality, God is host and we are all invited by the Spirit to participate with humility and mutuality in God's mission.[14]

A reminder of the linguistic roots of hospitality in the Christian tradition will help at this point develop the kind of hospitality that is being imagined here. In both Greek, *xenos*, and Latin, *hospes*, the same word has a broad semantic domain that includes the idea of both host and guest and this is vital to any theological development of hospitality. Alongside the sense of welcome, generosity and attentiveness, which is at the heart of offering hospitality, sits the risk, vulnerability and dependency of being the guest. In order to avoid the control that can develop when you understand yourself always as the host it is necessary to embrace the de-centering experience of the guest. Being hospitable as this third aspect of a pastoral imagination, rooted in the mission and vulnerability of God, will express itself

---

11. See Bretherton, *Hospitality as Holiness*.

12. See Justes, *Hearing Beyond Words: How to Become a Listening Pastor*.

13. See Newman, "Who's Home Cooking? Hospitality, Christian Identity and Higher Education"; Marmon, "Teaching as Hospitality."

14. World Council of Churches, *Together Towards Life*, paragraph 71.

in both the way that those in ministry welcome and offer a place to others, especially those marginalized, with real attentiveness, and also in risk taking that accepts the welcome of others. Being hospitable will then both lead to and be shaped by specific hospitable practices. Pioneering offers an important example of this, for ministering without the "traditional" base of a building and established congregation, means a much greater dependence on the hospitality of others and a much more significant balancing of the dialectic between being host and guest.

My suggestion, then, is that this combination of being reflective, collaborative and hospitable is the pastoral imagination that for me, emerges, from an understanding of both the nature of the triune God and the particular Baptist tradition and which I seek intentionally to develop and shape in ministerial students. Any pastoral imagination that is intentionally owned will then have implications for practice.

THE PRACTICE OF PREPARATION

In order to develop such a pastoral imagination intentionally within a college, these three themes will shape the broader practice of preparation for ministry. There is also, it seems it me, a clear interplay between the practice of preparation understood within the formation paradigm and the kind of pastoral imagination for which I am arguing. To develop in being reflective, collaborative and hospitable is at the very core of who we are and how we relate to God and to others, which will impact on the skills we develop and the knowledge we gain but are much broader concepts rooted in the kind of people we aspire be as ministers. And whereas we can be trained in models of reflection and patterns of team work and in missional practice, more fundamentally we are being formed so that these qualities or virtues develop. As Goodliff suggests,

> the knowledge that is gained through community participation is not so much a series of self-contained units of cognitive capital, but rather the embodied ability to behave as community members . . . here is a powerful case for practice-based learning in ministerial formation.[15]

---

15. Goodliff, *Shaped for Service*, 46.

On this basis, that the whole of the curriculum forms the whole person, exploring three themes will lead to pedagogical reflections and developments.

Reflective

One of the challenges that emerged through the empirical research was the most appropriate pattern for teaching and facilitating theological reflection, and in my own experience it has been an area of fairly constant trial and development. We now teach most of our ministerial students through ether a BTh suite or an MTh that both explicitly name reflective practice as central to the course and include this in summative assessment. We have experimented with different kinds of group reflections, so that the collaborative aspect can be developed, individual reflective journals and the development of more reflection-based assessment. Creating the time and appropriate space to enable good practice and the virtue of theological reflection to develop remains one of the most significant challenges.

One way this has been done by some institutions is the development of a fully contextual degree, working on the wider belief that all theology is practical theology, and so practical theology methodologies become the overarching approach of the whole course within which the particular methodologies associated with some of the traditional sub-disciplines are taught and explored. In my own context the MTh is shaped much more in this way, whereas the BTh is still shaped around a more traditional pattern of biblical studies, history and doctrine and practical theology. On the one hand, pedagogically, there is a distinct appeal about a radical reworking of our current curriculum and its sub-divisions so that a variety of themes are taught drawing on biblical, historical and theological material within a practical theology methodology, as a way of embedding reflective practice in the whole of the course.

But, on the other hand, it may also, inadvertently, lead to greater struggles with the *theological* aspect of reflection. For theological reflection to be done well it requires a knowledge of the broader biblical, historical and theological tradition so that the reflection is not just pragmatic solutions. It is notable that while the Baptist colleges had, collectively, given more significant space in the curriculum for areas such as mission and were clearly committed to practical theology methodologies, there was also the danger that less space was given to those subjects that offer knowledge of the tradition. One of the clear dangers for Baptists, rooted in the more activist evangelical approach, is the acceptance of pragmatic solutions ahead of deeper theological reflection. With ongoing pressures on time and the curriculum one of the areas that could be in danger of being squeezed out too much is the broader biblical and theological tradition.

One of the first subjects our undergraduate first year ordinands take is on Early Church history and theology. Partly this is because I teach it and as Course Director I am eager for that early engagement with the students, but partly it is also seeking to model the way that the tradition acts positively as a structuring structure that offers resources for the practice of reflection. What often appears initially as arcane historical debate ends up, normally, being seen as significant resources for ongoing reflection on Christology, soteriology and theology. Thus I think we currently face this double challenge of teaching both the practice of theological reflection and the resources of the biblical and theological tradition to do this well.

A further very specific practice that emerged from the empirical research in two particular institutions was the requirement for students, who were developing their own patterns of theological reflection, perhaps for the first time, to quickly become the "tutors" by facilitating theological reflection with others. This seems to me to have much to commend it. It has been embraced in those institutions that have developed the most contextually shaped programs, where it may also be able to function as summative work. Not only does the need to teach, or at least facilitate others, become the context for significant personal learning, as is often the case, it also emphasizes the collaborative nature of the whole exercise. It seems an excellent example of learning in and from practice. What it requires is a clear, perhaps clearer, connection between the college and church as centers of formation.

We have seen that congregation-based patterns of ministerial formation, with this emphasis on practice-based learning, have become the dominant experience for most people preparing for Baptist ministry, although college-based approaches now draw to some degree on the same practice-based approach. For Baptist colleges, there can be no significant return to residential formation, which remains a possibility but in reality only for those who are commended for ministry at a young age before they have been to University. Some form of congregation-based pattern will continue to be dominant in the years ahead, with some contexts being more pioneering and others being bi-vocational. Yet while our espoused theology has been of two centers, and on the partnership in formation between college and placement church, the focus of attention seems to have been much on the college center, with the expectation, or trust, that formation is somehow happening in the church context. The challenge we face, especially given that the amount of time engaging in college has decreased, is how to develop further this pattern so that the placement is more than the exercising of ministry, or providing the material for reflection at college, but is itself increasingly a genuine center of formation. This will require a greater partnership, one I suggested will need to be understood in terms of covenant, with a concomitant time commitment, between college and church, and for tutors to work more closely with churches so they can reflect together on how the church experience can be formative.

While we have begun to work on this, it is an area that needs further development, particularly looking at ways that the experience and understanding college has gained can be shared with churches so that they can develop more as a center of formation. For a number of years, we have used "partnership agreements" which the college, the placement church and the student sign. I have felt some pressure from church placements to make this a more contractual document that sets out in more detail exactly what students and churches are expected to do. Yet my desire would be, in contrast, to make them more explicitly theological, so that the implicit covenantal understanding they contain can be made more explicit as the theological basis for formation in two centers. Working this covenant out in practice will then require more direct contact between college and partner churches.

Finally it is important for tutors intentionally to model the practice of theological reflection not simply in a more formal context, for example, in a class that is teaching theological reflection, but also in the way that other subjects are taught. My own practice, for example would be routinely to begin with practice and experience in areas such as preaching, leadership or disability, before exploring ways that the resources of the whole wider tradition might be brought to bear on the issue.

Collaborative

I have argued that the espoused and historic Baptist understanding of ministry is built on a dialectical model as responsibility flows between minister and members, between the few and the many, but that this has been challenged by other approaches and by voices within and without Baptist churches. One of the key challenges for Baptist colleges then is the teaching of this tradition, and these ecclesiologically shaped patterns of leadership, as fundamental sources for theological reflection. There is of course something of a tension here, made more noticeable in my own context, deeply rooted in Oxford's tutorial system in which the tutor seeks to expose the student to a variety of opinions and facilitate them in developing their own views.

The reality, of course, is that there will always be some shaping of the process through the tutor's own beliefs, their teaching and the bibliographies they set. We might then helpfully return to the idea discussed earlier that education should be both formative and critical. As a Baptist college, with those preparing for ministry in Baptist churches, we are engaging, unapologetically, in formative education within a particular tradition, which we own and celebrate, and while the Baptist Union struggles with a normative theology I have suggested there is a very clear representative theology. My own belief is that we should be explicitly seeking in all we do to develop a pastoral imagination based on a ministry rather than leadership *habitus*, drawing on the dialectical model of ministry which is deeply collaborative. This is something which goes beyond some specific classes that cover "Baptist Principles" but shapes the broader curriculum. Formative education in Baptist principles happens best when these are woven throughout the course and so returned to frequently. This would be true of course for any other tradition as well.

But such principles from any tradition are not static and their contours change and develop, so education always allows space for them to be critiqued and developed. A collaborative pedagogy will always intentionally provide space for the learning to be owned and shaped by the group, in which crucible some of the aspects of a particular approach to ministry are refined.

Finally, again, there is the importance of modelling such a collaborative approach in both teaching and in leadership within a college context. Two Baptist colleges now, and I sense somewhat uniquely, have adopted the practice of appointing co-principals, both as a way of exercising collaborative leadership and as a clear commitment to this as a Baptist understanding. They stand out as significant developments, but exemplify the necessary pedagogical and leadership approach. If we are to seek to develop a collaborative pastoral imagination then this must be experienced and inhabited within the college context itself. This might also help rethink the wider relationship between tutors and students. One of the patterns of ministerial formation that Goodliff explores is that of the apprenticeship model, recognizing that this is a model with historic roots before residential colleges including for Baptists, although he suggests fewer opportunities now exist in larger churches with team ministries.[16] Goodliff also draws inspiration from contemporary intern schemes for this model. Yet in the earliest apprenticeships there would have been the opportunity for learning Biblical studies, Biblical languages and theology, and a venture like the London Baptist Education Society in 1752 (which eventually led to Regent's Park College) brought promising young men to learn in very small groups, normally one or two, with and from a tutor who was a minister. Perhaps one way of expanding the idea of an apprenticeship model beyond Goodliff's suggestions, is to see the relationship between tutor and ministerial student's in apprenticeship terms. So Foster *et al.* suggest that

> students participate in a teacher's practice as apprentices to a master craftsperson . . . Over time the knowledge and skills required to participate in the practice become increasingly familiar, even comfortable and often unconscious.[17]

The activity of the "master craftsperson", if that language is not too grand, is fundamentally the practice of theological reflection and all that emerges from this. The tutor would be someone who was able to engage in theological reflection by drawing on all their knowledge of the tradition, but also able to use this knowledge to make connections with and to shape practice. This practice would of course be by its nature collaborative and hospitable, focused towards the mission of God and vulnerably welcoming others in so that their voices were heard. There would of course be other "ministerial" practices that a tutor would engage in, preaching and leading worship, pastoral care, teaching, but in particular a tutor would be modelling a pastoral imagination that is reflective, collaborative and hospitable and drawing others into this practice.

Hospitable

Developing hospitable ministers begins with an understanding of the triune God always welcoming others into the patterns of the divine dance, and so is something we first of all experience. In chapters 5 and 6 I included information from my research into patterns of worship and spirituality in

---

16. Goodliff, *Shaped for Service*, 110–21.
17. Foster *et al.*, *Educating Clergy*, 28–29.

the different theological colleges and courses, noting both the differences between them and the way worship functions as a central part of the implicit curriculum. What I was not able to do was comment on the content of those occasions of worship and how they were experienced. A significant immersive experience as a participant-observer in college worship would be a fascinating project. The worship I would argue that is necessary and appropriate is based on hospitality and grace, rather than being didactic and moralistic. The fundamental place of worship in the college curriculum is because these should be moments when we encounter the welcoming hospitality and grace of God which then allows the welcoming of each other.

But gathered worship in college is now comparatively infrequent, as the majority of students are congregation-based, and this model cannot emulate the residential colleges of the past or present. What is required is a different kind of gathered-dispersed model. In an Anglican context, for example, the daily office provides something of this model, whereas there is nothing within the Baptist tradition that works as such a structuring structure. There is this kind of material available now from the Order for Baptist Ministry and some ministers have drawn significantly on resources from both the Northumbria and Iona Communities, but there is also the possibility of a college developing its own patterns and rhythms as part of a covenantal approach to ministerial formation.

The language of hospitality then deeply resonates with spirituality, and while it is absolutely right that spirituality features on the explicit curriculum, especially offering students that opportunity to understand the breadth of spiritual tradition and practices from which they can draw, this is an important area in which the pastoral imagination is shaped by the whole of the broad explicit and implicit curricula. But we have also seen that it also deeply resonates with understandings of mission in a way that always takes us out into the world.

Yet hospitality is more than missional practice or an aspect of the explicit curriculum, but describes a way of life. A further challenge in making hospitality a central aspect of the pastoral imagination is for me to reflect on my own practice of hospitality, in the classroom, in my office and in my home, as I seek to pursue practices, in availability and vulnerability, that help model and develop this in others.[18] If worship, for example, is constructed in such a way as to stress participation in divine grace, then I clearly need to reflect on how such grace is experienced and mediated in the classroom

---

18. For further discussion see Call, "The Rough Trail to Authentic Pedagogy".

as well as the chapel, how those who disagree with me are welcomed and heard and encouraged. If the vulnerability of hospitality is expressed as much by being the guest as being the host then I need to reflect on the way that students are empowered to act as a host, both more literally and more metaphorically, alongside the desire to welcome them into my home.

CONTEXT

Drawing on the empirical research, one of the significant aspects of the uniqueness of each college or institution is its context, which inevitably is a mixture of the chosen and the contingent. This is one of the key issues that creates different experiences for students in the different colleges. My own unique context, for example, is formed from being at a Permanent Private Hall of Oxford University, which is a full part of the University and where a variety of subjects are taught to students of various faiths and none, and which is also a member of an ecumenical partnership, the Oxford Partnership for Theological Education and Training (OPTET) and a member of the Baptist Union of Great Britain. Together they form the unique structured tradition, which provides the context in which reflection happens, three covenant partners with whom the college seeks to work collaboratively and creatively, and opportunities for hospitality, as both host and guest. Such hospitality involves listening to and welcoming the voices of all three partners, which may of course be saying different things.

Based, fundamentally, on decisions made nearly a century ago, there is a significant givenness to this context—even though those making the decision to move the college to Oxford could not have foreseen the particular contextual shape of the early 21st century. But there is also in the college a significant embrace of this givenness. Regent's Park is not a seminary in the sense that all its students are preparing for ministry, or even studying theology or even coming from the Christian tradition, and this breath of context and hospitality is welcomed. Equally, it would be possible for the same kind of classes to be taught by the same tutors but without any ecumenical or university partnerships—just an "in-house" process of preparation. My sense would be that so much would be lost in such an experience, in which those who are welcomed are very much the same, without the need for wider collaboration and deep hospitality. It is this context then that helps make the experience not just an education in theology or training in skills but a rich process of formation.

CONCLUSION

These reflections suggest the kind of *habitus* or structuring structure appropriate for a Baptist college which is shared and cooperative with others as something distinctly Baptist, but also creative and distinct, and rightly remains a unique context in which to prepare for ministry. In significant ways the pastoral imagination proposed here already deeply shapes the understanding and practice of preparation as tutors seek to model reflection in their teaching and in their own approach to study, act collaboratively as a staff team and with the student body, and develop pedagogical practices shaped by the virtue of hospitality. Yet these practices and virtues rightly remain challenges for the on-going work of a college.

As I indicated in chapter 1, I embarked on this research project as a practitioner, with all my existing biases. I was already instinctively embracing more fully the language of formation, but in doing so I was becoming increasingly aware of both the debate about the practice of preparation and the persistent description of this as training. Equally, while seeking to teach classes on the nature of ministry with a stress on a collaborative approach I was routinely confronted with a strong leadership model emerging from the previous experience of students. The research I have undertaken has confirmed, for me, the instinctive approach I was taking around the issues of both formation and ministry, but also has allowed me to develop these more fully and defend them more strongly. For me then it is clear that both my own practice and, I have argued, the practice of preparation among Baptists, is better described as forming ministers rather than training leaders.

Within a methodology that sought to generate knowledge, which would impact my practice, as well as affirming that my own practice is best understood as forming ministers, I have sought so far to offer a number of new insights and perspectives.

In setting out a theoretical and methodical basis in chapter 1 I offered an understanding of practice and a more refined and developed concept of the pastoral imagination. I suggested that Dykstra offers a more theological, and so helpful understanding of practice than the influential definition of MacIntyre, by rooting it in the pursuit of a good beyond itself within God's self-giving grace.[19] While this understanding of practice has shaped the discussion, I would want to further develop this definition, in the light of

---

19. Bass and Dykstra, *For Life Abundant*, p. 30.

the trinitarian theology developed later on in the book. A trinitarian practice pursues a good beyond itself by participating in God's vulnerable and risk-taking self-giving grace, through which it develops trinitarian virtues.

Similarly, while offering in chapter 1 a new and refined understanding of the pastoral imagination, first set out by Dyskrta and developed by Foster *et al.*, I would also want to further refine this definition within a trinitarian perspective. The interplays it suggests both between the structured tradition, the shared co-operative approach and creative and individual agency, and between practice and theology are rooted in the fundamental interplay between trinitarian practices and virtues. So I would suggest that a pastoral imagination is then the fundamental way a minister understands and experiences their participating in the triune God that therefore shapes everything they think and do.

In chapter 2 I explored the way that contemporary Baptists understand the practice of ministry, highlighting the tension that currently exists between two distinct paradigms, named as ministry and leadership and arguing for a coherent historic and contemporary Baptist approach, which I have labelled as a dialectical model. Whereas there are certainly elements of this model in other writers I have sought to bring this material in the literature together and articulate it in a new and coherent way.

In chapter 3 I explored the history of the practice of preparation among Baptists over the last forty years and the way that it is currently understood. Whereas the development of a formation paradigm in other denominations has been narrated, this had not been offered before within a British Baptist context and therefore this is a distinct contribution. I have already published a version of this chapter in a peer-reviewed journal resulting in a number of further conversations.[20] These two chapters, by engaging with current and historic literature, have offered a *representative* understanding of the practice of preparation for Baptists—as formation for ministry—which is already theologically rich.

Building on this theoretical basis I engaged in research to explore the *espoused* and *operant* understanding of the practice of preparation in the other Baptist colleges, by focusing on the first of two empirical research questions: what is the pastoral imagination which the Baptist colleges individually are seeking to inculcate in their students?

Although there have been anecdotal discussions of the perceived biases and differences within the five Baptist colleges, no sustained empirical

---

20. Clarke, "How Did We End Up Here?"

research had been done in this area. Chapter 5, then, offers the most comprehensive research and clearest insight available into the practice of the other four Baptist colleges. In this chapter I have shown both significant similarities with a shared structured understanding and some particular creative differences. Future discussion about the work of the five Baptist colleges can now happen on a much firmer empirical basis. Exploring further the similarities found among the Baptist colleges I pursued a second empirical research question: is there a particular combination of practices and elements of a pastoral imagination that could be considered distinctly Baptist?

In the light of this, chapter 6 sets out in some detail the practice of five non-Baptist institutions. Some of the information contained here may be less useful in its own right because of its anonymized nature, but this aspect of the empirical research suggests that there is a distinctive combination of emphases that could be described as "Baptist", and so it broadens and deepens the knowledge of Baptist practice.

The empirical research focused on the intentions of the colleges and the pastoral imagination that they were seeking to develop, and did so by comparing Baptist and non-Baptist institutions. One of the consequences of this research decision is that the data gathered is stronger on the espoused theology of the colleges within their documentation and the operant theology of a college expressed in its explicit curriculum than on the wider implicit curriculum of the college. The research could then be extended in a number of ways.

Further research could take a more intensive immersive experience of participant observation into the life of the other four Baptist colleges, not simply considering documents and one key interview, but sharing in classes, meals and worship with the community over a period of time, interviewing a broad spectrum of staff and thus building a fuller and richer picture of each college. Alternatively, or additionally, a broader sample of non-Baptist institutions could be included, which would then test further some of the conclusions of this research. A much broader sample would also be able to test Baptist practice against institutions, for example, of a particular denomination or churchmanship. These options would pursue the same kind of questions in greater depth.

A different kind of agenda for further research would take a student-centered approach and explore the impact of the practice of a college on its ministerial students, so moving beyond the intentions of the college in its practice to exploring the actual pastoral imagination expressed in the ministry of its students. Such research could, further, explore the ways that different models of ministerial formation might impact upon student experience, for example, focusing on those who take a college-based or a congregation-based or a bi-vocational route. In addition, the impact of church contexts on formation could be explored with empirical evidence offered about the differences entailed in, for example, being placed in a small church as sole minister or a larger church as part of a team. All this would be valuable further research, but at present chapters 5 and 6 offer the frontier of empirical research on the practice of the Baptist colleges of the Baptist Union of Great Britain.

The *representative* voice from the literature review and the *espoused* and *operant* voices from the empirical research are both already theologically extensive, but I combined them with a third strand, the work of leading Baptist theologian Paul Fiddes, in order to extend the theological depth by explicitly engaging theory and practice with the doctrine of God. In Chapter 7 I offered a clear and explicit theology of formation for Baptists, which has sought to combine these three sources of knowledge. I am not aware of any other attempt to offer such a theology of ministerial formation and this is one of the distinct contributions to knowledge arising from my research. Some of the theology here has also already been explored in a published article, which develops a trinitarian theology of ministerial formation in dialogue with Paul Fiddes; what is unique about this chapter is the way it has sought to bring together the finished empirical research together with a wider review of the literature and the work of Fiddes. Finally in this chapter I have indicated some of my own learning and offered the explicit and intentional pastoral imagination that is shaping my own work as a college tutor.

9

Towards a Renewed Practice of Ministry

"What should I do now, first?" This was the question with which we began, and to which we returned at various times through this book, using it as a test for how ministry and ministerial formation is practiced. And through the book I have been arguing that practice, and in particular the practice of ministry, should be understood as something that is structured, cooperative and creative, so that ministry is not a set of unconnected individual actions but a participation with others in the mission and ministry of God that develops and persists over time. The main theme of my initial research and so this book was the practice of theological colleges in the preparation of men and women for ministry, but it seems appropriate as something of an afterword to offer the beginnings of an answer to this structuring question. And so using the framework of the pastoral imagination set out in the previous chapter, I offer here some personal experience and suggestions on how this question might be answered.

REFLECTIVE

If ministry is to be both structured and creative, then one of the first tasks of ministry is to engage with the tension between the uniqueness of the context and the givenness of the tradition. One of the lessons I quickly learnt in my second pastorate was that the successes of the first pastorate could not simply be repeated! Having moved from the borders of East London / Essex to Oxford, I was now in a very different place with a unique set of people. What I needed to do now was to reflect with a new group of people in a new way.

Pete Ward suggests that our ecclesial practice cannot simply be applied from an ideal vision of church and that "speech about the Church does not take the form of a 'blueprint' rather it is itself crucially influenced by and located in the lived." Drawing on a notion from Rowan Williams that the theologian always starts "in the middle of things" Ward then goes onto say that "theology of all kinds, and particularly theologies of the Church, arise from the 'middle.'"[1] This accurately describes what I had earlier experienced, that in beginning a new pastorate I had started in the middle of different things, in which this particular lived experience shaped both the way church was understood and practiced.

The Baptist Union has understood the process of initial ministerial formation (what is often described as IME—initial ministerial education by ecumenical partners) to be, normally, a six-year process: three years of more intense engagement with a college course followed by ordination and then a further three years of a comparatively light touch process of ongoing learning and study supervised by a College, as, in the language of the Baptist Union, Newly Accredited Ministers. In recent years one of the required elements of this further three-year period has been to engage in a Mission Audit of some description.

As we have noted earlier, one of the recent trends in ministerial formation is for more "Ministers-in-Training" (Formation) to stay in their placement churches after ordination, and also for more "Ministers-in-Training" to begin their college course staying in their sending churches. For some, engaging in a new context is brought forward to the start of their college course and for others this is delayed until some years later, and this is leading to a rethink of the Mission Audit requirement. Most ministers will at some time have the experience of starting in a new context; but even for those who stay in the same context, this context will itself change, it will in time be a different lived experience and so require fresh eyes.

Such a Mission Audit is located in the broader realm of congregational studies and is one expression of the rise in importance of ethnography in the development of ecclesiology, encouraged by the turn to practice here too; it is part of what Nicholas Healy refers to as the "turn to the concrete."[2]

---

1. Ward, "Blueprint Ecclesiology and the Lived," 89, drawing on Williams, *On Christian Theology*, xii.

2. See Healy, "Practices and the New Ecclesiology," 287–308.

Congregational studies as a description of a discrete area of studies has declined in the UK over recent years, although it is still more used in a US context, as have more general tools to allow congregations to undertake such an audit. But there has been a development in ethnographical studies,[3] and academic empirical research into congregational life has continued in doctoral studies.[4] But there remains a real need for resources to help congregations to be able to think carefully about their context in a way that is not limited either to academic writings or by consultant fees.[5]

This Mission Audit seeks to draw on both qualitative and quantitative data to combine with the theological tradition as the basis for reflection on ongoing practice. At its heart it is a process of double and careful listening, of engaging in hospitality as host and guest, paying attention both to the unique and particular context and also to the breadth of the theological tradition, and it is this double engagement that is always challenging about the reflection process in practice. Its challenging nature means that it is not always done well, but also why this practice of reflection is a fundamental part of the process of ministerial formation. The reason it is not always done well is that there are a number of temptations that might either short-circuit the reflection process or lead it down cul-de-sacs.

First, there is the temptation to assume too great a knowledge and awareness of the context already; in other words the genuine "lived" experience of that context is not taken seriously enough and so the response is not genuinely creative. If a key aspect of the response of ministry is to do what the context demands, then the reality of the lived context needs to be known. Even those who have lived in a local area for some time will probably only have heard a limited range of "voices" from within the context, voices filtered by an individual's own relationships and self-understanding. The challenge which may seem more obvious in a new context, but may be as important in an existing one, is to recognize where there are personal and corporate "blind spots" so that the fraction that is seen is not assumed to be the whole. This, of course, is not to suggest that an exercise like a Mission Audit will simply and straightforwardly reveal the whole, but it

---

3. The ecclesiology and ethnography network is perhaps the best example of this, https://www.ecclesiologyandethnography.net.

4. See, for example, the Ashgate series on explorations in practical, pastoral and empirical theology.

5. The Baptist Union's Re:focus material is one example of material that is still available, https://www.baptist.org.uk/Groups/220682/re_focus.aspx.

will offer a greater insight into a context that may challenge existing presuppositions and assumptions

Second, there is the temptation for a much more limited engagement with the theological tradition, one of the challenges in all *theological* reflection, and thus the response is not appropriately structured, that is it does not draw significantly enough on the underlying tradition. If one response in a new context is to do what ministers always do, a deep and rich understanding of ministry is here brought alongside the challenges of the new context. There will be some responses to issues that may be apparent or emerge through a process of Mission Audit that will be based on instinct and experience. This is not to suggest that these responses are not theological, because for all of us instinct and experience have already been shaped theologically as well as contextually; but they may be limited in their theological breadth and scope. One of the challenges for good theological reflection is to broaden its engagement with a theology of mission, or ecclesiology or the doctrine of God, and to avoid the temptation to, too quickly, take the off the shelf resource that has emerged from a very different lived experience.

To enable a local church to deepen its theological engagement seems to me to be a particular responsibility of those called to be ministers, and is part of the very nature of ministry itself, which is less about being visionary leaders and more being theologians-in-residence in a congregation, offering the structured resources of the tradition to enable the whole congregation to engage in a cooperative piece of reflective practice.

Third, there is the temptation for an over-optimistic expectation. Helen Cameron in a piece of research into tools for use in church and community audits, refers to "the over-optimistic models of managerialism" that emerge from the secular organizational change literature and concludes that in fact little is known about how congregations change.[6] While there has been more research in recent years on the way congregations change and develop, this remains an important note of caution. Of course God can work in significant ways and while stories of significant "success" from a minority of churches can inspire they can also demoralize; and what can best be described as "success" is itself of course theologically loaded language that needs careful exploration. Goodliff rightly points to the danger

---

6. Cameron, "Church Community and Change."

of a "frenzy of activity" that is "obsessed with numbers" as the British churches' response to the pressures of Late-capitalism and secularization.[7]

So, what do I do at the beginning? I engage in a careful, collaborative and structured process of double listening, to the context and to the tradition, so that the active dialogue between the structured and the creative might enable a faithful response to this context and situation.

COLLABORATIVE

If ministry is to be truly collaborative, following what I have argued is a dialectical approach and understanding, then this demands a strongly relational approach both within and beyond the church. If I think back to the beginnings of my first ministry then those early weeks were shaped by two significant activities: visiting the church members and planning for our gathered worship. It was a fairly small congregation and so perhaps the task was less daunting, but I took the membership list which was set out in alphabetical order and began working my way down it, visiting everyone on the list. This was an instructive process, for I learnt much by a careful listening to the members of the congregation, but it was also one that set a pattern for the following years.

Reflecting on the practice of ministry these seem to be two areas that would have been at the heart of a structured approach, for visiting and sharing in leading the congregation in worship would have been central parts of the tradition, which had clearly traditioned me both before and through ministerial formation to do the same; to visit and oversee worship is to do what ministers have always done. In some practices of ministry now these aspects feature much less significantly, with these two areas being the two most commonly delegated out to others, to a pastoral care team and a music group. This delegation seems to me to be to the detriment of the ministry that can then be exercised in the church. This delegated approach, of course, is not the same as taking a collaborative approach in which pastoral care, leading worship and preaching is the shared responsibility among a wider group in which the minister, or ministers, play a central role.

But these choices about engaging in particular activities will both reveal and be shaped by an underlying theology, and in particular whether the minister will be influenced by what I have named as the "leadership" or "ministry" paradigms. Goodliff goes even further and suggests that "the

7. Goodliff, *Shaped for Service*, 230.

absence of pastoral visitation, or leadership and responsibility for public worship" is not in fact "a valid option for able ministry."[8] For a minister to offer pastoral care at moments of crisis is important, but for this to be the limit of pastoral care turns ministry into a service provision, where the direction of travel of any pastoral conversation is one way. This is pastoral care in the "leadership" paradigm. When a minister sits, talks with, and listens to their congregation it is a truly collaborative act; collaboration in the "ministry" paradigm is more than a shared approach to leadership but enables whom I am and what I do as a minister to happen in a deep partnership with others.

If, as I have argued, the practice of ministry must be understood beginning with and arising from participation in the loving and self-giving relationships of the Triune God, then equally important is the role of minister as worship-leader. This is the supreme moment when the gathered congregation are drawn again into those movements of divine grace. For a minister to preach is important, for the idea of ministry as bearing the Word is a central part of the structuring tradition, but much preaching is very didactic and so direction of travel is again one way, part of the "leadership" paradigm. Preaching easily descends into moral and practical exhortation for the development of the church. To lead worship well is not about musicality but about a theological and pastoral sensitivity to patterns of divine grace, in which minister and members are drawn together; such worship is, of course, itself deeply pastoral.

Collaboration is something that goes beyond the local congregation, for the minister who is shaped by this collaborative approach will be instinctively looking for partners with whom to work, whether within the same denomination or ecumenically. This inevitably requires engaging in the sometimes encouraging and sometimes challenging world of relationships with other ministers and ministers' meetings. I still recall fondly a regular ministers' meeting in my first pastorate where four of us from churches very close together, who were in some ways as different as could be, met both for mutual support and to plan shared ministry and mission—helped it has to be said by the insistence from one of the other ministers that he host us with a splendid cooked breakfast each gathering. My overall experience, as I know has been the case for many others, is, however, rather mixed, with ministers' meetings sometime becoming places for the

---

8. Goodliff, *Shaped for Service*, 181.

boosting of egos rather than another opportunity in vulnerability and humility to be drawn into God's divine grace.

What do I do at the beginning? I collaborate with the congregation—and never "my congregation" in any kind of possessive way—in worship and in life, sharing in and overseeing the gathered worship of the church, as together we experience God's grace, and listening to the congregation as I visit them.

HOSPITABLE

If ministry is to be hospitable then it requires the careful navigation of being both host and guest, and developing the kind of vulnerability required for both roles to be practiced well. One of the things that surprised me in my first pastorate—and as someone still young who had prepared for ministry in a more traditional college-based pathway such pastoral ministry was still very new—was the very mixed experience and expectation of hospitality within the church. As someone who had also grown up in a manse this was something that had always been part of life, and so in a new pastorate I was keen to practice and experience hospitality in a very practical way. While this was clearly also the expectation of some, for others to offer hospitality or to think you might be invited by someone was not at all a routine part of their cultural experience. It meant learning by experience and mistakes—sometimes the hospitality we offered was too formal or too much—and trying gently to develop an evolving culture in the church. How could we all learn to be hosts and guests in this particular context?

Such hospitality of course goes beyond the congregation itself. I recall quite early on in my first ministry the head teacher of the local junior school phoned the church, from my perspective at least somewhat out of the blue, asking for me. The school were looking for more governors and it is not an uncommon role for ministers to take. Soon after that I was being welcomed into the school for the first time and offered a tour, which was the first step in a relationship that continued and developed through all my ministry in that church. What I very soon discovered was that listening carefully to what was being said in the school environment gave a perspective on the local context that I had simply not heard through quite deep conversations within the church; at primary school many of the daily struggles that shaped the lives of our neighbors were noticed and heard. Over the next few years I would visit the school often, sometimes to take assemblies and classes, sometimes to be involved in interviews or attend special events, but even later as chair of governors I always went as the guest, always with something to receive and take away.

Stuart Murray, among others, argues strongly that we are already living in the world of post-Christendom and this means that the church is necessarily moving back to the margins of society where she existed before the Constantinian settlement.[9] Murray welcomes such a move and the subsequent decentering of the church. This, I think, requires the church to think of hospitality more in terms of being the guest than the host. Slightly ironically, it may have been the perceived status of a church minister, back in the early 1990s, that prompted the initial invitation from the school head teacher, but it led to a relationship in which I willingly embraced the role of guest. For me at that time neither was it an invitation I looked for but one simply I received. Yet practicing hospitality means willingly embracing this role of guest both from where such invitations come and also in the positive initiatives we take and seems to me a vital role for contemporary ministry as part of our engagement in God's mission.

What do I do at the beginning? I look for appropriate opportunities to be both host and guest, willing for the church to be decentered in both scenarios, embracing the vulnerability that is central to true hospitality.

CONCLUSION

Having been a local church minister and a college tutor, I am committed both to this dialectical understanding of the practice of ministry and to an understanding of the practice of preparation as best expressed by the language of formation. Formation will involve theological education in which the structuring tradition is encountered and critiqued; it will involve the development of appropriate skills in areas such as preaching and leading worship, engaging in mission, and offering pastoral care; but all these will come together in the development of a *habitus*, one that is both corporately shaped and open to change. The ongoing practice of ministry will, therefore, be this constant negotiation between the givenness of ministry that is both structured *and* cooperative, and the creative performance through the individual minister's agency and actions. And the ongoing practice of ministry will continue to shape and develop an individual's *habitus*, through ongoing practice.

9. Murray, *Post-Christendom* and *A Vast Minority*.

Towards a Renewed Practice of Ministry

What do I do first and why does this matter? It matters because it sets up patterns which both express and develop a ministerial *habitus*; it matters because it both expresses and develops my understanding of ministry; it matters because it is fundamental to the way I, as a minister, engage with the structuring tradition and creatively respond to the unique context with a unique group of people. It matters because it is how I participate in the grace of the Triune God.

Appendix 1
Core Questions in Empirical Interviews

IN TERMS OF THE overall aims of the College in respect to preparing men and women for Baptist ministry: clearly those who leave your College to be ordained will be different to each other in many ways, but what words would you use to describe that which you hope will be true of all those who are prepared for ministry here?

- Where necessary can you explain these words further, and what you mean by them?
- What leads you to these words?
- Is this a view shared by all the teaching staff here?

What do you understand by describing a Baptist minister as a 'professional'?

- Is it language that you use?
- Do the BUGB core competencies connect here for you, and if so how?

Is a particular theological understanding of ordination taught or encouraged by the College?

- If a variety of views are presented, how wide is the variety?
- Are they given equal weight?

Appendix 1

There is much talk within church and society of the concept of leadership:

- Is a particular theological understanding of 'leadership' taught or encouraged by the College?
- If a variety of views are presented, how wide is this variety
- Are they given equal weight?
- What 'leadership style' best describes what students may see modelled at the College?

In terms of the self-understanding of the College's work: the various documents which you have and which you have to work with, eg Inspection requests, use a number of different words, in particular: formation, training and education.

- What do you understand by these words?
- What are their relationships to each other?
- Do you have a preference for describing your work and the work of the College in preparing men and women to be Baptist ministers?

Bibliography

ALONGSIDE ALL THE ITEMS normally on a bibliography, listed below, there have been two additional sources of information drawn on. First, there were a significant number of documents supplied to me by the nine other theological institutions, some of which were in the public domain but many were not; in addition there were transcripts I made of all the interviews. Generally I have footnoted the documents but not the interviews, but I have not listed all the documents in the bibliography, as mostly they are not accessible.

Second, there are private papers in the archive of the Angus Library at Regent's Park College, Oxford, to which I have had access, but which again are not in the public domain. I have given references to these documents but list them immediately below rather than in the main bibliography. These are:

Papers of Revd Dr Michael Taylor former Principal of Northern Baptist College and in particular:

Taylor, Michael. "The Free Churches Selection and Training."
———. "Ministerial Training at Northern College."
———. "The Theology of Spiritual Formation." Lectures at 14th Atlantic Seminar in Theological Education.
———. "West Midlands Area Ministers Conference, Essays in Ministry."

Papers of Revd Dr David Russell former General Secretary of the Baptist Union and in particular:

Russell, David. "The College and its Future." An address given on the retirement of L. G. Champion and the inauguration of W. M. S. West as President of Bristol Baptist College, 1971.
———. "Practical Training for the Ministry in Britain."
———. "Theological Education in the Free Church Tradition: The British Situation."

Bibliography

Minutes of the Regent's Park College Council and Executive.

Minutes of The Baptist Colleges' Staffs' Conference.

Adair, John. *The Leadership of Jesus and its Legacy Today*. Norwich: Canterbury, 2001.
Adair, John and John Nelson, eds. *Creative Church Leadership*. Norwich: Canterbury, 2004.
Allen, Bill. "Pathways to Leadership: The Provision of Education for Training for Leadership in the Ordained Ministry." PhD diss., University of Wales, 1999.
———. "Pathways to Leadership." In *Creative Church Leadership* edited by John Adair and John Nelson, 32–47. Norwich: Canterbury, 2004.
Astley, Jeff, ed. *Learning in the Way: Research and Reflection on Adult Christian Education*. Leominster: Gracewing, 2000.
———. *The Philosophy of Christian Religious Education*. Birmingham, AL: Religious Education, 1994.
———, Leslie Francis and Colin Crowder. *Theological Perspectives on Christian Formation: A Reader on Theology and Christian Education*. Leominster: Gracewing, 1996.
Atkinson, Paul and Amanda Jane Coffey. "Analyzing Documentary Realities." In *Qualitative Research: Theory Method and Practice* edited by David Silverman, 56–75. London: Sage, 2004.
Bacon, Fred. *Being a Christian Leader*. Didcot: BUGB, 1990.
Ballard, Paul. "The Emergence of Pastoral Studies." In *Foundations of Pastoral Studies and Practical Theology* edited by Paul Ballard, 9–17. Cardiff: University College, 1986.
———. "Moving on from Here." In *Foundations of Pastoral Studies and Practical Theology* edited by Paul Ballard, 146–50. Cardiff: University College, 1986.
———. *Practical Theology: Proliferation and Performance*. Cardiff: Religious and Theological Studies, Cardiff University, 2001.
Ballard, Paul and John Pritchard. *Practical Theology in Action*. London: SPCK, 2006.
Banks, Robert. *Revisioning Theological Education*. Grand Rapids, MI: Eerdmans, 1999.
——— and Bernice M. Ledbetter. *Reviewing Leadership: A Christian Evaluation of Current Approaches*. Grand Rapids, MI: Baker Academic, 2004.
Baptist Union of Great Britain. *The Baptist Doctrine of the Church (A Statement Approved by the Council of the Baptist Union of Great Britain and Ireland)*. 1948.
———. *Covenant 21*. 1999.
———. *The Doctrine of Ministry*. 1961.
———. *Five Core Values for a Gospel People*. 1999.
———. *Forms of Ministry Among Baptists: Towards an Understanding of Spiritual Leadership* (A discussion document by the Doctrine and Worship Committee). 1994.
———. "Forms of Ministry—Some Reflections" (Christopher J. Ellis for the Doctrine and Worship Committee). 1996.
———. *Ignite: Final Report*. 2015.
———. *The Meaning and Practice of Ordination Among Baptists*. 1957.
———. *Ministerial Recognition Rules*. 2019.
———. *Ministry Tomorrow (The Report of the Commission on the Ministry)*. 1969.
———. "Ministry: Towards a Consensus" (Nigel G. Wright for the Doctrine and Worship Committee). 2000.

Bibliography

———. "The Nature of Ministry and Ordination" (Brian Haymes for the Doctrine and Worship Committee). 1993.

———. "New Thoughts on Old Ministries" (Nigel G. Wright for the Doctrine and Worship Committee). 1993.

———. *One Vision: Seven Colleges*. Undated.

———. *Partners Together: The Colleges and the Rest of the Baptist Union of Great Britain—Report of the Union/Colleges Partnership Task Group*. 1998.

———. *Patterns of Ministry among Baptists: A Review of the 'Register of Covenanted Persons Accredited for Ministry*. 2010.

———. *Recommendations for the Recognition of Youth Specialists*. 1994.

———. *Reply to the Lambeth Appeal*. 1926.

———. *Reply to the Report of the World Conference on Faith and Order*. 1930.

———. *Reply to the WCC Faith and Order Paper Baptism, Eucharist and Ministry*. 1986.

———. *Review of Selection, Formation, Continuing Ministerial Development and Funding for Baptist Ministry*. 2014.

———. *Statement on Accreditation of Baptist Ministers*. 1953.

———. *Statement of BU Council on the Report of the Second World Conference of Faith and Order*. 1939.

———. *Statement of Ministry adopted by Annual Assembly*. 1923.

———. "Towards a New List: Proposals for the Restructuring of the List of Accredited Ministers of the Baptist Union of Great Britain" (Christopher J. Ellis and Malcolm Goodspeed for Doctrine and Worship Committee). 1997.

———. *Transforming Superintendency: TheRreport of the General Superintendency Review Group Presented to the BUGB Council*. 1996.

Barth, Karl, *Church Dogmatics* II/2. Edinburgh: T&T Clark, 1957.

Bass, Dorothy C., ed. *Practicing Faith: A Way of Life for a Searching People*. San Francisco, CA: Jossey-Bass, 1997.

———, and Craig Dykstra, eds. *For Life Abundant: Practical Theology, Theological Education and Christian Ministry*. Grand Rapids, MI: Eerdmans, 2008.

Beasley-Murray, Paul, ed. *Anyone for Ordination?* Tunbridge Wells: Marc, 1993.

———. *A Call to Excellence*. London: Hodder and Stoughton, 1995.

———. *Dynamic Leadership*. Eastbourne: Marc, 1991.

———. "Let's not be Afraid to Learn Lessons from New Zealand." *Ministry Today* 53 (2011) downloaded from website.

———. *Living Out the Call*. Self-published e-book in four volumes, 2015.

———. Review of *A New Kind of Baptist Church: Reframing Congregational Government for the 21st Century* by Brian Winslade. *Baptist Times*, February 18th 2011.

Bebbington, David. "An Historical Overview of Leadership in a Scottish Baptist Context." In *Transforming Leadership: Essays Exploring Leadership in a Baptist Context* edited by Andrew Rollinson, 15–20. Baptist Union of Scotland website download.

Bell, Judith. *Doing Your Research Project: A Guide for First-time Researchers in Education, Health and Social Science*. Maidenhead: Open University Press, 2010.

———, and Clive Opie. *Learning from Research*. Buckingham: Open University Press, 2002.

Bergmann, Jonathan and Aaron Sams. *Flip Your Classroom: Reach Every Student in Every Class Every Day*. Eugene, OR: ISTE, 2012.

Blyth, Myra and Christopher Ellis. *Gathering for Worship*. Norwich: Canterbury, 2005.

Boff, Leonardo. *Trinity and Society*. London: Burns and Oates, 1988.

Bibliography

Bosch, David. *Transforming Mission: Paradigm Shifts in the Theology of Mission.* Maryknoll, NY: Orbis, 1991.

Bourdieu, Pierre. *The Logic of Practice.* Cambridge: Polity, 1990.

Bretherton, Luke. *Hospitality as Holiness, Christian Witness Amid Moral Diversity.* Aldershot: Ashgate, 2006.

Brooks, T. M., "Spirituality and its Impact on Theological Education." *Ministerial Formation* 80 (1997) 39–41.

Brown, Jeannine and Carla M. Dahl and Wyndy Corbin Reuschling. *Becoming Whole and Holy: An Integrative Conversation about Christian Formation.* Grand Rapids, MI: Baker Academic, 2011.

Brydon-Miller, Mary and Davydd Greenwood and Patricia Maguire. "Why Action Research?" *Action Research* 1.1 (2003) 9–28.

Bryman, Alan. *Social Research Methods.* Oxford: Oxford University Press, 2012.

Burnard, Clive. "Transformational Servant Leadership as Exemplified in the Ministry of the Reverend Doctor David R. Coffey." DMin diss., University of Wales, 2014.

Buschart W. David and Kent D. Eliers, *Theology as Retrieval: Receiving the Past, Renewing the Church.* Downers Grove, IL: IVP, 2015.

Cadbury, Henry. *The Peril of Modernising Jesus.* London: SPCK, 1962.

Call, Carolyne. "The Rough Trail to Authentic Pedagogy: Incorporating Hospitality, Fellowship and Testimony into the Classroom." In *Teaching Christian Practices: Reshaping Faith and Learning,* edited by David I. Smith and James K. A. Smith, 61–79. Grand Rapids MI: Eerdmans, 2011.

Cameron, Helen. "Church Community and Change: Methods of Congregational Review and the Reality of Congregation-Community Relationship." A paper presented to BIAPT, Cardiff, 2003.

——— and Philip Richter and Douglas Davies, eds. *Studying Local Churches.* London: SCM, 2005.

———, Deborah Bhatti, Catherine Duce, James Sweeney and Clare Watkins. *Talking About God in Practice: Theological Action Research and Practical Theology.* London: SCM, 2010.

——— and Catherine Duce. *Researching Practice in Ministry and Mission.* London: SCM, 2013.

Campbell, Alastair. *The Elders: Seniority Within Earliest Christianity.* Edinburgh: T&T Clark, 1994.

Certuk, Virginia. S. *What to Expect in Seminary: Theological Education as Spiritual Formation.* Nashville TN: Abingdon Press, 1998.

Church of England. *Beginning Public Ministry: Guidelines for Ministerial Formation and Personal Development for the First Four Years After Ordination.* ABM, 1998.

———. *Common Awards: Education for Ministry and Mission: Direction of Travel: Report of the First Phase of Consultation with Theological Educators.* Ministry Division, 2012.

———. *Education for the Church's Ministry.* ACCM, 1987.

———. *Educating Ministers of Character: Approaching the Curricula for Common Awards.* Ministry Division, 2012.

———. *Formation for Ministry Within a Learning Church.* Archbishops' Council, 2003.

———. *Guidelines for the Professional Conduct of the Clergy.* Archbishops' Council, 2003.

———. *Integration and Assessment: The Report of an ABM Working Party on Educational Practice.* ABM, 1992.

Bibliography

———. *The Mission and Ministry of the Whole Church: Biblical, Theological and Contemporary Perspectives*. FOAG, 2007.
———. *Mission and Ministry. The Churches' Validation Framework for Theological Education*. ABM, 1999.
———. *Mission and Ministry. The Churches' Validation Framework for Theological Education* 2nd edition. ABM, 2003.
———. *Preface to the Common Awards in Theology, Ministry and Mission*. Ministry Division, 2012.
———. *Prolegomena to the Common Awards in Theology, Ministry and Mission*. Ministry Division, 2012.
———. *Residence—an Education*. ACCM, 1990.
———. *Shaping the Future: New Patterns of Training for Lay and Ordained*. Archbishops' Council, 2006.
———. *The Structure and Funding of Ordination Training: The Interim Report*. Archbishops' Council, 2002.
———. *Theological Education for Christian Ministry and Mission: Pedagogical Foundations*. Ministry Division, 2012.
———. *Theology in Practice*. ACCM, 1988.
Clark, Neville. "A Perspective on Christian Ministry." *Baptist Quarterly* 39.5 (2002) 222–23.
Clarke, Andrew D. *A Pauline Theology of Church Leadership*. Edinburgh: T&T Clark, 2008.
Clarke, Anthony. *A Cry in the Darkness: The Forsakenness of Jesus in Scripture, Theology and Experience*. Macon, GA: Smyth and Helwys, 2002.
———. "How Did We End Up Here? Theological Education as Ministerial Formation in the British Baptist Colleges." *Baptist Quarterly* 46:2 (2015) 69–97
———. 'A Trinitarian Theology of Ministerial Formation' in *For the Sake of the Church* edited by Anthony Clarke, 126–44. Oxford: Regent's Park College, 2014.
———and Paul Fiddes, *Dissenting Spirit: A History of Regent's Park College 1752–2017*. Oxford: Regent's Park College, 2017.
Coghlan, David and Teresa Brannick. *Doing Action Research in Your Own Organisation*. London: Sage, 2014.
Cohen, Louis, and Lawrence Manion and Keith Morrison. *Research Methods in Education*. London: Routledge, 2007.
Collins, John. *Diakonia: Re-interpreting the Ancient Sources*. Oxford: Oxford University Press, 1990.
Colwell, John E. *Promise and Presence: An Exploration of Sacramental Theology*. Milton Keynes: Paternoster, 2005.
———. "The Sacramental Nature of Ordination: An Attempt to Re-engage a Catholic Understanding and Practice." In *Baptist Sacramentalism* edited by Anthony Cross and Philip E. Thompson, 228–46. Carlisle: Paternoster, 2003.
Cooper, R. E., *From Stepney to St Giles': The Story of Regent's Park College 1810–960*. London: Carey Kingsgate, 1960.
Cooperrider, David L. and Suresh Srivasta. "Appreciative Inquiry in Organisational Life." *Research in Organisational Change and Development* 1 (1987) 129–69.
Creswell, John W. *Qualitative Inquiry and Research Design: Choosing from Five Traditions*. London: Sage, 1998.
———. *Research Design: Qualitative and Quantitative Approaches*. London: Sage, 1994.
Croft, Steven. *Ministry in Three Dimensions: Ordination and Leadership in the Local Church*. London: DLT, 2008.

Bibliography

——— and Roger Walton. *Learning for Ministry: Making the Most of Study and Training*. London: Church House Publishing, 2005.

Cunningham, David. *These Three are One: The Practice of Trinitarian Theology*. Oxford: Blackwell, 1998.

Dakin, Arthur *The Baptist View of the Church and Ministry*. London: BU Publication Department, 1944.

Dykstra, Craig R. *Growing in the Life of Faith: Education and Christian Practices*. Louisville, KY: Geneva, 1999.

———. *Vision and Character*. Mahwah, NJ: Paulist, 1981.

———. "The Pastoral Imagination." *Initiatives in Religion (A Newsletter of Lilly Endowment Inc* 9 (1) (2001) 1–2 and 15.

——— and Dorothy C. Bass. "A Theological Understanding of Christian Practices." In *Practicing Theology: Beliefs and Practices in Christian Life* edited by Miroslav Volf and Dorothy Bass, 13–32. Grand Rapids, MI: Eerdmans, 2002.

Edwards Jr, Tiden. "Spiritual Formation in Theological Schools: Ferment and Change." *Theological Education* 17 (1980) 7–52.

Eisner, Elliot W. *The Educational Imagination: On the Design and Evaluation of School Programs*. New York: Macmillan, 1985.

Ellis, Christopher J. "Being a Minister: Spirituality and the Pastor." In *Challenging to Change: Dialogues with a Radical Baptist Theologian. Essays presented to Dr Nigel G Wright on his Sixtieth Birthday* edited by Pieter J. Lalleman, 55–70. London: Spurgeon's College, 2009.

Ellis, Robert. "'The Leadership of Some . . .' Baptist Ministers as Leaders?" In *Challenging to Change: Dialogues with a Radical Baptist Theologian. Essays presented to Dr Nigel G Wright on his Sixtieth Birthday* edited by Pieter J. Lalleman, 71–86. London: Spurgeon's College, 2009.

Farley, Edward. "The Curricular Pattern and its Rationale as an Issue in the Reform of North American Theological Education." *Ministerial Formation* 14 (April 1981) 8–11.

———. *Theologia: The Fragmentation and Unity of Theological Education*. Philadelphia, PA: Augsburg Fortress, 1983.

———. *Practicing Gospel*. London: Westminster John Knox, 2003.

Fiddes, Paul S. "The Body as Site of Continuity and Change." in *New Topics in Feminist Philosophy of Religion: Contestations and Transcendence Incarnate* edited by Pamela Sue Anderson, 26–78. London: Springer, 2010.

———. "Christianity, Culture and Education: A Baptist Perspective." In *The Scholarly Vocation and the Baptist Academy* edited by Roger Ward and David P. Gushee, 1–25. Macon, Georgia, Mercer University, 2008.

———. *The Creative Suffering of God*. Oxford: Clarendon: 1988.

———, ed. *Doing Theology in a Baptist Way*. Oxford: Whitley, 2000.

———. *A Leading Question: The Structure and Authority of Leadership in the Local Church*. London: Baptist Union of Great Britain, 1981.

———. *Participating in God: A Pastoral Doctrine of the Trinity*. London: DLT, 2000.

———. *Tracks and Traces: Baptist Identity in Church and Theology*. Carlisle: Paternoster, 2003.

Flick, Uew. *An Introduction to Qualitative Research*. London: Sage, 2009.

Flinders, David J., Nel Noddings and Stephen J. Thornton. "The Null Curriculum: Its Theoretical Basis and Practical Implications." *Curriculum Inquiry* 16:1 (Spring 1986) 33–42.

Bibliography

Forrester, Duncan. *Truthful Action: Explorations in Practical Theology.* Edinburgh: T&T Clark, 2000.

Foster, Charles R., Lisa Dahill, Larry Goleman and Barbara Wang Tolentino. *Educating Clergy: Teaching Practices and Pastoral Imagination.* San Francisco, CA: Jossey-Bass, 2006.

Fox, Mark, Peter Martin and Gill Green. *Doing Practitioner Research.* London: Sage, 2013.

Freire, Paulo. *Pedagogy of the Oppressed.* New York: Herder and Herder, 1970.

Fuller, Michael and Kenneth Fleming. "Bridging the Gap: A Curriculum Uniting Competencies and Theological Disciplines." JATE 2.2 (2005) 163–78.

Garland, Gareth. "Anyone Can? An Exploration of Ordained Baptist Ministry as one of Word and Sacrament." MTh thesis, University of Oxford, 2014.

Gilmore, Alec, ed. *The Pattern of Church: A Baptist View.* London: Lutterworth, 1963.

Goodliff, Paul W. *Ministry, Sacrament and Representation: Ministry and Ordination in Contemporary Baptist Theology and the Rise of Sacramentalism.* Oxford: Regent's Park College, 2010.

———. *Shaped for Service: Ministerial Formation and Virtue Ethics.* Eugene, OR: Pickwick, 2017.

Green, Laurie. *Let's Do Theology.* London: Continuum, 1990.

Graham, Elaine. *Transforming Practice: Pastoral Theology in an Age of Uncertainty,* Eugene, OR: Wipf and Stock, 2002.

———, Heather Walton and Frances Ward. *Theological Reflection: Methods.* London: SCM, 2005.

———, Heather Walton and Frances Ward. *Theological Reflection: Sources.* London: SCM, 2007.

Greenleaf, Robert. *Servant Leadership: A Journey into the Nature of Legitimate Power and Greatness.* Mahwah, NJ: Paulist, 2002.

Greenslade, Philip. *Leadership: Reflections on Biblical Leadership.* London: Marshall, Morgan and Scott, 1984.

Greenwood, Robin. *Transforming Priesthood: A New Theology of Mission and Ministry.* London: SPCK, 1994.

Grundy, Malcolm. *What's New in Church Leadership? Creative Responses to the Changing Pattern of Church Life.* London: Canterbury Press, 2007.

Gummesson, Evert. *Qualitative Methods in Management Research.* London: Sage, 2000.

Hadsell, John S. "Faith's Understanding: A Review of Farley's *Theologia.*" *Ministerial Formation* 26 (May 1984) 3–9.

Hale, Ted. "Down with Leaders." *The Baptist Ministers' Journal* 276 (October 2001) 7–11.

Hall, Douglas J. "Theological Education as Character Formation." *Theological Education* 24 (1988) 153–79.

Haymes, Brian, Ruth Gouldbourne and Anthony Cross. *On Being the Church: Revisioning Baptist Identity.* Milton Keynes: Paternoster, 2008.

Healy, Nicholas. "Practices and the New Ecclesiology: Misplaced Concreteness?" *International Journal of Systematic Theology* 5:3 (November 2003) 287–308.

Herbert, George. *The Country Parson and Selected Poems.* London: SCM, 1956.

Higton, Mike. *A Theology of Higher Education.* Oxford: Oxford University Press, 2012.

———. *Vulnerable Learning: Thinking Theologically about Higher Education.* Cambridge: Grove, 2006.

Holmes, Stephen R. "A Brief Theological Account of Ministerial Employment." *Baptist Ministers' Journal* 282 (April 2003) 21–24.

Bibliography

———. "Towards a Baptist theology of Ordained Theology." In *Baptist Sacramentalism* edited by Anthony R. Cross and Philip E. Thompson, 228–46. Carlisle: Paternoster, 2003.

———. *Baptist Theology*. London: T&T Clark, 2012.

Housego, John. "Being a Minister." In *Bible, History and Ministry: Essays for L G Champion on his Ninetieth Birthday* edited by Roger Hayden and Brian Haymes, 169–82. Bristol: Bristol Baptist College, 1997.

Hughes, Alfred C. *Preparing for Church Ministry. A Practical Guide to Spiritual Formation*. Denville, NJ: Dimension, 1979.

Hütter, Reinhard. "Hospitality and Truth: The Disclosure of Practices in Worship and Doctrine." In *Practicing Theology: Beliefs and Practices in Christian Life* edited by Miroslav Volf and Dorothy C. Bass, 206–27. Grand Rapids, MI: Eerdmans, 2002.

Hybels, Bill. *Courageous Leadership*. Grand Rapids, MI: Zondervan, 2002.

Jarvis, Peter. *Adult Education and Lifelong Learning: Theory and Practice*. London: Routledge Farmer, 2004.

Jones, L. Gregory and Stephanie Paulsell, eds. *The Scope of our Art: The Vocation of the Theological Teacher*. Grand Rapids, MI: Eerdmans, 2002.

Kelsey, David H. *Between Athens and Berlin: The Theological Education Debate*. Grand Rapids, MI: Eerdmans, 1993.

Knott, Kim. "Insider / outsider Perspectives." In *The Routledge Companion to the Study of Religion* edited by John R. Hinnells, 243–58. Abingdon: Routledge, 2010.

Lumpkin, William L. *Baptist Confessions of Faith*. Valley Forge, PA: Judson, 1959.

MacIntyre, Alasdair. *After Virtue: A Study in Moral Theology*. London: Duckworth, 1985.

Marmon, Ellen L. "Teaching as Hospitality." *Asbury Theological Journal* 63 no. 2 (Fall 2008) 33–39.

Maxwell, Joseph A. *A Critical Approach for Qualitative Research*. London: Sage, 2012.

Mayes, Andrew D. *Spirituality in Ministerial Formation*. Cardiff: University of Wales Press, 2009.

Methodist Ministerial Training Policy Working Group, *The Making of Ministry*. Peterborough: Methodist Publishing House, 1996.

Ministries Committee of Methodist Church. *The Fruitful Field: A Consultation Document*. 2011.

Moltmann, Jürgen. *The Crucified God: The Cross of Christ as the Foundation and Criticism of Christian Theology*. London: SCM, 1974.

———. *The Trinity and the Kingdom of God*. London: SCM, 1981.

Moon, Norman. *Education for Ministry*. Bristol: Bristol Baptist College, 1979.

Moschella, Mary Clark. "Ethnography." In *The Wiley Blackwell Companion to Practical Theology* edited by Bonnie J. Miller-McLemore, 224–33. Chichester: Wiley and Sons, 2014.

Murray, Stuart. *Post-Christendom: Church and Mission in a Strange New World*. Carlisle: Paternoster, 2004.

———. *A Vast Minority: Church and Mission in a Plural Culture*. Milton Keynes: Paternoster, 2015.

Myers, Ched. "Between the Seminary, the Sanctuary and the Streets: Reflections on Alternative Theological Education." *Ministerial Formation* (July 2001) 49–52.

———. *Binding the Strong Man: A Political Reading of Mark's Story of Jesus*. Maryknoll, NY: Orbis, 2008.

Bibliography

Neuhaus, Richard John, *Theological Education and Moral Formation*. Grand Rapids, MI: Eerdmans, 1959.

Newbigin, Lesslie. "Theological Education in a World Perspective." *Ministerial Formation* 4 (October 1978) 3–8.

Newman, Elizabeth. "Who's Home Cooking? Hospitality, Christian Identity and Higher Education." *Perspectives in Religious Studies* 26 no 1 (September 1999) 7–16.

Newman, John Henry. *The Idea of a University*. New York: Image Books, 1959.

Nicholls, Mike. "An Evaluation of Church-based Training." *Baptist Ministers' Journal* 234 (April 1991) 9–14.

———. *Lights to the World: A History of Spurgeon's College 1856–1992*. Harpenden: Nuprint, 1994.

———. "Ministry—Mean What You Say." *Baptist Ministers' Journal* 230 (April 1990) 12–14.

———. "Patterns of Ministry." In *A Perspective on Baptist Identity* edited by David Slater, 47–59. Kingsbridge: Mainstream, 1987.

Nicholson, John F. V. *Ministry: A Baptist View*. London: Baptist Publications, 1979.

Nicole, Jacques. "The So-called Classical Model of Theological Education: A Brief History." *Ministerial Formation* 67 (October 1994) 33–34.

Norman, Ralph. "Theological Foundations of Action Research for Learning and Teaching." *Discourse* 8.1 (2011) 114–40.

Nouwen, Henri. *Reaching Out, The Three Movements of the Spiritual Life*. Glasgow: William Collins, 1976.

Pattison, Stephen. *A Critique of Pastoral Care*. London: SCM, 2000.

———. *The Faith of the Managers*. London: Cassell, 1997.

———. "Management and Pastoral Theology." In *The Blackwell Reader in Pastoral and Practical Theology* edited by James Woodward and Stephen Pattison, 283–93. Oxford: Blackwell, 2000

———. "Research, Resources and Threats." In *Foundations of Pastoral Studies and Practical Theology* edited by Paul Ballard, 144–45. Cardiff: University College, 1986.

———. "Some Straw for the Bricks: A Basic Introduction to Theological Reflection." *Context* 99/2 (1989) 2–9.

———, Judith Thompson and John Green. "Theological Reflection for the Real World: Time to Think Again." *British Journal of Theological Education* 13.2 (2003) 119–31.

Payne, Ernest. *The Fellowship of Believers: Baptist Thought and Practice Yesterday and Today*. London: Carey Kingsgate, 1952.

Peterson, Eugene. *The Contemplative Pastor: Returning to the Art of Spiritual Direction*. Grand Rapids, MI: Eerdmans, 1993.

———. *Working the Angles: The Shape of Pastoral Integrity*. Grand Rapids: Eerdmans, 1994.

Pettifer, Brian. "Education and the Knowledge of God: Towards a Model of Theology as a Practical Discipline." In *Foundations of Pastoral Studies and Practical Theology* edited by Paul Ballard, 65–77. Cardiff: University College, 1986.

Pickard, Stephen. *Theological Foundations for Collaborative Ministry*. Farnham: Ashgate, 2009.

Pohl, Christine. *Making Room, Recovering Hospitality as a Christian Tradition*. Grand Rapids, MI: Eerdmans, 1999.

Bibliography

Quality in Formation Panel. *Quality Assurance and Enhancement in Ministerial Education: Inspection, Curriculum Approval, Moderation.* London: Church House Publishing, 2010.

———. *Quality Assurance and Enhancement in Ministerial Formation: A Guide for Inspectors and Training Institutions.* London: Church House Publishing, 2012.

Quicke, Michael. *360-degree Leadership: Preaching to Transform Congregations.* Grand Rapids, MI: Baker, 2006.

Raiser, Konrad. "Fifty years of ecumenical formation: Where are we? Where are we going." *Ecumenical Review* 48 (1996) 440–51.

Reason, Peter and Hilary Bradbury. *Handbook of Action Research: Participative Inquiry and Practice.* London: Sage, 2001.

Randall, Ian M. *English Baptists of the Twentieth Century.* Didcot: Baptist Historical Society, 2005.

Rollinson, Andrew, ed. *Transforming Leadership: Essays Exploring Leadership in a Baptist Context.* Baptist Union of Scotland, downloaded from website.

Sapsezian, Aharon. "Exploring the Nature of Ministerial Formation: An Invitation to Dialogue." *Ministerial Formation* 5 (1979) 20–24.

Schön, Donald A. *Educating the Reflective Practitioner.* London: Jossey-Bass, 1988.

Shaw, Perry. *Transforming Theological Education: A Practical Handbook for Integrative Learning.* Carlisle: Langham Global Library, 2014.

Sheldrake, Philip. *Spirituality and Theology.* London: DLT, 1998.

Shepherd, Peter. *The Making of a northern College.* Manchester: Northern Baptist College, 2004.

Shier-Jones, Angela, ed. *The Making of Ministry.* Peterborough: Epworth, 2008.

Silverman, David. *Interpreting Qualitative Data.* London: Sage, 2006.

———. *Qualitative Research: Theory Method and Practice.* London: Sage, 2004.

Smith, James. K. A. *Desiring the Kingdom: Worship, Worldview and Cultural Formation.* Grand Rapids, MI: Baker Academic, 2009.

Smith, David I. and James K. A. Smith, eds. *Teaching and Christian Practices: Reshaping Faith and Learning.* Grand Rapids, MI: Eerdmans, 2011.

Smyth, John, *Differences of the Churches of the Separation.* In *The Works of John Smyth, Fellow of Christ's College 1594–98.* Cambridge: Cambridge University Press, 1915.

Sparkes, Douglas. *An Accredited Ministry.* Didcot: Baptist Historical Society, 1996.

Swinton, John. "Is theological reflection a technique or a virtue?" BIAPT conference paper, http://www.biapt.org.uk/tr5.shtml.

Swinton John and Harriet Mowatt. *Practical Theology and Qualitative Research.* London: SCM, 2006.

Thomas, Viv. *Future Leader.* Carlisle: Paternoster, 1999.

———. *Paper Boys: A Vision for the Contemporary Church.* Milton Keynes: Paternoster, 2004.

———. *The Spectacular Ordinary Life.* Milton Keynes: Authentic Media, 2008.

Tidball, Derek. *Builders and Fools: Leadership the Bible Way.* Nottingham: IVP, 1999.

———. *Ministry by the Book: New Testament Patterns for Pastoral Leadership.* Nottingham: Apollos, 2008.

Toulmin, Stephen. "Theology in the Context of the University." In *Theological Perspectives on Christian Formation: A Reader on Theology and Christian Education* edited by Jeff Astley, Leslie Francis and Colin Crowder, 393–405. Leominster: Gracewing 1996.

Bibliography

Treier, Daniel J. *Virtue and the Voice of God: Towards Theology as Wisdom.* Grand Rapids, MI: Eerdmans, 2006.
Tucker, Ruth A. *Leadership Reconsidered: Becoming a Person of Influence.* Grand Rapids, MI: Baker, 2008.
Vincent, John. "Theological Education in the 1980s in Britain: Adaption or Alternatives." *Ministerial Formation* 10 (April 1980) 9–13.
Volf, Miroslav. *After Our Likeness: The Church in the Image of the Trinity.* Grand Rapids, MI: Eerdmans, 1998.
———. "The Trinity is our Social Program: The Doctrine of the Trinity and the Shape of Social Engagement." *Modern Theology* 14 (1998) 403–23.
———. "We are the Church: New Congregationalism—A Protestant Response." *Concilium* (1996) 347–44.
Volf, Miroslav and Michael Welker, eds. *God's Life in Trinity.* Minneapolis, MN: Augsburg Fortress, 2006.
Walls Andrew and Cathy Ross, *Mission in the 21st Century: Exploring the Five Marks of Global Mission.* Maryknoll, NY: Orbis, 2008.
Walker, Simon P. *Leading Out of Who You Are: Discovering the Secret of Undefended Leadership.* Carlisle: Piquant, 2007.
Ward, Frances. *Lifelong Learning: Theological Education and Supervision.* London: SCM, 2005.
Ward, Pete. "Blueprint Ecclesiology and the Lived: Normativity as a Perilous Faithfulness", *Ecclesial Practices* 2 (2015) 74–90.
Warner, Rob. *Reinventing English Evangelicalism, 1996–2001: A Theological and Sociological Study.* Milton Keynes: Paternoster, 2007.
Weaver, John. "Developing Patterns of Ministerial Training." *Baptist Ministers' Journal* 250 (April 1995) 3–8.
Wesson, John. "How Cinderella Must go to the Ball: Pastoral Studies and its Relation to Theology." In *Foundations of Pastoral Studies and Practical Theology* edited by Paul Ballard, 53–64. Cardiff: University College, 1986.
West, W. M. S. and Michael J Quicke. *Church, Ministry and Baptism: Two Essays on Current Questions.* London: Baptist Union of Great Britain and Ireland, 1981.
Wickett, Reg. "Adult Theories and Theological Education." *JATE* 2.2 (2005) 153–61.
———. "The Learning Covenant." In *Addressing the Spiritual Dimensions of Adult Learning: What Educators Can Do* edited by Leona M. English and Marie A. Gillen, 39–48. San Francisco, CA: Jossey-Bass, 2000.
Williams, Rowan. *On Christian Theology.* Oxford: Blackwell 2000.
Winslade, Brian. *A New Kind of Baptist Church: Reframing Congregational Government for the 21st Century.* Macquarrie Park, NSW: Morling, 2010.
Wood, Charles M. "Theological Enquiry and Theological Education." In *Theological Perspectives on Christian Formation: A Reader on Theology and Christian Education* edited by Jeff Astley, Leslie Francis and Colin Crowder, 342–58. Leominster: Gracewing, 1996.
World Council of Churches, *Baptism, Eucharist and Ministry.* Geneva: WCC, 1982.
———. *Spiritual Formation in Theological Education.* Geneva: WCC, 1987.
———. "Theological Education for Ministerial Formation: The Statement from the European Consultation on Theological Education." *Ministerial Formation* 12 (October 1980) 3–9.

Bibliography

———. *Together Towards Life: Mission and Evangelism in Changing Landscapes*. Website download, 2013.

Worthen, Jeremy. "A Model of Ministerial Formation: Conceptual Framework and Practical Implications." In *The Making of Ministry*, edited by Angela Shier-Jones, 38–54. Peterborough: Epworth, 2008.

———. *Responding to God's Call: Christian Formation Today*. Norwich: Canterbury Press, 2012.

Wright, Nigel G. *Challenge to Change: A Radical Agenda for Baptists*. Eastbourne: Kingsway, 1991.

———. *Free Church, Free State: The Positive Baptist Vision*. Milton Keynes: Paternoster, 2005.

———. "Inclusive Representation: Towards a Doctrine of Christian Ministry." *Baptist Quarterly* 39.4 (October 2001) 159–74.

———. *New Baptists New Agenda*. Carlisle: Paternoster, 2002.

Index

action-research, 4, 15, 16, 17, 18, 21
Allen, Bill, 31, 50, 63, 64, 151
Angus Library, 56, 57, 58, 59
Astley, Jeff, 44, 50, 137, 138, 154

Ballard, Paul, 56, 58, 59, 60, 63
Banks, Robert, 5, 29, 35
Baptist colleges, 5, 15, 19–20, 21, 42–44,
    49, 51, 52, 55–69, 71–77, 80,
    83, 84, 85, 94–100, 104, 107–9,
    121–24, 128–34, 138–40, 143–52,
    155–57, 161, 164–70, 172–74
Baptist Union of Great Britain, 4, 5, 15,
    19, 20, 24, 25, 27, 31, 38, 39, 40,
    43, 45, 51, 52, 55–57, 61, 63–68,
    72–73, 82–83, 87, 89, 91, 92, 94,
    95, 99, 108, 133, 140–43, 146,
    147, 148, 158, 161, 167, 170, 174,
    176, 177, 185
Barth, Karl, 147
Bass, Dorothy, 7, 8, 159, 171
Beasley-Murray, Paul, 29–31, 33, 39–40,
    63, 88, 98
Bebbington, David, 25, 26
Bell, Judith, 76, 77, 78
Biblical studies, 4, 59, 96, 103–4, 114,
    117, 128–29, 132, 164, 168
Blyth, Myra, xiii, 67
BMS World Mission, 68, 93, 145
Bourdieu, Pierre, 8–10
Bosch, David, 147
Bretherton, Luke, 148, 162
Bristol Baptist College, 27, 42, 49, 54,
    56, 65, 68, 72, 90–92, 94, 98, 99,
    100–101, 103–6, 150

Burnard, Clive, 31

Cameron, Helen, 14, 15, 17–20, 73, 134,
    178
character, 45–46, 50–51, 54, 58, 63, 64,
    69, 70, 88, 90, 91, 92, 96, 104, 108,
    112, 113, 115, 116, 120, 135, 138,
    147, 151, 154, 157–59, 161, 162
Church of England, 3, 5, 28, 33, 47–48,
    51, 52, 58, 61
Churches Together in England, 66
Coghlan, David, 4, 15, 16, 17
collaborative, 16, 18, 55, 73, 86–87, 91–
    92, 97–98, 107, 115, 159, 160–63,
    164–65, 166–68, 170, 171, 179–81
college-based courses, 2, 4, 62, 89, 103–4,
    108, 132, 165, 174, 181
Colwell, John, 37
Common Awards, 5, 51, 90, 146
competence, 48, 57, 63, 91, 116, 154
competencies, 63–64, 67, 91, 113, 152,
    154, 158, 185
congregation-based courses, 49, 61–63,
    103–4, 124, 132, 138–39, 142–43,
    165, 169, 174
congregational studies, 176–77
context, ix, xiv, 1, 3–5, 7, 9, 13–15, 20, 21,
    23, 25, 30, 32, 34, 38, 40, 43, 49,
    59, 61, 63, 65, 68, 72, 76, 85–86,
    91–93, 96, 97–99, 104, 106–8,
    110–12, 115, 119, 120, 123–24,
    132, 136–38, 144–46, 149,
    155–57, 160, 161, 164–67, 169,
    170–72, 174, 175–79, 181, 183
Cooper, R E, 58

Index

cooperative, 7, 9, 10–13, 19, 38, 40, 42, 55, 60, 69, 71–72, 96, 134, 137, 147, 151, 155, 157, 159, 171, 172, 175, 178, 182
Cooperrider, David, 15, 17
covenant, 143–46, 153, 166, 169, 170
creative, 9–11, 13, 23, 24, 28, 38, 50, 55, 71, 95, 115, 134, 140, 144, 148, 149, 154, 155, 157, 160, 170, 171–73, 175, 177, 179, 182, 183
Cronshaw, Darren, 5
Cunningham, David, 153–54
curriculum, 47, 52, 57, 58, 60, 63, 77, 79, 84, 86, 96, 108–10, 115, 117, 121, 122, 132, 139, 149, 150, 164, 165, 167, 169
curriculum, explicit, 79–81, 100–105, 108, 114, 125–30, 139, 158, 169, 173
curriculum, implicit, 79, 81–82, 105–8, 130–31, 169, 173
curriculum, null, 79

Declaration of Principle, 19, 97
dialectical, x, 8, 13, 18, 25–29, 31, 34, 37, 38, 40, 41, 97, 107, 136, 140–43, 145, 154, 155, 160, 163, 166, 167, 172, 179, 182
discipleship, 33, 87, 89, 91, 92, 111, 135, 140–43, 150, 151
Dykstra, Craig, 7, 8, 11–13, 154, 155, 159, 171

ecclesiology, 11, 19, 20, 28, 30–35, 48, 62, 75, 139, 140–43, 161, 167, 176–78
ecumenical, 3, 5, 10, 20, 21, 26, 28, 37, 43, 44, 45, 52, 59, 65, 66, 68, 74, 75, 77, 82, 86, 88, 97, 99, 106, 107, 110, 111, 114, 115, 118, 121, 124, 129, 131, 144, 145, 146, 161, 170, 176, 180
education, ix, x, xiv, 2, 3, 5, 6, 12, 20, 43, 44–62, 63, 65, 69, 76, 79, 85, 87, 88, 90, 92, 94, 96, 98, 108, 110–14, 116, 118, 119, 121, 122, 135, 137–39, 141, 143, 144, 148, 150, 151, 154, 159, 162, 167, 170, 176, 182, 186
education, critical, 137–38, 141, 159, 167
education, formative, 137–38, 141, 167
Edwards Jr, Tiden, 46, 47
Eisner, Elliot, 79, 81
Ellis, Chris, 49, 54, 67, 91, 150–51
Ellis Rob, xiii, 26, 28–29, 37
espoused voice, 18–19, 21, 73–76, 78, 79, 83–84, 85–94, 97, 103, 107, 109, 110–120, 121, 122, 129, 134, 145, 146, 147, 150, 155, 156, 157, 165, 166, 172, 173, 174
ethnography, 14, 15, 18, 21, 176, 177
evangelical, 29, 32, 33, 35, 37, 49, 52, 88, 89, 90, 91, 93, 97, 112, 116, 121, 122, 152, 165

Farley, Edward, 47
Fiddes, Paul, xiii, xiv, 9, 20, 22, 24–28, 37, 57, 99, 134–36, 139–40, 143–45, 147, 150, 153–54, 157, 174
Flick, Uew, 82
Freire, Paulo, 61, 85, 87, 96
formal voice, 18, 20, 21, 134, 135
Foster, Charles, 11, 12–13, 50, 52, 53, 69, 70, 88, 96, 98, 168
four voices methodology, 17–20, 73, 83, 134
Fox, Mark, 4, 16, 17
Free Churches, 44, 49, 57, 88, 98, 140

Garland, Gareth, 39
God, as Trinity, xi, xiii, 22, 26, 134–36, 138, 140, 141, 144, 147–50, 153–55, 162–63, 168, 172, 174, 180, 183
God, divine dance as metaphor, 135, 147, 149, 168
God, grace of, 7, 144, 148, 153–54, 169, 171–72, 180–81, 183
God, hospitality of, 144, 147–49, 162, 169
God, mission of, 9, 10, 14, 17, 53, 90, 147–49, 162, 168, 175, 182
God, vulnerability of, 153–55, 162
Goodliff, Paul, 3, 19, 20, 23, 24, 26–29, 32, 35–37, 39, 42, 44, 55, 82, 133,

Index

142, 152, 156, 159, 163, 167, 168, 178–80
Graham, Elaine, 8–9, 150, 158, 160
Grundy, Malcolm, 29
Gummesson, Evert, 77

habitus, 8–10, 13, 21, 38, 42, 69–71, 94, 95, 97, 121, 140, 144, 149, 151, 152, 154, 155, 158, 167, 171, 182–83
Hale, Ted, 29
Haymes, Brian, 26, 49
Healy, Nicholas, 176–77
Helwys, Thomas, 25
Herbert, George, 153
Higher Education, 5, 6, 20, 46, 57, 58, 96, 113, 144, 148
Higton, Mike, 46, 148
Hind Report, 48, 64
Holmes, Stephen, 32, 37, 66
hospitality, 144, 146–49, 162–63, 169–71, 177, 181–82
Hughes, Alfred, 46
Hybels, Bill, 33–34

Ignite Report, 5, 43, 51, 64, 82, 95, 143, 152
integration, 67, 69, 86, 88, 90, 95, 96, 103, 107, 112, 114, 117, 119, 121, 122, 131, 149–52
integrity, 12, 46, 64, 69, 86, 88, 95, 107, 111, 131, 152
interviews, x, 15, 52, 73–84, 86, 94, 109, 141, 153, 182, 185, 187
Iona Community, 139, 169

Justes, Emma, 162

Keeble, Bruce, 60, 95
Knott, Kim, 73
knowledge, 4, 9, 14–15, 17, 21, 34, 44, 45, 50, 59, 64, 70, 73, 88, 96, 104, 117, 120, 135, 150, 151, 153, 159, 163, 164, 168, 171, 173, 174, 177

laity, 28, 32, 45
Leach, Jane, 159

Luther King House, 65, 85, 86, 99

MacIntyre, Alasdair, 7, 8, 10, 12, 35, 137, 171
Marks of Ministry, 64, 152, 154, 158, 161
Marmon, Ellen, 162
maturity, 54, 58, 61, 111, 113, 115, 116, 120, 135, 152, 158, 161
Mayes, Andrew, 3, 42, 44, 45, 46, 48, 49, 51, 52, 53, 54, 69, 135, 151
Methodist Church, 5, 48, 52, 65, 85, 137
ministers-in-training, ix, 44, 142, 176
mission, 5, 9, 10, 14, 17, 31, 39, 53, 56, 64, 66, 69, 85, 86, 88–91, 93, 98, 100–104, 107, 112, 117, 123, 125, 127, 129, 132, 135, 144, 145, 146–49, 162, 163, 164, 168, 169, 175, 180, 182
Mission Audit, 176–78
Moltmann, Jürgen, 140
Moon, Norman, 54, 56
Moschella, Mary Clark, 14–15
Murray, Carol, xiii
Murray, Stuart, 182

Neuhaus, Richard, 47
Newbigin, Lesslie, 61
Newman, Elizabeth, 148, 162
Newman, John Henry, 46
Nicholls, Mike, 30, 49, 56
normative voice, 18–19, 49–50, 53, 67, 79, 114, 152
Northern Baptist College, 58–63, 65, 68, 72, 85–87, 95–99, 102–4, 106
Northumbria Community, 139, 169
Nouwen, Henri, 148

operant voice, 18–21, 34, 73, 78–82, 83, 84, 100–107, 109, 125–31, 134, 146, 155–57, 172, 173, 174
Order for Baptist Ministry, 169
organizational studies, 14, 15, 18
OPTET, 65, 170
oversight, 25, 28, 32, 35, 38, 39, 40, 92, 141, 145, 151, 160
Oxford University, 4, 6, 96, 99, 170

201

Index

paideia, 159
participant observation, 14–15, 20, 73, 78, 81, 83, 169, 173
pastoral care, 38, 39, 64, 89, 100, 102, 103, 105, 126, 127, 129, 150, 162, 168, 179, 180, 182
pastoral imagination, 11–13, 16, 18, 19, 21–24, 38–43, 52, 55, 64, 68–70, 71–72, 81, 84, 86, 89, 90, 91, 93, 97–99, 107, 109–11, 113, 115, 117, 119, 120, 122–23, 124, 129, 131, 134, 136, 145, 146, 152, 156–74
Pattison, Stephen, 36, 57, 60, 151
Payne, Ernest, 26, 27
pedagogy, 58, 62, 149–52, 167, 169
Peterson, Eugene, 37, 41
phronesis, 111, 159
Pickard, Stephen, 160
Pohl, Christine, 147
prayer, 69, 82, 101, 102, 106, 111, 115, 126, 127, 130, 131, 138, 151, 152
preaching, 38, 39, 80, 89, 93, 100, 102, 103, 105, 117, 122, 125, 127, 129, 131, 158, 166, 168, 179, 180, 182
preparation, x, xiii, 1–5, 10–13, 15, 18, 20–22, 37, 42–45, 48–55, 61–64, 69–71, 73–79, 82, 85–88, 90, 92, 94, 95, 97, 98, 107–10, 114, 117–22, 131–35, 138, 141, 142, 147–50, 152–57, 161, 163, 170–72, 175, 182
priesthood of all believers, 25, 28, 30, 32, 40
professional, ix, xiii, 11, 12, 46, 50, 58, 63–64, 70, 87, 89, 90, 92, 97, 98, 107, 110, 112, 113, 114, 119, 123, 131, 140, 142, 159, 185

QAA, 105, 112, 113, 116, 124
QiFP (Quality in Formation Panel), 5, 21, 52, 53, 76, 86, 89, 110, 114, 119
Quicke, Michael, 29, 31, 33, 98

Randall, Ian, 56, 57, 63, 66
Rasier, Konrad, 45

reflection, x, xiii, xiv, 4–5, 7, 16–19, 29, 35, 39, 46, 48–55, 60, 62, 64, 73, 74, 77, 80, 86, 88, 96, 100, 102, 105, 109, 114–16, 119–21, 128–28, 133, 137, 138, 149–52, 157–60, 163–68, 170, 171, 177, 178
reflective, 59–61, 68, 86, 93, 97, 111, 115, 119, 137, 138, 157–60, 163, 164, 168, 175–79
reflexive, 20, 86, 111, 120, 157–60
Register of Nationally Accredited Ministers, 42, 43, 45, 148, 161
representative voice, 20–22, 24, 27, 34, 38, 67, 71, 72, 82, 83, 134, 150, 152, 155, 160, 167, 172, 174
Regent's Park College, ix, xiii, 3, 4, 15, 20, 22, 27, 57–60, 62, 65, 68, 72, 83, 94, 96, 98, 99, 104–6, 153, 155, 168, 170
Russell, David, 54, 56, 57, 58, 59, 65

sacramental, 3, 23, 36–37, 39, 98
sacraments, 24, 28, 38, 67, 82, 86, 102, 130, 150
sapiential, 159
Sapsezian, Aharon, 47
Schleiermachian, 60, 63, 80
servant leadership, 31, 32, 35, 39, 40, 92
Shepherd, Peter, 59, 62, 65, 86
Shier-Jones, Angela, 45, 141
Silverman, David, 74, 75, 76, 78
skills, 44, 45, 47, 49, 50, 57, 58, 64, 69, 70, 85, 88, 89, 90, 104, 105, 112, 113, 116, 119, 120, 122, 131, 135, 138, 151, 167, 168, 170, 182
Smith, James K A, 47, 139
Smyth, John, 25
South Wales Baptist College, 65, 72, 92–95, 102–6, 144
Spurgeon's College, 30, 31, 37, 50, 56, 59, 62, 63, 65, 66, 67, 68, 72, 87–90, 94, 95, 97, 98, 99, 100–101, 103–7, 150
Stevenson, Peter, 95
structured, 8–13, 19, 23, 38, 40, 55, 65, 70–71, 84, 95, 97–98, 108, 134,

Index

137, 138, 140, 143, 144, 151, 152, 154, 155, 157, 159–61, 165, 169–73, 175, 178, 179, 182
Swinton, John, 14, 74, 157, 158

Taylor, Michael, 44, 49, 54, 59–63, 65–66, 95, 98
theology, applied, 69, 93, 112, 113, 151
theology, contextual, 59, 85, 93, 96–97, 112
theology, historical, 96, 103, 117, 160
theology, liberation, 58–59, 61, 87, 96, 98
theology, practical 17, 58–60, 62, 80, 85, 88, 93, 96, 103, 107, 111, 114, 118, 122, 129, 132, 152, 164
theology, systematic, 59, 96, 103, 117, 132, 160
Thomas, Viv, 31
Tidball, Derek, 3, 31–32
Treier, Daniel, 159

United Reformed Church, 52, 65, 85

virtue, 37, 46, 58, 64, 69, 120, 133, 148, 152–55, 157–60, 162–64, 171
Volf, Miroslav, 140
vulnerability, xiv, 74, 148, 152--55, 162, 169, 170, 181, 182

Walls, Andrew, 91
Ward, Frances, 48
Ward, Pete, 176
Weaver, John, 49
Williams, Rowan, 158, 176
Winslade, Brian, 31–34, 36, 40
wischenshaft, 159
Wood, Nick, xiii
World Council of Churches, 28, 45, 46, 49, 162
worship, 6, 39, 80–81, 84, 89, 100, 102, 105–7, 109, 111, 114, 119, 120, 125, 127, 129, 130, 131, 138, 139, 150, 168, 169, 173, 179–82
Worthen, Jeremy, 45, 141
Wright, Nigel, xiii, 26, 31, 37, 51

www.ingramcontent.com/pod-product-compliance
Lightning Source LLC
Chambersburg PA
CBHW051050160426
43193CB00010B/1134